POWER, COMMUNITY
AND THE CITY

Volume 1

D1607452

POWER, COMMUNITY
AND THE CITY

Comparative Urban and Community Research
Volume 1

Edited by

Michael Peter Smith

Transaction Books
New Brunswick (USA) and Oxford (UK)

ISSN: 0892-5569
ISBN: 0-88738-734-9
Printed in the United States of America

Volume 1 comprises volume 12 of *Comparative Urban Research*.

POWER, COMMUNITY AND THE CITY

Contents

John Friedmann and Mauricio Salguero The Barrio Economy and Collective Self-Empowerment in Latin America: A Framework and Agenda for Research 3

David R. Meyer and Kyonghee Min Concentration and Specialization of Manufacturing in Core and Peripheral Cities during Rapid Industrialization: Korea, 1960-1970 38

Philip Cooke The Postmodern Condition and the City 62

Barry Wellman The Community Question Re-Evaluated 81

Barbara Frankel The City in Black Kinship: A Comparison of Rural Past and Urban Present 108

Adolph Reed, Jr. The Black Urban Regime: Structural Origins and Constraints 138

Comparative Urban and Community Research, an annual review succeeding the journal Comparative Urban Research is devoted to theoretical, empirical and applied research on the processes of urbanization and community change throughout the world. The format of Comparative Urban and Community Research enables the publication of manuscripts that are longer and more richly textured than the articles a quarterly journal can feature.

Future issues of this annual will address the following topics: power and symbol in the city; socialist city/capitalist city: does it matter?; world cities, the new urban class structure?; and Asian cities in the world economy. The editorial board welcomes manuscripts on these topics and suggestions from readers willing to help develop special issues devoted to these topics.

This volume was prepared with support from the Department of Applied Behavioral Sciences of the University of California, Davis. Editorial correspondence should be addressed to Comparative Urban and Community Research, Department of Applied Behavioral Sciences, University of California, Davis 95616.

Michael Peter Smith, Editor
University of California, Davis

Evelyn Harris, Editorial Assistant

THE BARRIO ECONOMY AND
COLLECTIVE SELF-EMPOWERMENT IN LATIN AMERICA:
A FRAMEWORK AND AGENDA FOR RESEARCH

John Friedmann
Mauricio Salguero
University of California, Los Angeles

This paper proposes a conceptual framework and research agenda for the study of the popular sector of civil society in Latin America from a perspective of self-renewal and emancipation. The paper sketches some salient dimensions of Latin American development history from the 50s through the current period of crisis. As unemployment reaches unprecedented levels, many households confront the challenge of survival through a complex system of "informal" activities, many of which occur in popular collective organizations. The paper employs a model of the barrio economy to examine the activities of these organizations and their potential for transformation.

Introduction

In many ways, the most hopeful sign in a Latin America widely perceived as a continent "without a future," where traditional development models have been all but exhausted, and the word "crisis" is used so pervasively that it is no longer capable of arousing consternation, is the new activism of civil society which we have come to know as social movements.[1] This phenomenon is not unique to the region; it is part of a world-wide awakening of social forces which are neither of the state nor of the corporate economy but are rooted in household formations and their immediate organizations. In Latin America, this resurgence of civil society in the public domain has had specific proximate causes: the utter inability of the modern production sectors to provide a sufficient livelihood for any but a minor fraction of the working population and a state whose repeated attempts at countervailing policies have proved ineffective even as it has, in country after country, applied the stern principle of *mano dura* to shore up its crumbling authority (Singer and Brandt, 1982).[2]

There is much uncertainty about what these new grassroots movements really mean. In a highly original interpretation, colored by the European politics of the New Left, Tilman Evers proposes an essentially utopian view. He sees the movements as the carriers of a new collective identity:

In a way, the new socio-cultural patterns of everyday sociability that germinate within the new social movements are part of [the bitter need for a founding project to reconstruct hegemony]. They are the embryos of a popular counter-foundation, in response to the ill-fated efforts from above. The dissolution of established socio-economic structures and socio-cultural orientations has had the effect, coupled with a devastating social disintegration, of "setting free" what remained of a constructive potential to find new, self-determined orientations and openings (Evers, 1985, 63).

Latin American sociologist Ruth Cardoso argues as persuasively that the "new" social movements are neither new nor radical; that by their very nature they are easily co-opted by the state, and that neither in their intentions nor in their effects are they transformative of existing relations of power (Cardoso cited in Vink, 1985). Urban social movements have existed for quite some time, responsible for uncounted *invasiones* and *reivindicaciones* for at least 30 years (Goldrich et al., 1967-68; Castells, 1976).

Sociologists have pointed out, however, that their success tends to weaken and exhaust these movements; once land has been successfully claimed, once a particular demand for public services has ben met, they dissolve as a social force, leaving material accomplishments as the only trace of their former existence. Some grassroots movements in Latin America are admittedly new, such as the movement for human rights in Chile or the Ecclesiastical Base Communities (EBCs) in Brazil. They too must be seen as a response to a specific historical situation that will pass into oblivion once the conditions that gave rise to it are rectified. The return to democracy in Argentina all but ended the human rights movement in that country and the recent economic upsurge in Brazil, coinciding with a return to civilian rule and the persistent efforts of conservative factions of the Catholic Church to regain lost terrain, have sharply curtailed the political significance of the EBCs (Mainwaring, 1986). More fundamentally, many have argued that in the absence of formal political organization civil society lacks the capacity for sustained mobilization and transformative actions.[3]

If this apparently realistic appraisal is valid, the study of the new civil activism would be at most of historical interest. We propose to go by a different road, however. The perspective of the past is valid and has in its favor that the past is past; its record is complete. With equal justification, however, we can claim a perspective from the unique vantage point of a possible future. Here the future speaks to our actions in the present: the record has still to be made. We are dealing, then, with possibilities invested with hope. Although it is unlikely that the possible future we imagine will emerge just as we think, to envision it at all does light a beacon in whose direction we can set forth.

The possible future we propose to bring into relation with current grassroots movements in Latin America has economic and political dimensions. We shall discuss each in turn.

Global Crisis and the Political Economy of Survival

What is happening now in Latin American cities must be seen in historical perspective. Figure 1 sketches some salient dimensions of Latin American urban history since the early fifties. By not differentiating among specific national histories, our account inevitably distorts reality. National experiences are by no means uniform throughout, nor does the timing of change necessarily coincide with our periodization. There are, however, sufficient similarities in the separate stories of cities in the region to allow some conditional generalizations.

The table illustrates cycles of successive doctrine.[4] The first cycle spans the two decades after World War II. In Latin America, this is the period of the Keynesian state and is associated with the rise of national planning and the Alliance for Progress during the Kennedy administration. The reigning development doctrines are promulgated by Raúl Prebisch and W.W. Rostow: industrialization through import-substitution and the "stages of growth" leading to the material utopia of a mass consumption society. With the massive transfer of rural population to the city, urbanization is accelerated with population growth rates more than double the natural increase. The inability of the "modern sector" to adequately absorb the influx of rural migrants gives rise to the phenomenon of "marginality" (for a critical review, see Sabatini, 1986). Marginality is broadly defined as non-participation in the emerging consumer society. With some 20-30% of the urban population living in shanty towns and *tugurios* (inner-city slums), the state launches major programs of redistribution, especially in housing. These expenditures seem only to augment the flood of political demands on a state increasingly unable to respond to them with available resources. This concatenation of events, marked by the increased deterioration of living standards among an already impoverished population, made doubly burdensome by runaway inflation, leads to a breakdown of the model and rising urban violence.

With the tacit support and occasional active connivance of the United States, military-civilian dictatorships are established in Brazil, Argentina, Uruguay, Chile, Bolivia, Ecuador and Peru. While dissident elements are repressed, official terror is spreading (Linz and Stepan, 1986).[5] Economically, the development model of Period I is replaced by a frank accumulation regime in which the growth of GNP is the overriding objective. State policies to bring hyper-inflation under control are used to bring about an upward redistribution of income. Amid an orgy of deregulation, free trade euphoria, and reliance on monetary controls for maintaining essential macro-economic equilibria, the neo-liberal model of the state enjoys momentary popularity. With the massive influx of foreign private capital, indebtedness rises, the state acting as the ultimate guarantor of foreign loans. Although industrialization continues to be the first priority, the emphasis is now

Years	Social Policy	State	Development Model	The Urban Domain
50s-60s	-reforms -redistributive policies (e.g. low cost housing) -directed popular participation	-liberal (Keynesian) welfare -economic and social planning	-economic growth and development -the consumer society (passive) -industrialization through import substitution (foreign capital) restricted predominantly to elite markets -capitalist transformation of rural areas: agribusiness -massive expulsion from rural areas	-high rates of urban growth -the phenomenon of "marginality" (appx. 20-30% of urban population) -stepped-up demand-making (reivindicaciones) for items of collective consumption exceeds capacity of the state -deterioration of living conditions

Breakdown of Model I: Violence

Years	Social Policy	State	Development Model	The Urban Domain
60s-80s	-violent repression -income redistribution towards the more affluent sectors	-military and civil dictatorship -neo-liberal	-GNP cult/free market -rapid accumulation/-privatization -increased reliance on transnational capital -industrialization for export (new international division of labor) -increased indebtedness	-explosion of informal sector -employment and unemployment (30-50%) -massive impoverishment including middle strata -hyper-inflation -social polarization

Breakdown of Model II: Global Crisis and New Beginnings

Years	Social Policy	State	Development Model	The Urban Domain
80s-90s	-support of self-reliant practices -decentralization of services and of planning -deconcentration of power to local actors	-re-democratization (return of civilians to power), but the forms of democratization are not yet clearly defined (post-liberal model)	-walking on two legs: integration into the global economy AND a politics of basic needs at the level of the local community -expansion of internal markets through support of cooperatives and small enterprises	-resurgence of civil society: self-organization, self-reliance, self-governance, (empowerment) -liberation of territorial space for autonomous action -mobilization of non-conventional resources (e.g. mutual aid, dialogue, donation of labor time) -structural change from below: towards new forms of the local state -claim-making for expanded civil and economic rights

Fig. 1 The Urban Domain and the State, 1950-2000

on the promotion of production for export. For a few years, economic "miracles" make newspapers headlines, adding fuel to the ideological debate, but after the oil shock of 1973 and especially after 1978, with the dramatic slow-down of the international economy, "miracles" gradually yield to a sense of panic. The first almost automatic response is to meet rising economic problems at home by going overseas to borrow more money from willing creditors of petro-dollars. By the early 80s, however, the major borrowers, Brazil, Mexico, Argentina, Chile and Peru, are in no condition to meet even the interest payments on their loans. The notorious debt crisis has arrived.

Meanwhile, in urban areas, unemployment reaches unprecedented levels, with 30 to 50 percent of the population living at close to subsistence levels (rising incidence of hunger, infant mortality, etc.). This situation crests in 1982-83 but, with the exception of Brazil whose economy rebounds in 1984, fails to show significant improvements thereafter. In some countries, such as Mexico, the deterioration of living standards continues. As states adopt IMF-imposed austerity regimes, impoverishment begins to spread even to the urban middle sectors. Social polarization increases. Large-scale capital flight, huge interest payments, and the drying up of foreign investments lead to actual disinvestment in many cases and to absolute declines in the real value of production. All this takes place in a context of global economic "restructuring," with new technologies coming on line, rising levels of unemployment even in the core countries of world capitalism, and increasingly loud demands in these same countries for protecting employment in the declining older industries and regions.

By the mid-1980s, the neo-liberal model of the state has collapsed. Military regimes are again replaced with civilian governments in a process hailed as democratization, and official terror gives way to a resumption of party politics and periodic elections. Only Chile and Paraguay hold on to the discredited model, while Central American states are gripped in the turmoil of civil war and U.S.-sponsored aggression. Another cycle is beginning.

In Figure 1 we have attempted to link the mobilization of civil society and more specifically its popular sector with a new bifurcated development model that promotes both the integration of national economies with the global economic system and a politics of self-empowerment at the level of the local community (see Bitar, 1985; Friedmann, 1986; Geisse, 1986; Max-Neef, et al., 1986). This model has not yet been widely discussed, but in some countries such as Peru, it appears close to becoming reality. Beyond question is the surge of new activities in the barrios of large Latin American cities: a growing capacity for self-organization, self-reliance and self-governance in a process of collective self-empowerment. In the course of this historical evolution some barrios, such as in Chile, have even become a kind of "liberated" zone where non-conventional resources based on mutual aid, dialogue, and donation of labor time are mobilized (Max-Neef, 1985). As the community becomes increasingly empowered, the local state, inevitably implicated in this self-generated form of barrio development, is itself subject to transformation; its structures are being adapted to the demands of a participatory process. At the same time, the demand-making so prominent during Period I escalates to the claim-making of Period III (Singer, 1982). Underwritten with moral passion, claims are being staked out for expanded civil rights (local autonomy, participatory democracy) and economic rights (a decent livelihood and the collective provision of basic needs).

The preceding paragraph is written in a spirit of hope for a way out of the present impasse. It presupposes a structural reading of the economic crisis that points to a situation in which upwards of 50% of the urban population lives a marginalized existence (Sunkel, 1985; Aguilar, 1985). The familiar models of industrialization and "modernization," tied as they are to an emerging world economic order, are viewed as incapable of providing a satisfactory livelihood for any but a shrinking minority. This is true even for Brazil, which is currently enjoying an economic boom (Reicher and Madeira, 1986). Faced with the likelihood of permanent crisis, household adaptations must be regarded as more than make-shift arrangements. For many households, the road to survival will lead them into a complex system of "informal" activities, where every peso must be carefully weighed in balance with the effort (calories) necessary to produce it (Fass, forthcoming). This rationale conforms to the individual model of neoclassical economic theory; the system itself is not being challenged. For many others, however, the road will lead to new forms of cooperative activity with neighbors, the primary participants often being women, in which a new sociability is recovered in the teeth of continual assaults on one's identity as a social failure, a *marginado* (Hardy, 1984; 1985).

The vital connection of these responses to the political dimension remains to be considered. Poor people gain greater access to the bases for social (not yet political) power primarily by joining in collective, community-based efforts of struggling for survival in difficult times. Empowerment is one aspect of larger social processes in which the future is foreshadowed. More precisely, with their emphasis on reciprocity, mutual aid, solidarity, social learning, participation and egalitarianism, they are counter-hegemonic processes in the Gramscian sense (Gramsci, 1971; Evers, 1985).

The prime example of this new politics at the level of the barrio is found in the Ecclesiastical Base Communities of Brazil, Mexico and elsewhere (Betto, 1984; Gómez-Hermosillo, 1986). The intellectual leadership of the EBCs is particularly conscious of the break with hegemonic relations and practices within the sphere of the EBCs themselves. Beginning with a transformation of self through direct involvement with community work (including festivities and celebrations), EBCs go on to collective tasks that deal directly with the survival problems of its members, but radiate outward to the rest of the local community, who are not in principle excluded from the benefits of collective action. At this point also contact is made with the agents of the state, particularly the local state, and this in turn creates pressures for the transformation of local state structures towards greater independence from the center and more participatory practices of governance (Jacobi, 1985; Pease García, 1986). Beyond this lie still further transformative actions on the national plane that will require the formation of political parties with roots sunk deep into the popular barrio movement and other people's organizations, including the labor movement and the mobilized peasantry. Such parties have yet to appear in Latin America, though the Partido dos Trabalhadores in Brazil may turn out to be the first example of this kind.[6]

As stated earlier, our vantage point is the possible future, a future embodying hope. There are, of course, other possibilities less pleasant to contemplate. Latin American social formations can degenerate into anarchy, civil war, authoritarianism, and massive immiseration. Or civil society can return to a state of passive acquiescence, punctuated with periodic and essentially senseless outbursts of popular anger in which authoritarian accumulation regimes function in an essentially depoliticized environment for the benefit of privileged elites. Given these options, we frankly opt for a future promising a genuine social and political renewal from below. It is not a great hope we nourish, but it is a hope grounded in some, admittedly selective, realities of the present day.

Our objective in writing this paper, then, is to propose a conceptual framework for research that will lead us to a deeper understanding of the transformative forces that are coming together in the popular barrios of Latin American cities as they confront the double challenge of survival (necessity) and political practice (freedom).[7]

Households and the Barrio Economy

Central to the concept of civil society is the household and, more specifically, from a point of view of the production of life, the household economy (Borsotti, 1978; Razeto, 1984; Schmink, 1984). In this concept, households are viewed as pro-active units, achieving their goals in free association with other similar households. Households engage in the production of goods and services for both use and exchange. Both efforts bring satisfaction in return. How households use available resources -- the time, energy, and skills of their members -- depends on how they perceive their environment, the goals to which they aspire, and their expectations about the benefits they will receive for their effort.

The objective conditions of their environment, the more intimate environment of the barrio and the wider spheres of the market economy, are also relevant.

Households, then, will be treated as fundamental units in the political economy of survival. Despite increasing reference to "household survival strategies," the definition of households for purposes of research has become quite problematic (Schmink, 1984). As irreducible social units, households are neverthe-less preferable as a unit of study to the atomized individual. We shall therefore define households as *any group of related and/or unrelated individuals who, while living under the same roof and "eating from the same pot," constitute an economic decision-making unit.* By this definition, a single woman, living in the same dwelling and sharing meals with her three children, a distant cousin and her lover, would be considered a household, whereas a lodging house would not. The objective of any household is 1) to ensure its own reproduction as a unit within a given socio-cultural context, and 2) to improve its material condition. Households will thus devise "strategies" of both simple and extended social reproduction (Fass, forthcoming).

Households are not homogeneous entities, however. They are composed of individuals whose objectives may or may not be identical with those of the house-hold taken as a whole and who may or may not be willing to subordinate them-selves to a common strategy. Moreover, they will enter into social relations with other households, forming proximate networks of reciprocity with neighbors and kin (Lomnitz, 1977). They may also join in cooperative types of enterprise and mutual aid associations (Hardy, 1984). Finally, households are physically located in and part of an encompassing territorial community (the neighborhood or barrio) whose objectives are evolved through more or less democratic procedures, but whose interests are not necessarily identical with those of any of its component units: individuals, households, or community organizations. The entire complex forms an articulated social whole that interacts with its environment in ways that give rise to multiple conflicts and contradictions (Capecchi and Pesce, 1984).

Household resources can be invested in a number of sectors:

* The *household economy* itself (housing construction, food preparation, child care, care for sick or disabled, small livestock, etc.);
* The *territorial community* or *barrio* (participation in social networks and mutual aid efforts, participation in community-based organizations, and Church activities, sporting events, community celebrations, etc.);
* The *political community* as the counterpart of civil society in the political sphere (demonstrations, civil strikes, membership in political parties, labor unions, and politically oriented social movements);

* The *cooperative economy*, typically located within the barrio and, though selling in external markets, organized very differently from either the informal sector or the private corporate sector, providing benefits to member households -- and to the barrio as a whole -- that, beyond monetary returns, are based on solidarity relations;
* The *informal economy* (sometimes referred to as the unenumerated economy), frequently linked into the formal/official economy at the end of a long production chain, ranging from individual piecework production -- home industry -- to small business enterprise, but also including domestic work, street vending, the underground economy, etc.;[8]
* The *formal (or enumerated) economy*, including both corporations and the state as employer;
* The *state* (e.g. primary and secondary education, jail, obligatory military service).

Of these seven domains of action, only the last two are not under the immediate control of the household economy, though the degree to which households actually control these domains will vary greatly.

In a household perspective, the barrio constitutes the space for the production and reproduction of its life, because it is here, in the immediacy of their everyday social relations, that households are able to increase their capacity for action by gaining improved access to social power (Friedmann, 1987, ch. 9). As the habitat for the vast majority of the popular sectors, barrios typically have a name, a sense of their own identity, a history still fresh in the memory of its older inhabitants, dense social networks, a formal or informal structure of governance, and other attributes of a spatially defined political community. Although households may remain in their respective barrios for many years, the barrio's salience as a life space for its households will fluctuate with the relative attractiveness of the market economy. Accordingly, we shall hypothesize that, *as employment in the exchange economy declines and/or becomes less productive, households will tend to favor strategies that lead to an increased investment of their resources in the territorial community of the barrio and its component organizations.* The reverse of this hypothesis is also expected to hold true.

The relations between the household economy, its territorial base, and the market economy are shown schematically in Figure 2. This configuration is one of several possible ones, and the pattern shown is greatly simplified. Nevertheless, Figure 2 helps identify some critical dimensions of the problem.

The model shows households in four different relationships: among themselves (social networks); with the market economy in both formal and informal arrangements; with multiple household or cooperative enterprises located within

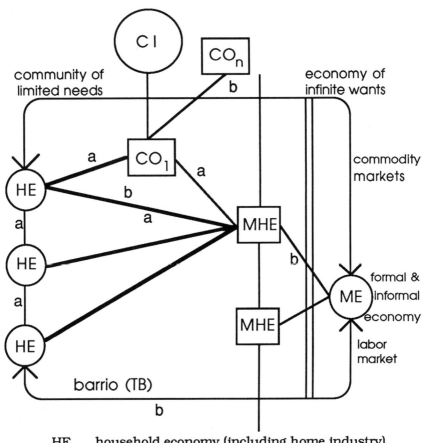

HE	household economy (including home industry)
MHE	multiple household enterprise (cooperative)
CO	community (self-help) organization
ME	market economy
CI	civil institutions (church, political parties, foundations, etc.)
a	reciprocity (solidarity) relations (use values predominate)
b	market exchange relations (commodified)
TB	territorial base or life space

Figure 2 A Schematic Model of Household Relations

the barrio; and with community (self-help) organizations. Any given household will display a certain pattern of resource allocation among these areas of household investment, but the pattern itself, i.e., the relative allocation of household resources, will be subject to frequent modification and adjustment.[9] In making decisions, households will generally be aware that they are dealing with two very different modes of production: inside the barrio, expected returns are measured primarily in terms of the direct *use value* of particular goods and services, feelings of good will, and social recognition, whereas in the market economy, where relations are commodified, returns are counted exclusively in terms of money. This distinction is drawn in Figure 2 by separately identifying solidarity and market exchange relations (a, b).

Related to this distinction is another which draws a line between the barrio viewed as a moral economy (Polanyi, 1977; Scott, 1976) and consequently as a *community of limited needs* and the *economy of infinite wants*, the market economy with which it continuously interacts. Within the community of limited needs of the barrio, households tend to focus on tasks of simple reproduction or economic survival. The structure of this community and thus of the barrio as a whole is cellular, being articulated through networks of solidarity relations (Lomnitz, 1977). In the form of its governance it is participatory and egalitarian, but as linkages to the market economy increase in importance, and differences in household incomes become more pronounced, solidarity relations tend to weaken.

Relations between the community of limited needs and the market are therefore central to our analysis. Within the barrio economy of Figure 2, we have shown several multiple household (cooperative) enterprises that maintain a dual relation to households based on both reciprocities and market exchange. These enterprises contain within themselves one of the major contradictions of the model. At the same time they offer the one possibility within the barrio of expanding production beyond simple reproduction. In studying territorially-based cooperatives, therefore, purists will be disappointed. The contradiction in its own structural relationships must be resolved for a variety of reasons, but results will rarely, if ever, correspond to the idealized model of cooperation (Tendler, 1983).

The pattern of household relations shown in Figure 2 points to several sources of contradiction. In addition to the contradiction between solidarity and market relations, there are contradictions within the household itself. These can be seen in the relations between genders, as women escape from traditional roles into new roles of leadership and household support; between multiple household enterprises and the market economy, particularly where they contract with more powerful corporate firms on the outside; and between the community of limited needs -- the barrio viewed as a collectivity -- and the economy of unlimited wants which appeals to the acquisitive urge of individuals and households. As the market economy increases the range of opportunities for remunerative employment, individual households will tend to shift their resources away from the community economy of the barrio to earn more money in the economy outside. Under these conditions, accumulation will tend to accelerate beyond the confines of the barrio, and individualist calculations will begin to replace the collectivist criteria of barrio economics. If economic growth continues, other changes are likely to follow: the bureaucratic state will reassert its control over the life space of working class households, economic exploitation of workers will increase, wealth will be progressively transferred out of the barrio, hierarchical relations will become more pronounced even within it, and participatory processes will atrophy.

The community of limited needs is thus an exceedingly vulnerable construction. At the personal level, participation in it can be a highly satisfying experience, but households will tend to see it as a community of "last resort." As their own material situation improves, they will tend to reduce their involvement in community-based organizations, because these organizations do not promise to lead them out of poverty (according to the hegemonic definition of poverty, a life at or below a certain subsistence income).

This somewhat cynical conclusion must be tempered by two additional observations. First, we do not expect a dramatic reversal in the conditions of Latin American urban economies. Although there may be local upsurges in formal employment possibilities, the prospects for a general resumption of high rates of economic growth on a long-term, secular basis, generating large numbers of new jobs in the modern sector, appears an unlikely prospect. For most countries the existing economic crisis is likely to become the normal situation. This prospect, regarded as dismal by some, is nevertheless encouraging for the emergence of a new type of development from within the barrio communities themselves.

Second, a great deal will depend on the success of multiple household enterprises, such as worker-controlled cooperatives, because they alone, and not the micro-enterprises of the informal sector, harbor the possibility of a genuine counter-hegemonic praxis. For this reason, we propose to focus our work on production activities within the barrio. It is through these activities and their linkages into the community, that we hope to capture the elusive phenomenon of collective self-empowerment which is at the heart of our research.

Specification of the Model and Questions for Research

In studying multiple household enterprises and micro-enterprises inside the barrio, one must always be aware of the contradictory nature of their external relations: their *forward linkages* (primarily marketing and purchasing arrangements in the larger economy) and their *backward linkages* (strengthening solidarity relations, the convivial society, the role of women) into the community. It is also useful to look at *lateral link-ups* among multiple household enterprises within a given barrio, such as barrio cooperative associations, as well as between two or more barrios (confederations) within the same city. A study of the broad social and political implications of the new forms of production within barrio communities is helpful. What can present initiatives tell us about the future of an "alternative" development engendered by conditions of prolonged, structural crisis? Very little information is available on any of these questions. The remainder of this paper will specify the many questions for research in more detail, based on our still limited knowledge.

1.   The Barrio Economy: Households, Cooperatives, and the Informal Sector

Much of what we shall refer to as the *barrio economy*, the territorial base of household activities sustaining life and livelihood, remains invisible to the observer because of the imprecise use of the informal sector as an umbrella term to cover the great variety of officially unenumerated income-generating activities. Among the activities often lumped together in this sector are home-based industries (artisan production, textiles, knitware, electronic assembly), personal and repair services, small-scale manufacturing (micro-enterprises), casual labor, domestic work, prostitution, and many other diverse trades. Some informal sector workers produce directly for the final consumer while others, possibly the majority, are situated at the end of long production chains, working for capitalist firms that control important shares of the consumer market (Portes, 1984). It has frequently been observed that formal and informal sectors are linked to each other not only through relations of production but also in a more general, functional sense. Informal production, for example, tends to lower overall wage-costs, offer flexibility to corporate management in weathering fluctuations in demand and, by absorbing large quantities of labor at subsistence and below subsistence levels, serves as a kind of buffer for the corporate economy.

This role of the informal sector leads to a curious result. During periods of economic recession, the number of informal workers may actually increase, while the income earned per worker declines (Murillo and Lanzetta 1984; Hardy 1985). Thus, open unemployment tends to be less than it would otherwise be, even though the material condition of workers deteriorates to a point where households may be driven to adopt a new strategy in order to eke out an existence (Ross and Usher 1986).

Unable to earn a living in the informal economy, supplemented by such formal-sector income as may still come their way, many households turn for support to the *cooperative household sector* or *sector asociativo* within working class barrios (Hardy 1984; Edy Chonchol 1984; Razeto 1983, 1984; Hirschman 1985; Hardy and Razeto 1986; Guimaraes 1986). In this bifurcated sector, some services are produced cooperatively for the common benefit of its associated members (e.g., through community self-help organizations such as housing cooperatives and soup kitchens), while other organized labor processes are producing chiefly for sale in outside markets (Hardy, 1986; Molina and Henao, 1986). Although both are fundamentally organized on the basis of solidarity relations, production for outside markets imposes special conditions which lead to the formation of multiple household enterprises (MHEs). MHEs are neither cooperatives in the traditional sense nor micro-enterprises organized according to proto-capitalist principles. They represent a mode of production *sui generis*. The Chilean term for them is *organizaciones económicas populares* (OEP) (Razeto, 1985).[10] They occupy a special place in the barrio economy. The typical multiple household enterprise:

* is based within the social and physical space of the barrio, displaying strong "backward" linkages into individual households and community (self-help) organizations (solidarity linkages);
* is small-scale, with fewer than 50 workers, but may be linked into larger, barrio-wide associations of similar enterprises;
* practices a form of collective decision-making in which hierarchical relations are minimized;
* abides by the principle of equal pay for equal work;
* is not primarily devoted to profit maximization but more to meeting the basic economic needs of its members (i.e., does not extract surplus value and therefore accumulates very little, if anything);
* tends to attract a predominantly female labor force;
* practices mutual aid among its members;
* tends to be relatively short-lived, but easily regroups and reestablishes itself.

Although not all MHEs are alike in all respects, they contrast sharply with the so-called micro-enterprises of the informal sector which are not territorial but individual in organization, lacking the close solidarity relations of the former (Strassmann, 1986).[11]

This relatively simple typology of barrio economic activities is summed up in the chart below (for a comparison, see Fig. 2):

The Barrio Economy

a.   Formal (capitalist) sector activities: for the most part, income earned outside the barrio. Accumulation is concentrated in this sector. Income may be spent inside the barrio.

b. Informal (proto-capitalist) sector:
1) micro-enterprises, producing both inside and outside the barrio but selling primarily outside the barrio.
2) other, such as domestic work, prostitution, ambulant trading, etc., carried out mostly outside the barrio. May be further subdivided into semi-legal and illegal activities, including those customarily defined as "criminal."

c. Cooperative household (non-capitalist) sector:
1) community (self-help) organizations
2) multiple household enterprise (MHE)

Individual households must devise a survival strategy appropriate for their specific situation that will optimize their time, labor, and skill resources over the array of potentially productive activities, with their specific rates of return in money and/or kind. These resource allocations are not likely to remain stable, as households endeavor to optimize their economic situation in a series of adaptive moves among the three sectors and their respective sub-sectors. For our purposes, however, it is the cooperative household sector, especially the multiple household enterprise, which is of interest. Economically, it is the weakest of the three sectors and the one that brings the lowest monetary return. From a political and counter-hegemonic perspective, on the other hand, it is also the sector that holds the greatest prospects for the future.

The best way to study MHEs in the context of the barrio economy is to look at how they are articulated, in a forward direction with capitalist markets and in a backward direction with the network of reciprocal relations within the barrio. Forward (market) linkages may have a disintegrating effect on solidarity relations, undermining the incipient counter-hegemonic practices of households. These two sets of linkages and their interrelations therefore require the closest possible attention.

2. Forward Linkages: Marketing Relations

Like the informal economy, the cooperative household sector produces for markets. Although the question of how these markets are organized is of the utmost importance, very little information exists on the subject. Hardy (1984) reports how women's cooperatives in the Santiago suburb of Conchalí were initially assisted by the Church, acting through a beneficent foundation, in marketing their products in Santiago and export markets abroad. When, after a number of years, responsibility for marketing was shifted to the cooperative itself, a crisis ensued, and many members dropped out. There is no information about subsequent events, but the changeover undoubtedly had far-reaching effects on the incipient cooperative movement.

More pertinent information is available on the informal sector. For example, whether formally organized or not, small-scale production is often tied into larger production ensembles through subcontracting arrangements (Portes, 1984; Murillo and Lanzetta, 1984; Holmes, 1986). The resulting marketing relations tend to impose a harsh discipline on small producers and are inherently exploitative. A monopolistic buyer may set up one or more micro-enterprises with working capital and a supply of raw materials, while retaining key operational control. Thus, the supply network is arranged as an informally organized, dispersed "factory" (Piore and Sabel 1984). The buyer decides on the appropriate division of labor, imposes design and quality standards, sets delivery schedules convenient for himself, and establishes piece work rates. Unless multiple household enterprises organize their own marketing, they will sooner or later be forced into similar arrangements, losing their autonomy and, indeed, much of their cooperative character as well. Within a very short time, they will turn into proto-capitalist micro-enterprises.

To retain their integrity as part of the cooperative household economy, MHEs must associate into larger entities and, in this new form, struggle to establish themselves in the market (Egana n.d.).[12] Associations may be required at both barrio and city-wide levels. Through a system of cooperative stores, for example, or through cooperatively organized production ensembles, some of the essential features of the cooperative household sector can be preserved.[13] Even a change of scale, however, will tend to alter the relations of production from non-hierarchical solidarity at the base to relations articulated through the nexus of the market. Still, it is only by associating among themselves that MHEs can hope to preserve the essentials of cooperation, creating possibilities beyond the horizon of mere survival. We have no knowledge of the extent of associative relations in Latin American barrios, and the subject calls for thorough investigation.

3. Backward Linkages: Solidarity Relations and Social Mobilization

The new barrio movements represent a collective response to the deepening economic crisis in Latin America. A coalescence of diverse household strategies, they represent a new form of collective action. This much was already evident in the early 1980s. Writing of the Christian Base Communities (*Communidades Eclesiais de Base*) which were then beginning to be active in Sao Paulo and elsewhere in Brazil, Paul Singer found them to be "rooted in an ideological position completely different from that which inspired the movements of the previous decade" (1982, 290). He went on to explain:

Instead of assuming that the needs of the peripheral barrios and impoverished populations stem from the negligence of the authorities, and that this might be overcome by an adequate mobilization of interested parties, privation is attributed to the very social organization inherent in capitalism. This, according to the CEBs, tends to trap individuals within the narrow circle of their personal interests and to prevent the development of a mutual solidarity which might unify the population and enable it to divide the fruits of its common efforts in a more equitable manner.

The point of departure places an extremely high value on the participation of all members in the life of the Community as also in the protest movements which it comes to inspire. The exchange of votes for concessions on the part of the authorities--which is the essence of the so-called *politica de clientel* or clientelist politics--is from the point of view of this ideology, immoral at best. Access to public services can only reinforce a system which is responsible for the injustices in the first place (ibid).

As this passage suggests, the Latin American barrio movement may represent much more than an act of sheer desperation in the face of economic decline and massive unemployment. It is making a larger claim, which Singer calls "unity in self-help," which demands a new relationship between the local state and a self-organized citizenry. At the same time the new movements, building on traditional reciprocity networks, display an extended sociability. Ivan Illich spoke of it as the *convivial society* and imagined it as a utopian alternative to capitalist relations (Illich 1975). What is novel about the extended sociability that we actually encounter is that it grows out of working people's experience with active intervention in their own environments to ensure the collective provisioning of basic survival needs. Some form of social learning is evidently taking place, and the experience of autonomous community-based action is having positive effects on its participants, changing their very perceptions of the world and the possibilities it holds for them.

Nevertheless, organized citizen movements do not, as a rule, occur spontaneously, requiring instead the catalytic action of an outside agency. In some instances, the agent may be a political party. In the case of Brazil's Ecclesiastical Base Communities, it is the radical wing of the Catholic Church (Mainwaring 1986). This has been true of barrio movements in Chile as well, where the Church has played a key role in organizing local communities, strengthening their capacity to resist.

Though the Church has been the most visible, it has not been the only or even the principal agent of social mobilization. In Colombia, for example, it is the state itself which, through its recently formed Institute of Natural Resources and the Environment (INDERENA), is promoting new forms of self-reliant community action.[14] Elsewhere, research collectives have taken a leading role. In Bogotá, for example, the Center for Research and Popular Education (CINEP) declares its purpose to be "to contribute to changing the country's social, political, and economic structures through action research and popular education" (personal communication, Manuel Uribe Ramón, April 1986). Within the last ten years, research institutes similar to CINEP have proliferated throughout the continent. Outside intervention of whatever origin raises fundamental questions concerning leadership, financial support, and the long-term goals of intervention. Very little systematic information exists on any of these topics. We can therefore do no more than specify some of the questions that need to be asked.

A. **Leadership**
    1) Is it the objective of the intervention to encourage the development of an "organic" leadership from within the community itself, or to exert control indirectly through accommodationist community leaders? In other words, does the mobilizing agent aspire to lead the community himself or to plan to withdraw from the effort in the measure that an effective local leadership emerges?
    2) Is the leadership style personalistic in the traditional manner or broadly democratic, participatory, and inclusive?
    3) Are women encouraged to take a leading part in the mobilization effort? Is their presence in leadership councils in proportion to their numbers in the community?
    4) What methods of community organization are being used? Are practical problems being addressed as a matter of priority? Is due attention being given to the question of collective self-empowerment and therefore to a dynamic process of change involving social learning, or is the emphasis instead on traditional demand-making (*reivindicaciones*)?

B. **Financial Support**
    1) How much outside support is made available to community action groups, from what sources, and for what purposes?
    2) Are counterpart resources being generated, and in what proportion to outside assistance?
    3) Is aid made available in the form of grants, loans, or payments in kind, such as services, materials, etc.? How much accountability is required in the use of external resources?
    4) Does external financial assistance lead to new forms of patronage and dependency?

5) Is there an expectation that local projects will ultimately become self-supporting and, if so, how? Over what period of time?

C. Ultimate Objectives of the Intervention

No external intervention is ever naive in the sense of being completely disinterested in the outcome. Objectives may be simple or complex and are, at any rate, always difficult to ascertain. Often they have to be imputed, since self-declarations may be designed to mislead. An objective of social pacification, for example, might never be publicly declared, though it may well be the major motivation behind a specific external intervention. Other possible objectives include providing for the basic survival needs of the population, progressing towards a convivial society with some autonomy vis-a-vis the state, or creating new social relations of production with a view towards a future democratic socialism in a productive economy beyond the limits of simple reproduction.

The limited evidence we now have, chiefly from Brazil, Chile, Peru and Colombia, is that a great deal of effort is expended to create new relations of solidarity within the cooperative household sector of the barrio economy. Solidarity, mutual aid, and conviviality are the incentive goods the community offers in addition to the primary material benefits households can expect if they take part in the cooperative production of housing, local services, and commodities for sale.

Women are likely to be very active in community affairs and bring to them an organizational experience based on non-hierarchical relations, small groups, networks, dialogue, and mutual support. An intriguing question is whether this typically feminist style of social mobilization (Jagger 1983) carries over into the larger associative behavior required and the management of external market relations. It appears not to be the case, as men are likely to assume control whenever formal organizations emerge. Even so, important new roles for women and their newly won self-confidence and independence are having notable effects on gender relations within the household. In the longer term, they may well lead to a more assertive voice for women in the transformation of society and the local state.

4. Lateral Linkages and Political Practice: Transforming the Local State

Political articulations have typically been studied under the general category of urban social movements. The material interests defended by these movements tend to be narrowly defined, in the trade union manner, as housing, social infrastructure, and subsidies for transport and staple foods. When, in responding to popular pressure, the state would meet these demands, the movements soon subsided. In the specialized literature, urban social movements was merely a fashionable name for traditional interest politics.

In contrast to this a-spatial approach, we propose to make political practice a dimension of a territorially-based barrio politics. This should be done for three reasons: 1) self-reliant development, self-management, and claims for greater community autonomy have traditionally been identified with territorial politics; 2) the formation of barrio economies is the first essential step towards a trans-formation of the local state towards more decentralized, participatory structures; and 3) a territorial politics of the popular sectors is likely to have more staying power and a greater potential for change than either the interest politics dear to pluralists or the working class politics of the traditional left. With regard to the latter, the relative numbers of blue collar workers in modern factories and mining communities are so small that no significant action for structural change can be expected by organizing labor only at its place of work. Approximately half the workers in Latin American cities are now included in the informal and cooperative household sectors. Working, if at all, in hundreds of thousands of small busines-ses, this near majority of the population cannot be effectively organized *except at their place of residence*, which is increasingly becoming a place of production as well. The new class politics must be territorially defined.[15]

The step from the barrio economy to a politics of change is neither simple nor straightforward. A myriad microscopic *organizaciones económicas populares*, no matter how effective they might be in solving people's survival problems, do not necessarily lead to a transformative political practice. Lateral linkages must first be established among them, both within a given barrio and on a city-wide scale in barrio confederations, before they can gain the clout necessary to make a difference politically. They must also tie into progressive, politically organized forces -- political parties of the sort which do not yet exist in Latin America, with strong popular roots -- to gain a transformative vision beyond their own immediate interests and needs.[16] To translate economic interests into political practice, barrios need to step up their activism and political involvements to city, regional, and national levels.

The question of a territorially-based progressive politics of this sort has received little attention so far (but see Bitar, 1985). These are some of the more pertinent questions for future research:

a. Siege mentality vs. open democracy

It is sometimes said that the new barrio movement, for example in Brazil, flourished as a protest movement during the period of dictatorship, but now, with the return of democracy, is losing much of its earlier drive (see, for example, Mainwaring, 1986, who is careful to distinguish church-led communities from the barrio movement in general). According to this account, barrio politics is particularly intense when the popular sectors are placed under siege by the state. Normal bourgeois politics tends not only to be more populist but also allows individuals to seek satisfactions outside collective action, for example, through political parties or the traditional *política de clientela* mentioned by Paul Singer. If there were any truth in this, our arguments for a territorial politics would need to be sharply modified. But on the strength of admittedly limited evidence, we are inclined to doubt the hypothesis which strongly links barrio movements to a siege mentality. To deal successfully with structural crisis, bourgeois politics in Latin America must yield to a participatory and open democratic style rooted in the politics of the barrio (Friedmann, 1986). The simple reason for this is the demographics of the situation. From one-third to one-half the urban labor force subsists outside the state and corporate sectors and has no prospect of being incorporated into a national development program except on the strength of a revitalized barrio economy. The evidence from Brazil's Ecclesiastical Base Communities, corroborated in Peru, Colombia, and Chile, suggests that this hypothesis may have more validity than the first. Barrio movements throughout the region are beginning to assert comprehensive claims for change in the name of economic, political, and human rights. Further research, however, is required to lend support to or refute this hypothesis.

b. The barrio economy: Articulating modes of production and political culture

The barrio economy, as we have shown, is an expression of complex economic and social relations, involving formal, informal, and cooperative household sectors. Contrary to neoclassical economics, which separates economic functions from residentiary functions, the political economy approach sees them as interactive within the same territorial space. Production for exchange is directly related to household production for use and the solidarity relations of the barrio. To understand collective political responses at the barrio level, therefore, we must first gain a better understanding of how the articulation of different modes of production (formal capitalist, informal capitalist, cooperative, and household), particularly in barrios, is effectuated, and how this articulation, in turn, is reflected in the political behavior of the barrio, its collective strength, leadership, activism, and so forth. In part, this has to do with the assessment of collective experience by individual households: are new ideologies becoming accepted that reinforce a self-conscious political role? What new traits of political culture are becoming part of the normal political behavior? How much social learning is going on and what, specifically, is being learned? These questions are fundamental to our claim that the new barrio movement has the potential of becoming a counter-hegemonic movement, prefiguring social relations that may become more generally accepted throughout civil society, and which ultimately has the capacity not only to resist the state more effectively but also to transform it.

c. State control vs. collective self-empowerment

The tendency to formalize the informal sector by extending state assistance to micro-enterprises, as in Colombia and Brazil, has already been noted. Moreover, the idea seems to be gaining in popularity. A bill currently before the U.S. Congress, the Micro Enterprise Promotion Act, H.R. 4894, directs the U.S. Agency for International Development to commit a portion of its development assistance to the promotion of micro-enterprises owned by both the urban and rural poor. Assisting micro-enterprises may be officially seen as "encouraging individual entrepreneurs." In a more critical perspective, assistance to the informal sector may also be seen as the state seeking to extend its control over a large proto-capitalist sector, and thus help to ensure the reproduction of the system-in-dominance.

The question now is whether a similar process of formalization, involving control and cooperation, is not also in store for the cooperative household sector of the barrio economy. The answer is not immediately apparent. The barrio economy has considerable capacity for resistance, especially where it is closely linked into countervailing structures at the city level. The state, for its part, may see the cooperative household sector as less of a threat than its alternatives and may therefore treat it rather gently. But even where the state comes in ostensibly to assist the cooperative sector, the resulting empowerment of barrio residents may outweigh the state's ability to control its performance. The presence of the state is inevitably problematical. But it does not automatically spell the doom of counter-hegemonic praxis. As Laclau and Mouffe (1985) point out, hegemony is itself a terrain of struggle.

d. Organization vs. spontaneity in social movements

This question brings us to the limits not only of barrio politics but also of the present research agenda. If planning for open democracy is indeed a necessary option for Latin America, it is likely that political parties will begin to compete for the favors of barrio voters, seeking to capture barrio movements and hitch them to their own purposes. They may, when in power, set up political bosses in the barrios, as the PRI has done in Mexico (Veliz, 1978). Or they may try to establish a political base within the barrio, as the Chilean parties of the Center and Left did during the Frei government in the 1960s. If this were to happen again, would the community autonomy be undermined? Would it divide and fragment the popular sector? Or would it provide citizens with new channels for carrying their movement to the national scene? Opinions on these questions are divided, carrying forward an old argument within classical Marxism. On one side, there are those who, following Gramsci, strongly favor the politicization of urban social movements (Castells, 1983; Laclau and Mouffe, 1985). There are others who, like Piven and Cloward (1979), in a faint echo of Rosa Luxemburg, assert that only the spontaneous eruptions of citizen anger will bring results benefitting the urban poor. We side with those who argue that social movements must be organized politically, but the question itself requires closer attention than it has received and lends itself particularly well to comparative research.

Toward an International Agenda for Collaborative Research

The conceptual framework sketched here for understanding the movement for social and political empowerment in the barrios of large Latin American cities is a first attempt to make sense out of the welter of empirical information that has become available over the last half dozen or so years. As events continue to develop, and as the framework is tested in specific settings, there will almost certainly arise a need to revise it. An attempt has been made to identify the many facets and dimensions of a phenomenon of historical proportions--the emergence in the region of the so-called popular sectors of civil society as an active force for social transformation. This social movement, if it can be called that, may be seen as a response of working class households to a persistent economic crisis whose most obvious characteristic is the lack of productive work for as much as 50% of the urban labor force. But the response has taken many forms and reflects, among other things, the severity of the economic crisis, the nature of the political regime in particular countries, political culture and traditions, and the specific local situation. It is extremely difficult to systematically relate these structural conditions to particular forms of civil action; nevertheless, their importance must be recognized. It is because of the variability in the specific national and local conditions that a broadly comparative, international approach to the research is essential. A great deal of relevant research is already underway in Latin America, sponsored primarily by private research institutes such as the Academía de Humanismo Cristiano in Chile, DESCO in Peru, CINEP in Colombia, CEDES in Argentina, and CEDAC, along with other centers, in

Brazil.[17] Although studying the same broad phenomenon, researchers in different countries are not in close communication with each other nor with scholars in Western Europe and North America. Yet it is obvious that it is only through the constant exchange of information and insight, and the persistent critical review of work in progress, that an adequate understanding of the urban survival economy and the progressive self-empowerment of the popular sectors can be gained in all of its rich diversity, and that its ultimate significance for political order and national development can be grasped. In the interest of such future collaboration, we propose to structure research around five focal concepts.

a. *The household economy.* Individual households may be viewed as social units engaged in the production of their life (see below) and thus as being both rational and political in the pursuit of their own objectives. As the smallest social unit having some stability over time, households can be studied in terms of their social, political, economic, cultural, and spatial relations within the micro-environment of the household itself as well as with other households and the world outside. In the context of household strategies for survival and material betterment, these five dimensions must each be separately taken into account. Key research areas are the relations of gender within the household and women's struggles against traditional relations of male dominance.

b. *The territorial economy of the barrio.* Household relations are initially constrained by distance. Household networks, therefore, are found primarily within an easy walking radius from one's home. This fact is decisive for the formation of the barrio economy as the first step up from the household economy itself. Within the barrio, the micro-enterprises of the informal sector and the multiple household enterprises of the cooperative sector are dominant. What distinguishes the barrio from all other territorially-based economies, however, is the remarkable coexistence within it of both market and non-market (reciprocity) relations. Though in many ways complementary, these two forms of relation stand in fundamental contradiction to each other. Success in the market place tends to undercut the more fragile relations of reciprocity and mutual trust. These relationships are best studied at two levels: that of the household itself, with a focus on its strategies of survival, and that of the cooperative sector, with emphasis on production linkages forward into markets, backwards into the community, and laterally to other production units in the formation of cooperative and other worker-controlled associations.

c. *The self-production of life.* This concept is introduced for three reasons. First, as a counterweight to the predominant perception of households as more or less passive consuming units engaged in the art of spending money; second, because it allows us to accept direct production for use (for the most part work performed by women) as regular work; and third, because it raises dramatically the question of collective self-empowerment. The self-production of life leads to household strategies for the allocation and use of its available resource of time, energy, skills, and knowledge. At the barrio level, it conduces to political claims for democratic self-governance, participatory decision-making and the formation of cooperative associations.

d. *Collective self-empowerment.* This concept focuses on the relative access of household, multiple household enterprises, and other collective units within the barrio to the many bases of social power: time above survival needs, a secure activity space, social organization and networks, knowledge, skills and information, tools of production, and financial resources. In a household perspective, development is largely about empowerment; about gaining greater access to these bases of social power in successive rounds of individual and/or collective struggle. The latter, however, requires social mobilization as a decisive step towards self-empowerment and raises a number of relevant questions for research, such as the role of external agents, contending ideologies, alternative leadership styles, and the choice of strategy.

e. *Political practice and the local state.* For individual working class households, the room for successful maneuver tends to be restricted. More choice is possible when households engage in political practice. What seems to have been set alongside the old Latin American politics of *revindicaciones* is the assertion of fundamental citizen rights for basic necessities, empowerment, self-governance, political participation, and women's rights. Coinciding as it does with the current preoccupation of the national state with crisis management, this "politics of claims" (Peattie and Rein, 1983) is beginning to have positive results, as the state is forced to take seriously old arguments for decentralization. Especially significant is the concurrent and increasingly insistent demand for an inclusive democratic order and the softening of hierarchical relations. This movement toward democratization requires a full-scale political analysis, with a view toward restructuring the local state as it encounters an increasingly self-confident barrio movement pressing its claims for greater autonomy, state assistance, and civil rights.[18]

This brief summary clearly shows that the study of the new civic (popular) activism in its territorial, economic, political, and cultural dimensions is no small assignment. Clearly, it cannot be done by one individual working alone or even by a single research unit, but requires long-term collaboration and comparative research over a period of years. This paper therefore closes with a plea for such collaboration among research centers and individuals in countries where the movement appears to have progressed the furthest, including Brazil, Argentina, Chile, Peru, Colombia, and Mexico.

Conclusion

The object of this essay has been to propose a conceptual frame for the study of civil society in Latin America, particularly its popular sector, from a perspective of self-renewal and emancipation. We have argued that the empirical focus of such a study must be the barrio economy as the center of possible counter-hegemonic praxis, that is, as a potentially political praxis, neither colonized by capital nor subservient to the state. The transformative model we have in mind has as its main theoretical terms the self-production of life, taking the household as the smallest unit of production, and collective self-empowerment, meaning the process through which households gain greater access to the several bases of social power. The third term in our model, or the movement from social to political power, remains for now little more than a possibility; the evidence for its existence is still very thin.

Why, of all possible objects for the study of civil society, have we settled on the barrio economy? There are two primary reasons. The first is empirical. The barrio economy internalizes a great deal of what we have called the self-production of life. To study the articulation of market and non-market forces in the self-production of life, the barrio economy is preferable as an object of study to, say, the household economy or, worse yet, the fate of isolated individuals. As a territorial economy, the barrio internalizes more articulations than the household sector and has the ever-present possibility of becoming a political subject, a self-conscious actor in the public domain.

The second reason is praxis-related and pragmatic. In Latin America, factory labor in the large-scale, modern sector is a relatively small and, in some countries, declining fraction of the total work force. If civil society is to be mobilized for political ends, the factory cannot thus remain as the primary locus. As the home terrain for the self-production of life, the barrio economy is the more inclusive alternative. It brings in the long-term unemployed, the young first-time job seekers, women without steady remunerative work, the workers active in the informal (non-enumerated) sector, older folks, and even small children. In short, it includes *the entire working class sector of civil society* with their multiple needs and concerns, not only for "better wages and working conditions" but also for a better, more facilitative environment as the setting for the self-production of life. The possibility of a counter-hegemonic mobilization in the popular barrios of Latin American cities is certainly only a latent possibility at this time, though there is growing evidence for it from a wide spread of cities, from Sao Paulo to Santiago to Lima and Medellín. The actual extent of mobilization is not known. In a fluid struggle, the zone of battle is indeterminate and subject to rapid fluctuations. At least we know, though, that a struggle is underway. A unified struggle on many fronts, it will decide the future of the continent.

Acknowledgements

We are especially grateful for the many thoughtful comments we received on an earlier draft of this essay. At a meeting convened at the University of California, Los Angeles in October 1986, an earlier draft was the focus of an extended critical discussion of the subject. Participants included Manuel Castells, Lisa Fuentes, Larissa Lomnitz, David Lopez, Lisa Peattie, Keith Pezzoli, Charles Reilly, Francisco Sabatini, John Walton, and Maurice Zeitlin. Additional extensive comments were received from José Luis Coraggio. To all of them, our thanks. And of course the usual caveats apply. Whatever faults remain, they are clearly our joint responsibility.

Notes

1. The term civil society frequently appears in discussions of social trends, especially by Latin American authors, and presumably refers, leaning on Gramsci's (1971) writings, to a realm of action that is at least potentially autonomous of both the state and corporate economy. With the urban household as its central institution, civil society can be further divided into sectors and classes. For the present, we shall use a simple division into "bourgeois" and "popular." This paper will be primarily concerned with the latter. By focusing on civil society, the emphasis is placed on the domestic sphere of "reproduction" (which is broadened by referring to it as the "production of life"), where it is the woman and not generally the man of the household who plays the privileged role. There are other implications of this choice of concepts of both a theoretical and practical nature, which will later become apparent.

2. For the best and most recent treatment of Latin American social movements in English, see Slater (1985).

3. In their book on the poverty struggles of the 1960s, Piven and Cloward (1979) maintain just the opposite. Only the spontaneous uprisings of the poor, they argue, confronting bourgeois order with the specter of anarchy, are able to produce gains for the poor. These gains, they would be the first

to admit, are a far cry from the "structural transformation" proclaimed and hoped for by many Latin American intellectuals, but they are the only thing the poor can reasonably expect.

4.   The term "development" is intended to cover normative dimensions that are broader than simple economic growth or expansion in the volume of production. Specifically, it is meant to hint at an equitable distribution of income and positive gain in social indicators. In some of its meanings, however, it comes perilously close to the 19th century idea of Progress (always capitalized) and may well be destined to suffer a similar fate. It might indeed be safer to speak exclusively of economic growth, conceived as the "engine" of development, but development is the ideological coin of discourse. A related term is "modernization," but its meaning is even more slippery than that of development and seems ultimately to be derived from the cultural experience of advanced capitalist countries in Western Europe and North America.

5.   Peru is the one exception to this statement. Its military regime for at least a number of years was social reformist without, however, destroying the power base of the traditional elites.

6.   For an argument along this line, with specific reference to Nicaragua, see Coraggio (1985).

7.   Although the focus of this research is urban, there is growing evidence that the phenomenon takes place in semi-rural and rural settings as well.

8.   The concept of informal economy has become increasingly unpopular, and many scholars counsel against using it (see, for example, Breman, 1985). Two reasons are usually given. First, dualistic formulations, of which the informal/formal dichotomy is one, can be grossly misleading by polarizing discussion around "ideal types," and second, because the informal category is imprecise. We accept these criticisms. Still, the term "informal" (alternatively unenumerated or unofficial) can be quite useful to distinguish a category of economic activities which are small-scale, market-oriented and labor-intensive. For a recent summary on research, see Castells and Portes (1986).

9.   Not shown here are investments in its own sphere of activities, in education, and in political action.

10. Hardy and Razeto define *organizaciones económicas populares* as follows:

> In general terms we understand by "popular economic organizations" the different forms of association which are formed in order to confront the problem of subsistence or to satisfy specific economic needs among the popular sectors (especially among those having lower incomes) in order to develope specific economic activities or functions, such as the production and marketing of goods and services, the procurement, supply or consumption of daily necessities for their associated membership, etc. In general, they consist of small groups of people who share the same situation and similar problems [of deprivation]; find themselves linked by residing in the same firm, by belonging to the same religious community, or be sharing the same ideological persuasion; and who decide to confront their immediate problems [of survival] jointly through an action which is meant to lead to a solution of these problems. (Hardy and Razeto, 1986, 162; our translation.)

Among OEPs, Hardy and Razeto identify the following general types: workshops (*talleres laborales*), organizations of the unemployed (*organizaciónes de cesantes*), organizations for the satisfaction of basic consumption needs, housing organizations, and other community service organizations. About 20% of Santiago's working class population participates in one or more of these self-help organizations.

11. Additional differences include hierarchical organization and individual decision-making: patriarchy and bossism; the extensive use of family labor (self-exploitation); unequal pay for equal work; competitive behavior; and profit-orientation.

12. Logically, there is a prior step to association. Before they can associate, MHEs must first consolidate and stabilize their business. This may require special training in the different tasks of self-management, stabilizing cash flow, securing regular market outlets, etc.

13. A famous example of cooperative production which may be relevant to the Latin American case is Mondragon in the Basque country of Spain. See Oakeshott (1978), Thomas and Logan (1982), and Jackall and Levin (1984).

14. In October 1985, INDERENA initiated a so-called Campaña Verde or Green Campaign, aiming to contribute to the development of a process of social

participation. The objective of such a campaign is, in the long run, to go beyond ecological issues by promoting self-help initiatives of the local community, developing mechanisms for local democracy, and consolidating the empowerment of citizens. The idea is to create the mechanisms which will allow the organized community to take responsibility of all the natural and social aspects that make up its environment (Ungar and Barrera, 1986).

As of January 1986, 280 Green Councils (*Consejos Verdes*) had been set up by different municipalities in Colombia. Although INDERENA is initiating the campaign, the project must be undertaken by civil society itself. INDERENA is prepared to give technical advice and share its modest resources, while local authorities constitute the bridge to help such resources reach their destination: civil society and the local community, which must take in their own hands, in an autonomous way, the control, organization and management of the environment.

15. For a parallel argument relating to U.S. urban politics, see Katznelson (1981) and for Australia, Sandercock (1985). Because ethnic divisions are less of a factor in Latin American political life than in North America, the coalescence of barrio-based social movements in the major Latin American cities is conceivable, whereas in the U.S. it is not.

16. The need for a new form of political practice in Latin America should be fairly evident to those who follow the politics of the region. The majority of parties are elite-based and lack political organization at the grassroots.

17. Academía de Humanismo Cristiano, Catedral 1063, Piso 5, Santiago, Chile; DESCO (Centro de Estudios y Promoción del Desarrollo), Av. Salaverry 1945, Lima 14, Peru; CINEP (Fundación Centro de Investigación y Educación Popular), Apartado Aereo 25916, Bogotá, D.E., Colombia; CEDES (Centro de Estudios de Estado y Sociedad), Av. Pueyrredón 510, 7° Piso, 1032 Buenos Aires, Argentina; CEDAC (Centro de Estudos e Documentaçao para Açao Communitaria), Rua dos Ingleses 325, Bela Vista, 01329 Sao Paulo, S.P., Brazil.

18. For a case study of barrio politics carried out to the city-wide level where it claimed the right to participate in policies affecting *favelados* see Rezende Afonso and Azevedo (1985).

References

Aguilar, Alonso M. (1985) Crisis and development strategies in Latin America, *Development and Peace, 6*, 17-32.

Betto, Frei (1984) O que é communidade eclesial de base. 5th ed., Sao Paulo: Ed. Brasilienese.

Bitar, Sergio (1985) The nature of the Latin American crisis, *Cepal Review, 27* (December), 159-164.

Borsotti, Carlos A. (1978) Notas sobre la familia como unidad socioeconomica. *Cuadernos de la CEPAL.* Santiago (Chile): CEPAL/ILPES.

Breman, Jan (1985) A dualistic labour system? A critique of the 'informal sector' concept. In R. Bromley (Ed.), *Planning for Small Enterprises in Third World Countries.* New York: Pergamon Press. (Orig. 1976)

Bruneau, Thomas C. (1982) *The Church in Brazil.* Austin: University of Texas Press.

Capecchi, V., and A. Pesce (1984) Reconsidering diversity to contend with dualism, *Ecodevelopment News, 31.* Paris: International Research Center on Ecodevelopment and Development.

Castells, Manuel (1976) *Movemientos Sociales Urbanos in America Latina: Tendencias Historicas y Problemas Teoricas.* Lima: Pontífica Universidad Católica.

Castells, Manuel (1983) *The City and the Grassroots.* London: E. Arnold.

Castells, Manuel and Alejandro Portes (1986) World underneath: The origins, dynamics, and effects of the informal economy. Written for presentation at the Conference on the Study of the Informal Sector, Harper's Ferry, VA, October 2-6.

Corragio, José Luis (1985) Social movements and revolution: The case of Nicaragua. In D. Slater (Ed.), *New Social Movements and the State in Latin America.* Amsterdam: CEDLA (Center for Latin American Research and Documentation), 203-232.

Corragio, José Luis (1986a) *Nicaragua: Revolution and Democracy.* Boston: Allen and Unwin.

Corragio, José Luis (1986b) Economics and politics in the transition to socialism: Reflections on the Nicaragua experience. In Richard R. Fagen, Carmen Diana Deere, and José Luis Corragio (Eds.), *Transition and Development: Problems of Third World Socialism.* New York: Monthly Review Press.

Edy Chonchol, Maria (1984) Unofficial sector and social creativity in Chile and Brazil, *Ecodevelopment News, 31* (December), 25-30.

Egana, Rodrigo (n.d.) *De Taller a Empresa de Trabajadores: La Experienca de Servatec.* Santiago (Chile): Academía de Humanismo Cristiano.

Evers, Tilman (1985) Identity: The hidden side of new social movements in Latin America. In D. Slater (Ed.), *New Social Movements and the State in Latin America.* Amsterdam: CEDLA (Center for Latin American Research and Documentation), 43-72.

Fass, Simon (forthcoming) *The Political Economy of Survival.* Manuscript, Hubert Humphrey Institute of Public Affairs, University of Minnesota.

Friedmann, John (1986) Planning in Latin America: From Technocratic Illusion to Open Democracy. GSAUP Discussion Paper 204.

Friedmann, John (1987) *Planning in the Public Domain: From Knowledge to Action.* Princeton: Princeton University Press.

Geisse, Guillermo (1986) Desarrollo de ciudades medianas a travel del sector de sobreviviencia, *Revista Interamericana de Planificacion, 20*(80) 62-77.

Goldrich, D., R.B. Pratt, and C.R. Schuller (1967-68) The political integration of lower-class urban settlements in Chile and Peru, *Studies in International Development, 3,* 1-22.

Gómez-Hermosillo, Rogelio M. (1986) La Iglesia del lado del pueblo? CEB's y MUP in la región metropolitana, *El Cotidiano (Cd. de Mexico), 2,* 11, 54-61.

Guimaraes, Roberto P. (1986) Cooperativismo y participación popular: Nuevas consideraciones respecto de un viejo tema, *Revista de la Cepal* (28) (April), 181-194.

Gramsci, Antonio (1971) *Selections from the prison notebooks,* Q. Hoare and G. Nowell Smith (Eds.), London.

Hardy, Clarisa (1984) *Los Talleres Artesanales de Conchali.* Santiago (Chile): Academía de Humanismo Cristiano. Colección de Experiencias Populares.

Hardy, Clarisa (1985) Estrategias organizadas de subsistencia: Los sectores populares frente a sus necesidades en Chile. Documento de Trabajo 41. Santiago: Academía de Humanismo Cristiano, Programa de Economía del Trabajo.

Hardy, Clarisa (1986) *Hambre and Dignidad = Ollas Comunes.* Santiago (Chile): Programa de Economía de Trabajo (PET) Academía de Humanismo Cristiano. Colección de Experiencias Populares.

Hardy, Clarisa and Luis Razeto (1986) Sector informal y concertación social. (source unknown)

Hirschman, Albert O. (1984) *Getting Ahead Collectively: Grassroots Experiences in Latin America.* New York: Pergamon Press

Holmes (1986) The organization and location of production subcontracting. In Allen J. Scott and Michael Storper (Eds.), *Production, Work, Territory: The Geographical Anatomy of Industrial Capitalism.* Boston: Allen and Unwin.

Illich, Evan (1975) *Tools for Conviviality.* London: Fontana/Collins.

Jackall, Robert and Henry M. Levin (Eds.) (1984) *Worker Cooperatives in America.* Berkeley: University of California Press.

Jacobi, Pedro (1985) Movimentos sociais urbanos e a crise: Da explosao social a participação popular, *Politica e Administração, 1*(2) (July-September), 223-238.

Jaggar, Allison M. (1983) *Feminist Politics and Human Nature.* Totowa, N.J.: Rowan and Allanheld.

Katznelson, Ira (1981) *City Trenches: Urban Politics and the Patterning of Class in the United States.* New York: Pantheon.

Laclau, Ernesto and Chantal Mouffe (1985) *Hegemony and Socialist Strategy: Towards a Radical Democratic Politics.* London: Verso.

Linz, Juan J. and Alfred Stepan (Eds.) (1986) *The Breakdown of Democratic Regimes: Latin America.* Baltimore: The Johns Hopkins Press.

Lomnitz, Larissa Adler (1977) *Networks and Marginality: Life in a Mexican Shantytown.* New York: Academic Press.

Mainwaring, Scott (1986) *The Catholic Church and Politics in Brazil, 1916-1985.* Stanford, CA: Stanford Univesity Press.

Max-Neef, Manfred (1985) Another development under repressive rule, *Development Dialogue (Uppsala),* (1), 30-55.

Max-Neef, Manfred et al. (1986) Desarollo a escala humano: Una opción para el futuro. *Development Dialogue (Uppsala),* Special number.

Molina, Humberto G. and Carlos Arturo Henao R. (1986) *Censo Nacional de Proyectos Asociativos de Vivienda.* Bogotá: CPU - Universidad de los Andes.

Murillo, Gabriel and Morica Lanzetta de Pardo (1984) La articulación entre el sector informal y el sector formal de la economía urbana: El caso de Bogotá. In *Clacso, Ciudades y Sistemsa Urbanos Economía Informal y Desorden Espacial.* Buenos Aires: CLACSO

Oakeshott, Robert (1978) *The Case for Workers' Co-ops.* Boston: Routledge and Kegan Paul.

Pease García, Henry (1986) Experiencias para democratizar la gestión de la ciudad. Manuscript. Washington, D.C.: The Woodrow Wilson Center.

Peattie, Lisa and Martin Rein (1983) *Women's Claims: A Study in Political Economy.* New York: Oxford University Press.

Piore, Michael and Charles F. Sabel (1984) *The Second Industrial Divide: Possibilities for Prosperity.* New York: Basic Books.

Piven, Frances Fox and Richard A. Cloward (1979) *Poor People's Movements: Why they Succeed, How they Fail.* New York: Vintage Books.

Polanyi, Karl (1977) *The Livelihood of Man.* New York: Academic Press.

Portes, Alejandro (1984) El sector informal: Definicion, controversias, relaciones con el desarrollo nacional. In *Ciudades y Sistemas Urbanos: Economía Informal y Desorden Espacial.* Buenos Aires: CLACSO.

Razeto, Luis et al. (1983) *La Organizaciones Económicas Populares.* Santiago: Academía de Cristianismo Humano.

Razeto, Luis (1984) *Economía de Solidaridad y Mercado Democratico*, Vol. 1. Santiago: Academía de Cristianismo Humano.

Razeto, Luis (1985) *Las Empresas Alternativas*. Santiago: Academía de Cristianismo Humano. Programa de Economia del Trabajo.

Reicher Madeira, Felicia (1986) Los jovenes en el Brasil: Antiguos supuestos y nuevos derroteros, *Revista de la Cepal, 29* (August), 57-80.

Rezende Alfonso, Mariza and Sérgio de Azevedo (1985) Cidade, poder público e movimento de favelados. Rio de Janeiro (UNU - Projeto Movimentos Sociais na América Latina).

Ross, David P. and Peter J. Usher (1986) *From the Roots Up: Economic Development as if Community Mattered.* Croton-on-the-Hudson (New York): The Bootstrap Press.

Sabatini, Francisco (1986) Knowledge for planning: Marginality theories in Latin America, manuscript. UCLA, Graduate School of Architecture and Urban Planning.

Sanchez León, Abelardo (1986) Lima y los hijos del desorden, manuscript. Lima: DESCO. Washington, D.C.: The Woodrow Wilson Center.

Sandercock, Leonie (1985) The importance of place and a politics of place: From Wollongong to Bondi Beach. Paper presented at the Conference on Place and Place-Making, Melbourne, Victoria, Australia.

Schmink, Marianne (1984) Household economic strategies: Review and research agenda, *Latin American Research Review, 19*(3), 87-101.

Scott, James C. (1976) *The Moral Economy of the Peasant: Rebellion and Subsistence in Southeast Asia.* New Haven: Yale University Press.

Singer, Paul (1982) Neighborhood Movements in Sao Paulo. In Helen Safa (Ed.), *Towards a Political Economy of Urbanization in Third World Countries.* Delhi: Oxford University Press.

Singer, Paul and Vinicius Caldeira Brandt (Eds.) (1982) *Sao Paulo: O Povo em Movimento.* 3rd ed. Petropolis: Vozes Ltda.

Slater, David (Ed.) (1985) *New Social Movements and the State in Latin America.* Amsterdam: CEDLA (Center for Latin American Research and Documentation).

Strassmann, W. Paul (1986) Types of neighbors and home-based enterprises: Evidence from Lima, Peru, manuscript. Forthcoming, *Urban Studies.*

Sunkel, Osvaldo (1985) *America Latina y la Crisis Económica Internacional: Ocho Tesis y una Propuesta.* Buenos Aires: HEL. Colección Cuadernos del RIAL.

Tendler, Judith (1983) *What to Think about Cooperatives: A Guide from Bolivia.* Rosslyn, VA: The Inter-American Foundation.

Thomas, Hank T. and Chris Logan (1982) *Mondragon: An Economic Analysis.* Boston: Allen and Unwin.

Ungar, Elizabeth and Cristina Barrera (1986) Participación popular y Ecología: La Campaña Verde. Bogotá: Universitad de los Andes, Depto. de Ciencia Política.

Veliz-I, Carlos G. (1978) Amigos políticos o amigos sociales: The politics of putting someone in your pocket, *Human Organization, 37*(4), 368-377.

Vink, Nico (1985) Base communities and urban social movements: A case study of the metalworkers' strike 1980, Sao Bernardo, Brazil. In D. Slater (Ed.), *New Social Movements and the State in Latin America.* Amsterdam: CEDLA (Center for Latin American Research and Documentation), 95-126.

Williams, Raymond (1983) *The Year 2000.* New York: Pantheon.

CONCENTRATION AND SPECIALIZATION OF MANUFACTURING IN CORE AND PERIPHERAL CITIES DURING RAPID INDUSTRIALIZATION: KOREA, 1960-1970

David R. Meyer
Brown University

Kyonghee Min
Chung Bug University

Theories of systems of cities in less-developed nations -- modernization, ecological, dependency, and world-system -- have focused on increasing primacy and polarization of development in the core region. This study examines the change in manufacturing concentration and specialization of 31 Korean cities during the 1960s, a period of increasing primacy, polarized development, and rapid urban-industrial growth. A dramatic increase in concentration of most industries occurred in Seoul, the national metropolis, during the export industrial growth of the 1960s. Cities remained moderately specialized in various industries, but the individual specialties of cities changed and non-core cities grew rapidly. Core and peripheral cities exhibited few differences in specializations. Future research on systems of cities in developing nations, especially those which industrialize, needs to move beyond a focus on the national metropolis to consider the complexity of the entire system of cities.

The industrialization of Asian nations such as Korea, Malaysia, and Taiwan poses a challenge to existing theories of systems of cities in less developed nations. These theories can be divided into two groups: modernization and ecological theories; and dependency and world-system theories. Members of both groups claim that the early stages of national economic growth are characterized by polarized development (that is, the growing concentration of economic development in the core region) and by increasing primacy of the system of cities (that is, a growing percentage of the nation's urban population concentrated in the largest city) (Gilbert and Gugler, 1980:31-38; Richardson, 1977; Smith, 1985a).

Primacy is defined as the case when the largest city of a nation is disproportionately large relative to other cities (Walters, 1985:63). Because increasing primacy in less-developed nations has been associated typically with population and economic imbalances which can inhibit their development, researchers have attempted both to explain why primacy emerges and changes over time and to propose policies to counteract increasing primacy (Berry, 1971; Smith 1985a). The finding that primacy is not necessarily associated with level of economic development (that is, primacy may or may not occur in developed or less developed nations) has not deterred researchers from continuing to focus on primacy in less developed nations (Ettlinger, 1981, 1984).

The focus on primacy, however, does not adequately explain the dynamics of systems of cities in the newly industrializing Asian nations of Korea, Malaysia and Taiwan. They do not have highly primate city size distributions, and in each nation industrial cities grew which were not simply satellites of the national metropolis (Chan and Lian, 1984; Ho, 1978; Mills and Song, 1979; Pannell, 1973; Smith, et al., 1983; Tsai, 1984). The industrial dynamics of these cities have not been examined systematically. An analysis of their industrial change, as well as of the primate city and its satellites, therefore, will contribute to creating a broader theory of system of cities dynamics in developing nations.

This study examines change in manufacturing concentration and specialization in Korean cities during the 1960s, a period of increasing primacy and extraordinary urban-industrial growth. Research on city manufacturing in developing nations and on urban-industrial growth in Korea is reviewed. Changes in manufacturing concentration and specialization in Korean cities are then analyzed with data for 31 cities in 1960 and 1970. Three issues are addressed: 1) increasing concentration of industries in the national metropolis and its satellites; 2) industrial specialization of cities; and 3) specialization of cities in core versus the periphery. Finally, the theories of systems of cities dynamics in developing nations are reassessed. A revised theory might draw on the best insights of each (e.g., see Hawley, 1984; London, 1987).

City Manufacturing in Developing Nations

Although both groups of theories, modernization/ecological and dependency/world-system, provide different explanations of economic development or underdevelopment, their descriptions of early stages of systems of cities in developing nations are similar on several important points (Smith, 1985a). Under colonial rule the agglomeration of political, military and economic elites created a primate city. This primacy was exacerbated after independence because reliance on natural resource exports remained significant. Commodities were collected at one port (often the primate city) for export. Under government stimulus, import substitution industries expanded rapidly, and the concentrated market of the primate city was the optimal location for them. Continued transformation of export agriculture into a plantation wage-labor organizational form undermined traditional farming, and growth of import substitution industries undermined small-scale, local firms; the rural periphery, therefore, declined. Rural dwellers migrated to the primate city and its adjacent region (nation's core) because it had the most job opportunities. The result was increasing primacy of the system of cities and polarization of development in the core region.

Modernization researchers claim this is a normal feature of development which will lead eventually to the diffusion of development to the periphery and result in decreasing primacy and polarization reversal (Berry, 1971; Friedmann, 1966, 1973), but few examples of polarization reversal exist in developing nations (Richardson, 1980). In the absence of polarization reversal, however, modernization theorists have no basis for explaining the emergence of specialized industrial cities outside the core region of less-developed nations. This is because the ecological ideas of modernization theory are rooted in research on a highly developed nation, the United States, where population primacy does not exist. Ecologists use the term dominance to discuss the role of metropolises in the system of cities. It is a functional term which embodies the concepts both of control/coordination by large metropolises over economic exchange and of the importance of these metropolises in other economic activities. Manufacturing dominance, therefore, expresses the idea that metropolises are pivotal industrial centers, but this does not mean necessarily that most manufacturing is located in the largest metropolises (Boguc, 1950; Duncan and Lieberson, 1970; Duncan et al., 1960; Pred, 1966). At the same time, a significant number of small, specialized industrial cities exist (Kass, 1973; Wanner, 1977). Because these are characteristics of a highly developed nation, which presumably has experienced polarization reversal, most urban ecological research heretofore has not provided a basis for examining stages of increasing primacy in the systems of cities in developing nations. This, of course, is not a claim that ecological theory is irrelevant for urban research on developing nations; it has explicitly formed a basis for some research (see Hawley, 1971:265-315; London, 1987; Meyer, 1986; Nemeth and Smith, 1985).

Dependency and world-system researchers, in contrast to modernization and ecological researchers, view increasing primacy and polarized development as a result of an exploitative process by which developed nations extract surpluses from developing nations; polarization reversal is considered unlikely (Frank, 1967; Gilbert and Gugler, 1982; Smith, 1985a). Dependency researchers argue strongly that primacy is a long-term condition facing less-developed nations, whereas world-system researchers recognize this possibility, but stress also that less-developed nations exist in a more complex matrix of a capitalist world economy. These nations may experience different levels of development. For example, they may be semi-peripheral or peripheral, and internal forces may lead to urban development away from the primate city (Chase-Dunn, 1984; Gilbert and Gugler, 1982: 35-38; Nemeth and Smith, 1985). The cumulative effects of external and internal forces on the concentration of industries in the primate city and on industrial specialization of cities outside the core region, however, have not been specified systematically by world-system researchers.

The characteristics of city manufacturing in developing nations, as recognized by the different theoretical perspectives, can be summarized as follows. The modernization, dependency, and world-system paradigms agree that even if the level of primacy is not high, during the early stages of development import substitution industries concentrate increasingly in the national metropolis and secondarily in its satellites. This is associated with increasing primacy of population in the sense that an increasing proportion of the nation's urban population concentrates in the national metropolis. The national metropolis and its satellites have a greater percentage of their employment in manufacturing than smaller cities (Rondinelli, 1983). The latter may specialize in resource processing related to lumbering or mining (Alonso, 1971; Hackenberg and Hackenberg, 1971), but city specialization in non-resource processing industries away from the national metropolis, according to most researchers, seldom occurs during the import substitution stage.

None of the research paradigms systematically addresses the effect on a developing nation's cities of a shift to an export-manufacture economy. Several researchers, however, operating directly or indirectly in the world-system paradigm, but incorporating some ecological theory, argue that export industries can locate at all levels of the urban hierarchy (Nemeth and Smith, 1983, 1985; Santos, 1979). This presumably could result in a decreased concentration of industries in the national metropolis. The export industries may be owned by multinationals who obtain most commodity and service inputs within the firm and/or outside the nation, and government policies may encourage dispersal of export industries. In either case, export industries are oriented to location of factors of production such as natural resources or low-wage labor. The focus on industries of the core region, especially the primate city, hinders explanation of urban industrial growth in newly industrializing Asian nations such as Korea, Malaysia and Taiwan. An analysis of the change in concentration and specialization of industries in Korean cities, therefore, can contribute both to understanding changes in the systems of cities of these nations and to formulating a broader theory of systems of cities in developing nations.

Urban-Industrial Growth in Korea

Beginning in the late 1950s, Korea entered an era of rapid industrial growth. Its real gross national product grew at an annual rate of 4 percent from the mid-1950s to the early 1960s. The growth accelerated to 8 percent or more from the early 1960s to the mid-1970s; and it continued at almost 7 percent during the first half of the 1980s. Rapid industrialization was reflected in the dramatic rise in manufacturing as a percentage of gross domestic product; it increased from 11 percent in the mid-1950s to 35 percent in the early 1970s. By the mid-1980s, however, it had declined to 31 percent. Import substitution manufactures led the industrialization, but Korea switched to labor intensive export manufactures as the leading industrial sector by the late 1960s. During the 1970s, however, Korea switched its focus again. The heavy and chemical industries (ship-building, automobiles, steel and petrochemicals) were given strong support by the government. The jaebols (conglomerates) enhanced their growth dramatically, and some of them became multinationals. Initially, the industries were to be import substitution producers, but they were to be expanded to serve export markets. By the early 1980s they produced over 50 percent of all exports (Hasan, 1976; Kim, 1986; Kuznets, 1977, 1980; Mason, et al., 1980; Watanabe, 1972; Westphal, 1978). Korea's urbanization rate corresponded directly to its relative shift from agriculture into manufacturing. Its percent urban was 29, 43 and 57, respectively in 1960, 1970 and 1980 (Smith, et al., 1983).

Although Korea does not have a highly primate city size distribution (Mills and Song, 1979; Smith, et al., 1983; Song, 1981), most researchers agree that polarization processes were dominant during the 1960s. The percentage of the nation's urban population in the Seoul region increased sharply, and regional income disparities reached their peak. During the 1970s declines occurred in both the percentage of the nation's urban population in Seoul and regional income disparities. Manufacturing, however, concentrated increasingly in the Seoul and Busan regions between 1958 and 1977, but it deconcentrated within them. The industrial dispersal policies of the 1970s did not alter significantly long term relative concentration of industries except to increase the importance of southeastern Korea around Busan (Ho, 1980; Kim, 1978; Kwon, 1981; Lee, 1982; Mera, 1978; Nemeth and Smith, 1983, 1985; Park, 1981; Renaud, 1981; Rondinelli, 1984; Song, 1981).

Changes in manufacturing characteristics of Korean cities have not been examined in detail. Rondinelli (1983) studied total employment in cities, including agriculture, and concluded that manufacturing was a specialty of the largest cities in 1960; he did not examine 1970. By 1980 the percentage of manufacturing in most cities had increased significantly, and it was higher in the larger cities. He did not examine different types of industries, therefore, no evidence is available on the extent of and change in concentration and specialization of various industries in cities. Analysis of these changes during the 1960s, the first period of rapid industrial growth and a time of polarized development, would provide insights into city manufacturing concentration and specialization in newly industrializing nations.

Data

The data are drawn from 1 percent sample tapes of the Korean Population Censuses in 1960 and 1970. The 31 cities with 50,000 population or more in both 1960 and 1970 are included in the study. Based on three-digit SIC codes, most industries were aggregated into 13 groups. A few were eliminated because they could not be categorized meaningfully without creating a new group. It was decided not to create a large number of small groups because the focus is on those manufactures which were important in industrialization. A miscellaneous group was not used because it is too difficult to interpret. Because growth rates give misleading implications when the initial measure is small, the following formula was used:

$$G = (t2 - t1)/[(t1 + t2)/2]$$

The analyses focus on three issues: 1) increasing concentration of industries in the national metropolis and its satellites; 2) industrial specialization of cities; and 3) specialization of cities in core versus periphery.

Analyses

Increasing Concentration

A high degree of concentration of city industries and population occurred in the three largest cities (Seoul, Busan, and Daegu) and three smaller cities which were Seoul's industrial satellites in both 1960 and 1970, and the degree of concentration increased during the decade (see Table 1). Concentration for a city is measured as the percentage a variable comprises of the total for the 31 cities. Seoul, the capital and national metropolis, had a greater concentration than other cities in industrial employment and city population in 1960. It was the dominant industrial center and the leading national market for industries, but only two industries were more concentrated than population. Among individual sectors the employment concentration in Seoul ranged from 8 percent in textiles to 59 percent in printing/publishing; 11 of the 13 sectors had employment concentrations greater than 22 percent. Seoul's high concentration in printing/publishing and professional/scientific equipment fit the industries expected in a national metropolis. The former industry is closely allied to the information requirements of government, finance, and other office functions, while the latter industry requires the highly skilled personnel concentrated in the national metropolis of a developing country. Seoul also was a center of industries related directly or in-

Table 1. Percent Concentration of Manufacturing in Seoul and its Industrial Satellites and Busan and Daegu, for 1960 and 1970*

Variable	Seoul 1960	Seoul 1970	—Seoul's Industrial Satellites— Incheon 1960	Incheon 1970	Suweon 1960	Suweon 1970	Euijeongbu 1960	Euijeongbu 1970	Busan 1960	Busan 1970	Daegu 1960	Daegu 1970	Totals for 6 Cities 1960	Totals for 6 Cities 1970
Food	22.3	49.8	7.3	3.4	0.0	1.4	0.3	0.1	18.7	13.0	8.3	5.7	56.9	73.4
Textiles	8.0	35.9	5.6	2.3	2.5	2.1	0.0	0.6	23.9	15.7	40.9	23.4	80.9	80.0
Wearing apparel	31.8	45.7	2.9	3.3	1.9	0.5	1.0	0.3	16.1	17.2	17.0	8.9	70.7	75.9
Footwear	22.7	63.4	2.7	1.4	0.0	0.0	0.0	0.0	46.4	6.2	6.4	7.6	78.2	78.6
Wood & cork products	26.3	22.4	4.2	25.2	4.2	0.8	0.0	0.0	18.9	30.1	12.6	4.1	66.2	82.6
Paper & paper prod.	33.3	47.6	0.0	1.2	0.0	0.6	0.0	3.5	16.7	10.6	19.4	8.2	69.4	71.7
Chemicals & petroleum	33.5	47.0	4.7	6.5	1.6	0.8	2.1	0.4	17.8	17.1	6.8	4.3	66.5	76.1
Iron & steel	29.6	30.7	48.1	20.5	0.0	0.8	0.0	0.0	14.8	37.0	3.7	2.8	96.2	91.8
Metal fab. & mach.	32.7	46.7	9.5	4.6	0.4	0.5	0.0	0.2	15.6	17.8	16.0	13.2	74.2	83.0
Electrical machinery	31.8	62.8	0.0	3.7	0.0	1.9	9.1	0.4	45.5	17.1	9.1	3.0	95.5	88.9
Transport equipment	12.5	28.7	7.8	9.7	0.0	1.0	3.1	0.0	31.3	28.4	10.9	10.7	65.6	78.5
Printing & publishing	58.6	65.5	0.0	1.8	0.0	0.2	2.7	0.4	12.6	10.4	9.0	8.0	82.9	86.3
Prof/sci. equip.	50.0	92.3	0.0	0.0	0.0	3.8	0.0	1.9	0.0	1.9	25.0	0.0	75.0	99.9
Total mfg. empl.	25.3	44.3	5.7	5.1	1.1	1.2	0.6	0.4	20.5	17.8	18.2	11.0	71.4	79.8
City population	34.1	42.9	5.6	5.0	1.3	1.3	0.7	0.7	16.2	14.6	9.4	8.4	67.3	72.9

Computed from 1% samples of the Korean Population Censuses in 1960 and 1970.
*The percents are computed on the basis of the totals for 31 cities.

directly to raw material processing, such as wood/cork products, paper/paper products, chemicals/petroleum, and iron/steel.

Seoul's three industrial satellites had different industries (see Table 1). Incheon, whose industrial employment was the fourth largest in the nation, served as the port for Seoul. Based on its advantages for assembling raw materials, it was the leading producer of iron/steel. Mills in this industry, however, were still small as of 1960 (Korea Development Institute, 1975). The smaller cities of Suweon and Euijeongbu had their highest employment concentrations in wood/cork products and electrical machinery, respectively. Busan, the second largest city and a port in the southeast, was the leading producer of footwear, electrical machinery, and transport equipment, while Daegu, the third largest city, was Korea's major textile center. Textiles was a leading industry, but as of 1960 the majority of textile production came from small and medium-sized firms with under 500 employees (Kim, 1980).

Rapid industrial expansion during the 1960s resulted in polarized development; Seoul's population surged from 2.4 million (34 percent of total city population) in 1960 to 5.4 million (43 percent of total city population) in 1970. Its share of industrial employment grew even more dramatically from 25 percent to 44 percent. Total industrial employment in Seoul grew by 150 percent, over one and one-half times the average increase of 94 percent for all cities. By 1970, over two-thirds of the industries were more concentrated than population in Seoul (see Table 1). During the 1960s, export industries were the engine of industrial growth, and concentration of these in Seoul, textiles, wearing apparel, footwear, and electrical machinery, increased dramatically (see Table 1). Seoul did not increase its dominance of raw material related manufacturing to the same degree. The industries most concentrated in Seoul in 1960 - printing/publishing and professional/scientific equipment - retained their leading position in 1970. Seoul's growth in food and other industries suggests that its dominance of national market industries was maintained. The producer durables sector (metal fabrication and machinery) expanded commensurately with other industries, corresponding to its pivotal position as a provider of intermediate goods.

Some of Seoul's gains came at the relative expense of the second and third ranked cities Busan and Daegu (see Table 1). Their factory employment expanded 111 and 83 percent, respectively, far below Seoul's growth of 150 percent. Busan capitalized on its port status by increasing its concentration in industries related to raw material processing. In both wood/cork products and iron/steel, it became the leading national producer. Busan and Daegu, however, declined relatively in the other export sectors; Daegu in textile and Busan in footwear and electrical machinery. Seoul's industrial satellites also increased their employment, but they did not keep pace with Seoul; Incheon, Suweon, and Euijeongbu grew 112, 124 and

83 percent, respectively. Incheon maintained an emphasis on raw material-related industries. Suweon and Euijeongbu gained importance in professional/scientific equipment, probably a spillover from Seoul, which had most employment.

As expected by researchers who focus on increasing primacy of the system of cities and polarized development, Seoul, as the national metropolis, increased dramatically its dominance of city manufacturing. This polarized development in Seoul did not spill over significantly to its industrial satellites. Although their industries grew substantially, their share of total city industry was stable during the 1960s. Resource processing related industries did not increase in concentration in Seoul as much as other industries, but their moderately high concentration throughout the decade suggests that the advantages of the national metropolis were formidable during the polarization phase of development.

The stage of industrialization which is associated with this increasing concentration of industry in Seoul, however, is not the one expected by most researchers. The prevailing view is that import substitution industries are located in the primate city, and they contribute to increasing primacy. In 1960, during the period these industries grew, however, demand (indicated by population size) was more concentrated in Seoul than was both total manufacturing employment and all types except two. The increasing concentration of industries in Seoul occurred during the 1960s when export industries were the leading growth sector. The smaller cities declined relatively, the opposite of what some researchers expected (Nemeth and Smith, 1983, 1985; Santos, 1979). Their claim is that these industries are oriented to factors of production (raw materials, labor), not the national market. The smaller cities, therefore, should have increased their percentage of total city manufacturing, not declined as actually happened.

If the focus remains on the concentration of industry in Seoul and to a lesser extent in its satellites and several large cities, significant change in other cities is missed. The six cities discussed previously contained 71 and 80 percent of all industry in 1960 and 1970, respectively, but the typical city had a 94 percent increase in manufacturing employment during the decade. The potential existed, therefore, for the emergence of small specialized industrial cities; this specialization is examined now.

Industrial Specialization of Cities

Analyses based on location quotients and dissimilarity indexes are used to examine industrial specialization (Isserman, 1980; Sakoda, 1981). The distribution of cities among five categories of location quotients for each industry (see Table 2) suggests that some specialized cities existed by 1960. Cities with location quotients greater than 1.49 imply that they specialized in serving non-local

Table 2. Distribution of 31 Cities among Location Quotients
and Indexes of Dissimilarity for
Manufacturing Industries in Korea, 1960 and 1970

Variable	Location Quotients*										Index of Dissimilarity	
	0.0		0.01-0.49		0.50-1.49		1.50-2.99		3.0+			
	1960	1970	1960	1970	1960	1970	1960	1970	1960	1970	1960	1970
Food	1	1	2	2	13	19	11	6	4	3	.238	.160
Textiles	9	4	7	9	13	13	2	5	0	0	.388	.230
Wearing apparel	3	0	1	4	20	20	7	7	0	0	.191	.101
Footwear	15	13	3	3	5	7	5	7	3	1	.374	.283
Wood & cork prod.	13	8	1	4	10	14	4	3	3	2	.213	.404
Paper & paper prod.	25	13	0	4	3	7	0	3	3	4	.357	.237
Chemicals & petro.	10	1	3	5	12	22	3	0	3	3	.269	.155
Iron & steel	26	16	1	3	2	9	0	2	2	1	.505	.374
Metal fab/machinery	8	2	5	6	13	17	5	6	0	0	.212	.090
Electrical machinery	26	16	0	5	2	7	2	3	1	0	.421	.246
Transport equipment	13	11	1	3	5	9	8	5	4	3	.322	.262
Printing/publishing	17	4	1	8	7	18	2	1	4	0	.429	.237
Prof/sci. equipment	28	27	0	1	1	0	1	1	1	2	.539	.527

*Location Quotient is computed as $(CM_i/CM_t)/(TM_i/TM_t)$ where CM_i and CM_t are respectively a city's employment in industry i, and total manufacturing employment and TM_i and TM_t are respectively the total 31-city employment in industry i and total manufacturing employment.

markets (outside the city and its immediate environs), but not export markets because 1960 was still part of the era of import substitution. Paper/paper products, iron/steel, electrical machinery and professional/scientific equipment were highly concentrated in a few cities. At the other extreme, wearing apparel probably was represented in most cities by local industries; location quotients for most cities were in the group 0.50-1.49. Their percentages of employment in wearing apparel were close to the 31-city average; that is, a location quotient of about 1.00. Because the location quotient underestimates non-local manufacture, some of these cities also may have served non-local markets (Isserman, 1980). In other industries such as footwear, transport equipment and printing/publishing, a moderate number of cities served non-local markets, while about half the cities were under-represented; that is, they imported the products from other cities.

The uneven distribution of industries among cities in 1960 also is reflected in fairly high dissimilarity index values which ranged from 0.191 in wearing apparel to 0.539 in professional/scientific equipment (see Table 2). The dissimilarity index of 0.191 is a moderately high value, meaning that about 19 percent of the workers in wearing apparel must be moved to other cities to achieve an even distribution among cities. Industrial specializations were not limited to the four largest cities (Seoul, Busan, Daegu and Incheon). Among the most specialized cities (location quotient greater than 3.0) were small cities such as Masan, Weonju and Gunsan, which specialized in paper/paper products, or Chungmu and Pohang, which specialized in transport equipment. Other small cities had location quotients between 1.50-2.99. The huge iron and steel complex at Pohang did not begin production until 1973; its specialization in this industry, therefore, postdates 1970 (Korea Development Institute, 1975).

After a decade of rapid growth, numerous industries were important in many cities. In 1970 a larger number of cities had location quotients between 0.01 and 1.49 and a smaller number had location quotients of 0.0 (see Table 2). The number of specialized cities (location quotients 1.50 or more) changed in some industries, but the net result was only a small decline in the total number (summed over all industries) of specialized industrial cities. The addition of industries to cities which previously had little or none made the cities more similar; the dissimilarity indexes declined in most industries between 1960 and 1970 (see Table 2). Two of the important export industries, textiles and wearing apparel, illustrate these changes; they were the first and third largest employers in Korean cities in 1970. All cities engaged in production of wearing apparel and all but four cities produced textiles. Although the number of cities specializing (location quotients 1.50 or more) in them increased from 9 to 12 between 1960 and 1970, both industries' dissimilarity indexes decreased (see Table 2). This indicates a more even distribution of them among cities in 1970 than in 1960.

The sizes of firms in these industries increased dramatically during the 1960s; by the early 1970s a majority of production came from firms with over 500 employees. Most firms in these cities, however, were small; over 80 percent had fewer than 50 employees (Kim, 1980).

Selected examples of city specialization in 1970 illustrate the complex differentiation of cities which existed even while polarized development was occurring. Except for Seoul, cities with location quotients greater than 1.50 in a given industry are classified as specialized. Because Seoul had a large proportion of total manufacturing in the 31 cities, its specialization, measured by the location quotient, does not appear high. The criterion for Seoul's specialization, therefore, is set at 1.40. It specialized in printing/publishing, related to its metropolitan office functions, and in the national market and export industries of electrical machinery, footwear, and professional/scientific equipment. Seoul did not specialize in resource-related processing of imported raw materials, but its satellite and port, Incheon, specialized in iron/steel and wood/cork products. The small industrial cities distant from Seoul had diverse specialties including: 1) chemicals/petroleum in Ulsan, Chungju, and Jinhae; 2) electrical machinery in Gwangju and Iri; 3) footwear in Jeonju and Gimcheon; and 4) transport equipment in Sokcho and Chungmu. As more cities became industrial centers, the producer durables (metal fabrication/machinery) became more widely represented in cities. Its dissimilarity index was the lowest in 1970. Industrial city specializations sometimes were determined directly by Korean government actions. Ulsan, for example, was a target for extensive government investment during the 1960s, and the petrochemical industry with its characteristic large-scale plants was encouraged (Kim, 1978).

In summary, the analyses suggest that Korea had a significant number of cities in 1960 that specialized in different industries for domestic markets -- the era of import substitution -- and during industrial expansion of the 1960s cities continued to specialize. Because the location quotient is a conservative estimate of specialization, the degree of specialization probably was greater than indicated by these results. During the early stage of industrialization in a developing nation spread effects of industrial growth may occur as cities add industries in which they previously had little or no employment. These changes in Korea suggest that industrial specialties of cities were unstable during the rapid industrial growth of the 1960s.

Although manufacturing employment grew enormously in Korean cities, total employment was almost perfectly correlated ($r = 0.94$) between 1960 and 1970 (see Table 3). To a lesser degree this size stability also existed for individual industries; the correlations between sizes in 1960 and 1970 ranged from 0.87 in textiles to 0.67 in professional/scientific equipment. This indicates that the rank

Table 3. Pearson Correlations for Size of Manufacturing
Employment, Percent of Total Employment in Manufacturing
for each Industry, and Percent Employment in Manufacturing

	Size (log 10) 1970 versus Size (log 10) 1960	% Employment 1970 versus % Employment 1960
Food	.76*	.56*
Textiles	.87*	.71*
Wearing apparel	.84*	-.05
Footwear	.69*	-.09
Wood & cork products	.19*	-.04
Paper & paper products	.78*	.49*
Chemicals & petroleum	.81*	.39*
Iron & steel	.85*	.59*
Metal fab. & machinery	.87*	.26
Electrical machinery	.81*	.25
Transport equipment	.75*	-.06
Printing & publishing	.82*	.16
Prof & sci. equipment	.67*	-.01
TOTAL	.94*	.64*

----

*Significant at one-tail 0.05 level.

----

of cities in total and individual industries was established at an early stage of industrialization, and was relatively stable even under polarized development. Cities were less likely to maintain their percent employment (non-extractive) in manufacturing than they were to maintain their size-rank. The correlation between percent employment in 1960 and 1970 was 0.64 whereas the size correlation was 0.94 (see Table 3). The specialization of cities in individual industries was even more unstable. Only five correlations between percent employed in 1960 versus 1970 were positive and significant (0.05 level). The instability of most industries probably derives from at least two sources: the spread effects of industrial growth as cities added manufacturing employment in which they previously had little or none; and differential success and capitalization of firms.

Specialization of Cities: Core versus Periphery

Researchers have suggested that core cities are specialized in more industries than peripheral cities; the latter may specialize in resource processing. The final analyses examine this question. Based on previous research the following four-region division of Korea is used: 1) Seoul and its hinterland cities (Gyeonggi province); 2) Busan and its hinterland cities (Gyeongsangnam province); 3) the Seoul-Busan corridor; and 4) the other cities of Korea (Kim, 1978; Nemeth and Smith, 1983, 1985; Park, 1981; Song, 1981). Although Seoul and its hinterland cities comprise the main core of Korea, Busan and its hinterland cities are considered a secondary core. Differentiation of the two regions provides a finer division of the core. The Seoul-Busan corridor includes cities near the main highway and railroad linking the bipolar cores of Korea. Transportation improvements were made during the 1960s, therefore, cities in this corridor may have acquired industrial specialties. The "other cities" category is the periphery of Korea, although the Seoul-Busan corridor also may fit this characterization. Analyses of variance of the percent employed in each manufacture for the cities grouped by region were computed for 1960 and 1970 (see Tables 4 and 5).

Significant (0.10 level) regional differences among cities existed for only three industries in 1960 and 1970. The core was more specialized than the periphery in most significant cases. Seoul and its hinterland cities had greater percents employed than other cities in wearing apparel, iron/steel, and electrical machinery in 1960, and in electrical machinery and professional/scientific equipment in 1970. Wearing apparel also was a specialty of cities in the Seoul-Busan corridor in 1960 and 1970. In the latter year the highest percents employed in wearing apparel were in the peripheral cities ("other cities"). The failure of core cities to have greater percents employed in more industries than

Table 4. Analyses of Variance of Percent Employed in Manufactures, 1960
Regional Group Means[a]

	Seoul and Hinterland Cities	Busan and Hinterland Cities	Seoul-Busan Corridor	Other Cities	Grand Mean	F Signif. Level
Food	8.1 (6.4)	19.6 (18.8)	16.7 (7.0)	25.9 (15.0)	20.3 (14.4)	1.98 (0.14)
Textiles	17.8 (19.9)	15.1 (11.2)	16.1 (15.2)	7.6 (8.4)	12.2 (12.5)	1.27 (0.31)
Wearing apparel	15.6 (6.7)	10.2 (3.6)	18.2 (11.9)	9.0 (6.1)	12.1 (8.2)	2.73 (0.06)
Footwear	1.5 (1.9)	5.3 (3.7)	3.2 (7.4)	3.7 (5.3)	3.6 (5.2)	0.42 (0.74)
Wood/cork prod.	5.1 (6.0)	1.4 (1.7)	2.1 (2.8)	7.4 (11.6)	4.8 (8.4)	1.02 (0.40)
Paper/paper prod.	0.5 (0.9)	1.0 (2.0)	0.2 (0.6)	1.7 (4.9)	1.1 (3.4)	0.31 (0.82)
Chem/petroleum	13.3 (9.1)	8.3 (9.1)	4.0 (5.1)	9.8 (15.9)	8.7 (12.1)	0.57 (0.64)
Iron/steel	2.6 (4.3)	0.1 (0.3)	0.8 (2.1)	0.0 (0.0)	0.5 (1.9)	2.38 (0.09)
Metal fab/mach.	8.8 (8.5)	10.0 (9.6)	11.0 (6.0)	6.6 (6.4)	8.6 (7.2)	0.68 (0.57)
Elecrical mach.	3.6 (6.5)	0.3 (0.8)	0.1 (0.2)	0.1 (0.4)	0.6 (2.4)	2.88 (0.05)
Transport equip.	4.5 (6.1)	5.1 (3.8)	2.3 (4.6)	2.2 (2.4)	3.1 (3.8)	1.11 (0.36)
Printing/publish.	7.5 (9.6)	1.2 (2.0)	4.4 (7.2)	4.5 (8.0)	4.2 (7.2)	0.62 (0.61)
Prof/sci. equip.	0.1 (0.7)	0.3 (0.7)	0.0 (0.1)	0.0 (0.0)	0.1 (0.3)	1.25 (0.31)

[a] Standard deviations of means are enclosed in parentheses

Regional Groups: Seoul & hinterland cities: Seoul, Incheon, Suweon, Euijeongbu
Busan & hinterland cities: Busan, Masan, Ulsan, Jinju, Jinhae, Chungmu
Seoul-Busan corridor: Cheonan, Cheongju, Daejeon, Gimcheon, Daegu, Gyeongju, Pohang

Other cities: Gwangju, Jeonju, Mokpo, Weonju, Gunsan, Chuncheon, Yeosu, Chungju, Iri, Suncheon,
Gangneung, Andong, Jeju and Sokcho

Table 5. Analyses of Variance of Percent Employed in Manufactures, 1970 Regional Group Means[a]

	Seoul and Hinterland Cities	Busan and Hinterland Cities	Seoul-Busan Corridor	Other Cities	Grand Mean	F Signif. Level
Food	7.0 (3.4)	7.0 (2.2)	12.1 (11.1)	15.3 (8.3)	11.9 (8.4)	2.16 (0.12)
Textiles	23.8 (12.5)	20.4 (16.8)	24.1 (13.7)	12.0 (11.0)	17.9 (13.6)	1.84 (0.16)
Wearing apparel	7.9 (2.8)	8.5 (5.3)	12.2 (2.7)	17.1 (6.0)	13.1 (6.2)	6.17 (0.00)
Footwear	0.6 (1.0)	0.9 (1.2)	1.3 (1.6)	2.0 (2.4)	1.4 (1.9)	0.73 (0.54)
Wood/cork prod.	5.5 (8.3)	2.0 (2.5)	1.8 (1.5)	4.3 (5.7)	3.5 (4.9)	0.78 (0.51)
Paper/paper prod.	4.8 (7.6)	0.9 (1.6)	1.4 (1.5)	2.1 (3.2)	2.1 (3.5)	1.10 (0.37)
Chem/petroleum	7.7 (2.1)	17.9 (21.2)	5.0 (2.0)	7.1 (7.6)	8.8 (11.1)	1.90 (0.15)
Iron/steel	3.4 (4.6)	1.6 (2.1)	0.6 (0.8)	1.1 (1.7)	1.3 (2.2)	1.54 (0.23)
Metal fab/mach.	8.5 (4.0)	10.1 (6.6)	16.5 (11.5)	11.1 (7.0)	11.8 (8.0)	1.17 (0.34)
Electrical mach.	3.1 (1.0)	1.1 (1.4)	0.4 (0.6)	1.1 (2.0)	1.2 (1.7)	2.48 (0.08)
Transport equip.	2.4 (2.3)	5.0 (5.0)	1.1 (1.2)	3.5 (4.7)	3.1 (4.0)	1.11 (0.36)
Printing/pub.	3.8 (3.0)	2.2 (2.0)	2.6 (1.4)	3.6 (2.4)	3.1 (2.2)	0.79 (0.51)
Prof/sci. equip.	1.3 (1.1)	0.0 (0.0)	0.0 (0.0)	0.0 (0.0)	0.2 (0.6)	14.81 (0.00)

[a] Standard deviations of means are enclosed in parentheses. For list of cities in regional groups, see Table 4.

peripheral cities and the failure of peripheral cities to have greater percents employed in resource processing-related industries imply that the core-periphery conceptualization of specialization of cities has limited application to Korea during the 1960s.

Conclusions

The concentration of all industries and of most sectors increased dramatically in Seoul, the national metropolis, during the period of polarized development in the 1960s. The concentration in its industrial satellites, however, did not increase significantly. During the import substitution period industries were not as concentrated as population in Seoul, whereas during the export period they became more concentrated than population. Cities remained moderately specialized in various industries in both 1960 and 1970. Although the number of cities highly specialized in manufacturing did not increase with industrial growth, many cities added new industries or increased their employment in existing ones. These changes resulted in a high degree of instability in city specializations, but they maintained their rank order by size of industry. Core cities were more specialized than peripheral cities only in a few industries.

The results of this study underscore recent claims that systems of cities in developing nations are more complex than many researchers in the dominant paradigms recognize: 1) modernization and ecological theories; and 2) dependency and world-system theories (Ettlinger, 1981; Gilbert and Gugler, 1982; London, 1987; Nemeth and Smith, 1985; Roberts, 1978; Smith, 1985b; Walton, 1976, 1982). The standard claim by the modernization, dependency, and world-system paradigms that import substitution industries agglomerate in the primate city and contribute significantly, therefore, to increasing population primacy was not confirmed in the Korean case. First, Korea does not have a highly primate city size distribution. Second, in 1960, during the period when import substitution industries grew, Seoul had only one-fourth of total city manufacturing employment, and industry was significantly less concentrated than population. The increase in population primacy occurred during the export industrial expansion of the 1960s. By 1970 concentration of manufacturing employment had surpassed population in Seoul, and some of the increased employment was export-related. This latter result is unanticipated by world-system researchers who imply that export industries do not contribute to increasing primacy (Nemeth and Smith, 1983, 1985; Santos, 1979). The implication is that researchers in the modernization, dependency, and world-system paradigms need to reassess the effect of import substitution and export industries on the national metropolises of developing nations.

A focus on the concentration of industries in Seoul ignores the equally significant growth of smaller industrial cities. They already were specialized in 1960 during the import substitution period, grew significantly during the export-led industrial growth of the 1960s, and remained specialized in 1970. Growth of specialized industrial cities, therefore, is compatible with polarized development. Modernization, dependency, and world-system researchers have not adequately acknowledged this possibility, although the latter come closest to recognizing it. Ecological theorists, who have focused on the highly developed nations, would argue that the emergence of specialized industrial cities, synonymous with the evolution of an integrated system of cities, is a normal outgrowth of the economic development process. The dominance concept in ecological theory, however, refers to mutual interdependence (Duncan, et al., 1960:84). It is not suitably formulated for dealing with less-developed nations which have a high degree of centralization of political and economic decision-making in the national metropolis and which may be subservient (to some degree) to a metropolis in a developed nation. Ecological theory, therefore, has yet to explain how this centralization is compatible with the existence of specialized industrial cities. Growth and specialization of small industrial cities documented in this study confirm the suggestion by Nemeth and Smith (1983, 1985), based on secondary sources, that growth during the 1960s maintained a complex evenly distributed urban system. They did not anticipate, however, that industries simultaneously concentrated in Seoul.

Based on the world-system paradigm, Nemeth and Smith (1983, 1985) argue that the Korean urban system had its roots before 1950 in both internal political/economic and Japanese colonial decisions. Since 1950 the urban system has been affected by policy decisions of the Korean government made in the context of the nation's place in the world-system. During the 1960s one influence of these decisions on industrial location worked through construction of transportation and other infrastructure. Explicit government policies affecting industrial land use did not become important until the late 1970s (Rondinelli, 1984).

The results of this study have implications for predicting the effect of export-industrial expansion on cities in developing nations. During the early stages of this expansion, export industries concentrate in the national metropolis; increasing primacy of the system of cities results. These industries are not influenced in their location by the need for proximity to markets because their markets are in other nations. They are attracted to the national metropolis because its control/coordination functions such as finance, exporting, and importing provide important services and information about international market demands, and its high quality international transportation and communication services make it the low-cost location for distribution to export markets. To the extent lobbying the national government is important for gaining favors that support export firms, then single-plant firms will prefer location in the national metropolis so that the owner can both lobby government officials and supervise production.

Foreign multinational firms and indigenous multi-plant national and multinational firms are attracted to the national metropolis for these same reasons. The foreign multinationals, however, have much less familiarity with locational options in the nation. They are likely to concentrate much of their production in the national metropolis in order to reduce perceived risk, even though labor costs are higher. Indigenous multi-plant export firms, however, may locate some plants away from the national metropolis because they are better acquainted with the risk of alternative locations. The lower labor cost of the smaller cities becomes a major attraction. These indigenous multi-plant firms can retain their corporate offices in the national metropolis to have proximity to control/coordination functions and government officials. In Korea, for example, four of the largest jaebols (conglomerates), Daewoo, Hyundai, Lucky-Goldstar, and Samsung, are headquartered in Seoul (Kim, 1986).

To the extent the national government has improved the infrastructure, such as transportation, communication, and the electrical power grid, outside the core region, the location of export industries (especially low-wage) in the periphery will be accelerated. Other production factors become equal; the low wages in the periphery, therefore, become the pivotal location factor for labor intensive export firms. In fact, the national metropolis, with its high land, labor and congestion costs relative to peripheral cities, becomes an undesirable location for export firms. Foreign multinationals will increasingly locate their plants in these smaller cities. The national government can accelerate this dispersal process by establishing export processing zones which have all of the required infrastructure. Often these are in or near ports.

The effect of export industrial expansion on the system of cities, therefore, is to lead initially to greater concentration of industry in the national metropolis, but simultaneously to the growth of specialized industrial cities in the periphery. Over time, these latter cities capture a growing percentage of the export industrial expansion, while the national metropolis becomes relatively less important as an industrial center but more specialized in control/coordination functions such as finance, wholesaling, export/importing, and other high-level business services (law and accounting). In the Korean case, there are indications that these changes in the system of cities are now occurring (Corey, 1980; Kwon, 1981; Rondinelli, 1984).

Korea's system of cities has a long complex history; each stage has been influenced by the previous stage's characteristics. More recently, the post-1970 growth of industrial cities was built on a specialized industrial city base that already had changed significantly during the 1960s. These long-term dynamics of cities in developing nations need to be given greater attention. Future research on the systems of cities in developing nations might benefit from attempts to combine the best insights of the existing paradigms to derive a new theory.

Acknowledgements

Portions of this research were completed while Kyonghee Min was a post-doctoral fellow in the Population Studies and Training Center at Brown University. The authors are grateful for the Center's support. We thank James Sakoda for making available his computer program for computing dissimilarity indexes and for his advice concerning their interpretation. Also, we thank Nancy Ettlinger, Dennis Rondinelli, David Smith, and the anonymous referees for their comments on the paper.

References

Alonso, W. (1971) The location of industry in developing countries, *Industrial Location and Regional Development*, 3-36. New York: United Nations.

Berry, Brian J.L. (1971) City size and economic development: Conceptual synthesis and policy problems, with special reference to South and Southeast Asia. In L. Jacobson and V. Prakash (Eds.), *Urbanization and National Development*, 111-155. Beverly Hills, CA: Sage.

Bogue, Don J. (1950) *The Structure of the Metropolitan Community: A Study of Dominance and Subdominance.* Ann Arbor: University of Michigan Press.

Chan, Paul, and Kok Lian (1984) Urban development in Malaysia: Trends, patterns and policy issues, *Conference on Urban Growth and Economic Development in the Pacific Region*, 311-354. Taipei, Taiwan: Institute of Economics, Academia Sinica.

Chase-Dunn, Christopher (1984) Urbanization in the world-system: New directions for research. In Michael Peter Smith (Ed.), *Cities in Transformation: Class, Capital, and the State*, 111-120. Beverly Hills: Sage.

Corey, Kenneth E. (1980) Transactional forces and the metropolis: Towards a planning strategy for Seoul in the year 2000. In Won Kim (Ed.), *The Year 2000: Urban Growth & Perspectives for Seoul*, 54-88. Seoul: Korea Planners Association.

Duncan, Beverly, and Stanley Lieberson (1970) *Metropolis and Region in Transition.* Beverly Hills: Sage.

Duncan, Otis Dudley, Richard W. Scott, Stanley Lieberson, Beverly Duncan, and Hal H. Winsborough (1960) *Metropolis and Region.* Baltimore: Johns Hopkins University Press.

Ettlinger, Nancy (1981) Dependency and urban growth: A critical review and reformulation of the concepts of primacy and rank-size, *Environment and Planning A, 13,* 1389-1400.

Ettlinger, Nancy (1984) A note on rank-size and primacy: In pursuit of a parsimonious explanation, *Urban Studies, 21,* 195-197.

Frank, Andre Gunder (1967) *Capitalism and Underdevelopment in Latin America.* New York: Monthly Review Press.

Friedmann, John (1966) *Regional Development Policy: A Case Study of Venezuela.* Cambridge: M.I.T. Press.

Friedmann, John (1973) *Urbanization, Planning, and National Development.* Beverly Hills: Sage.

Gilbert, Alan and Josef Gugler (1982) *Cities, Poverty, and Development: Urbanization in the Third World.* Oxford: Oxford University Press.

Hackenberg, Robert A. and Beverly H. Hackenberg (1971) Secondary development and anticipatory urbanisation in Davao, Mindanao, *Pacific Viewpoint, 12,* 1-20.

Hasan, Parvez (1976) Korea: Problems and issues in a rapidly growing economy. Baltimore: Johns Hopkins University Press.

Hawley, Amos H. (1971) *Urban Society: An Ecological Approach.* New York: Ronald Press.

Hawley, Amos H. (1984) Human ecological and Marxian theories, *American Journal of Sociology, 89,* 904-917.

Ho, Samuel P.S. (1979) Decentralized industrialization and rural development: Evidence from Taiwan, *Economic Development and Cultural Change, 28,* 77-96.

Ho, Samuel P.S. (1980) *Small-Scale Enterprises in Korea and Taiwan.* World Bank Staff Working Paper No. 384. Washington, D.C.: World Bank.

Isserman, Andrew M. (1980) Estimating export activity in a regional economy: A theoretical and empirical analysis of alternative methods, *International Regional Science Review, 5,* 155-184.

Kass, Roy (1973) A functional classification of metropolitan communities. *Demography, 10,* 427-445.

Kim, An-Jae (1978) Industrialization and growth pole development in Korea: A case study of the Ulsan industrial complex. In Fu-Chen Lo and Kamal Salih (Eds.), *Growth Pole Strategy and Regional Development Policy,* 53-77. Oxford: Pergamon Press.

Kim, Kyong-Hae, Ed. (1986) *Business Korea: Yearbook on Korean Economy and Business.* Seoul: New Industry Management Academy.

Kim, Yung Bong (1980) The growth and structural change of textile industry. In Chong Kee Park (Ed.), *Macroeconomic and Industrial Development in Korea*, 185-276. Seoul: Korea Development Institute.

Korea Development Institute (1975) *Korea's Economy: Past and Present*. Seoul: Korea Development Institute.

Kuznets, Paul W. (1977) *Economic Growth and Structure in the Republic of Korea*. New Haven: Yale University Press.

Kuznets, Paul W. (1980) Accelerated economic growth and structural change. In Chang Yunshik (Ed.), *Korea: A Decade of Development*, 15-50. Seoul: Seoul National University Press.

Kwon, Won-Yong (1981) A study of the economic impact of industrial relocation: The case of Seoul, *Urban Studies, 18*, 73-90.

Lee, Ki-Suk (1982) The impact of national development strategies and industrialization on rapid urbanization of Korea. In Victor F.S. Sit and Koichi Mera (Eds.), *Urbanization and National Development in Asia*, 23-35. Hong Kong: Tai Dao.

London, Bruce (1987) Structural determinants of Third World urban change: An ecological and political economic analysis, *American Sociological Review, 52*, 28-43.

Mason, Edward S., Mahn Je Kim, Dwight H. Perkins, Kwang Suk Kim, and David C. Cole (1980) *The Economic and Social Modernization of the Republic of Korea*. Cambridge: Harvard University Press.

Mera, Koichi (1978) Population concentration and regional income disparities: A Comparative analysis of Japan and Korea. In Niles M. Hansen (Ed.), *Human Settlement Systems*, 155-175. Cambridge: Ballinger.

Meyer, David R. (1986) The world system of cities: Relations between international financial metropolises and South American cities, *Social Forces, 64*, 553-581.

Mills, Edwin S. and Byung-Nak Song (1979) *Urbanization and Urban Problems*. Cambridge: Harvard University Press.

Nemeth, Roger J. and David A. Smith (1983) Divergent patterns of urbanization in the Philippines and South Korea: A historical structural approach, *Comparative Urban Research, 10*, 21-45.

Nemeth, Roger J. and David A. Smith (1985) The political economy of contrasting urban hierarchies in South Korea and the Philippines. In Michael Timberlake (Ed.), *Urbanization in the World Economy*, 183-206. Orlando: Academic Press.

Pannell, Clifton W. (1973) *Tai-Chung, Taiwan: Structure and Function*. Department of Geography Research Paper No. 144. Chicago: University of Chicago.

Park, Sam Ock (1981) Locational change in manufacturing: A conceptual model and case studies. Unpublished Ph.D. dissertation, University of GA, Athens.

Pred, Allan (1966) *The Spatial Dynamics of U.S. Urban-Industrial Growth, 1800-1914*. Cambridge: MIT Press.

Renaud, Bertrand (1981) *National Urbanization Policy in Developing Countries.* New York: Oxford University Press.

Richardson, Harry W. (1977) *City Size and National Spatial Strategies in Developing Countries.* World Bank Staff Working Paper No. 252. Washington, D.C.: World Bank.

Richardson, Harry W. (1980) Polarization reversal in developing countries, *Papers of the Regional Science Association, 45,* 67-85.

Roberts, Bryan R. (1978) *Cities of Peasants: The Political Economy of Urbanization in the Third World.* Beverly Hills: Sage.

Rondinelli, Dennis (1983) *Secondary Cities in Developing Countries: Policies for Diffusing Urbanization.* Beverly Hills: Sage.

Rondinelli, Dennis (1984) Land-development policy in South Korea, *Geographical Review, 74,* 425-440.

Sakoda, James M. (1981) A generalized index of dissimilarity, *Demography, 18,* 245-250.

Santos, Milton (1979) *The Shared Space: The Two Circuits of the Urban Economy in Underdeveloped Countries.* London: Methuen.

Smith, Carol A. (1985a) Theories and measures of urban primacy: A critique. In Michael Timberlake (Ed.), *Urbanization in the World Economy,* 87-117. Orlando: Academic Press.

Smith, Carol A. (1985b) Class relations and urbanization in Guatemala: Toward an alternative theory of urban primacy. In Michael Timberlake (Ed.), *Urbanization in the World Economy,* 121-167. Orlando: Academic Press.

Smith, W. Randy, Wookung Huh, and George J. Demko (1983) Population concentration in an urban system: Korea 1949-1980, *Urban Geography, 4,* 63-79.

Song, Byung-Nak (1981) Economic growth and rural-urban relations in Korea. In Fu-Chen Lo (Ed.), *Rural-Urban Relations and Regional Development,* 45-77. Hong Kong: Maruzen Asia.

Tsai, Hsung-Hsiung (1984) Urban growth and the change of spatial structure in Taiwan. In *Conference on Urban Growth and Economic Development in the Pacific Region,* 577-615. Taipei, Taiwan: Institute of Economics, Academic Sinica.

Walters, Pamela Barnhouse (1985) Systems of cities and urban primacy: Problems of definition and measurement. In Michael Timberlake (Ed.), *Urbanization in the World Economy,* 63-85. Orlando: Academic Press.

Walton, John (1976) Political economy of world urban systems: Directions for comparative research. In John Walton and Louis H. Masotti (Eds.), *The City in Comparative Perspective,* 301-313. Beverly Hills: Sage.

Walton, John (1982) The international economy and peripheral urbanization. In Norman I. Fainstein and Susan S. Fainstein (Eds.), *Urban Policy Under Capitalism*, Urban Affairs Annual Reviews, Vol. 22, 119-135. Beverly Hills: Sage.

Wanner, Richard A. (1977) The dimensionality of the urban functional system, *Demography, 14*, 519-537.

Watanabe, Susumu (1972) Exports and employment: The case of the republic of Korea, *International Labor Review*, 106, 495-526.

Westphal, Larry E. (1978) The republic of Korea's experience with export-led industrial development, *World Development, 6*, 347-382.

THE POSTMODERN CONDITION
AND THE CITY

Philip Cooke
University of Wales
University of Minnesota

This paper explores the proposition that the era of modernity, set in motion by the onset of nineteenth century capitalism and expressed culturally in the aesthetic movements responsible for modernism, has become exhausted to be challenged by a new cultural aesthetic and socio-economic framework called postmodernism. The outlines of philosophical, aesthetic and architectural debates are provided and an attempt is made to ground changes in the contemporary aesthetic sphere in a greater flexibility found in the political economy. It is concluded that postmodernism does exist as a coherent, albeit paradoxical, mode of thought and action, that space and the locality are highlighted as its motifs, and that political struggle to appropriate its content is sited prominently in the contemporary city. The argument is illustrated by reference to present-day Los Angeles and London.

The Debate around Modernity and Postmodernity

Ever since the early 1970s, and sporadically even earlier, there has been a discernible rise in interest in the problem of modernity and its possible demise as a cultural framework in favor of something else, which for lack of a suitable name, is called postmodernity. The early stages of this interest were often characterized by the forming of antinomies, a profoundly modernist, rationalist approach to the development of knowledge, through the medium of critique. A good example appears in the work of the literary critic Ihab Hassan (1971, 1985) who is generally thought to have popularized the concept of "postmodernism" (if we ignore Toynbee's use of the term in 1947 or de Onis' in 1934). In his more recent works Hassan (1985) illustrates the differences between the cultures of modernism and postmodernism in a series of 32 oppositions, a selection of which is shown in Table 1.

Frederic Jameson writes about postmodernism as a Marxist aesthetician with a strong affinity to the modernist project. Jameson has considered the ideological diversity among those who write about postmodernism in a classically modernist, ideal-typical form. His typology is reproduced in Table 2, with each writer suffixed according to their politically progressive or regressive ideological viewpoints.

The pro-postmoderns include those such as Tom Wolfe (1981), journalist and author, whom Jameson characterizes as being both reactionary and facetious in his desire to get rid of the 1960s. Christopher Jencks (1977) is an architectural writer and critic who welcomes postmodernism for its attempt to make architecture comprehensible to the general public by its references to classical styles,

Table 1

Cultural Oppositions

Modernism	Postmodernism
Purpose	Play
Distance	Participation
Centering	Dispersal
Selection	Combination
Grand Narrative*	Local Narrative*
Paranoia	Schizophrenia
Metaphysics	Irony
Determinacy	Indeterminacy

After Hassan (1985), 123-124
*Hassan uses "Narrative/Grande Histoire" and "Anti-Narrative/Petite Histoire." I have rendered these terms into what has become their most common usage (see Lyotard, 1984).

Table 2

	Antimodernist	Promodernist
	Wolfe -	
Propostmodernist	Jencks +	Lyotard {±
	*Hassan {±	+Progressive
		-Reactionary
Antipostmodernist	Tafuri {±	Habermas+
		Kramer -

Based on Jameson (1984a)

*Hassan is classified thus by Jameson in the text of his article but does not appear in the table.

albeit in playful or parodic mood. Jean-Francois Lyotard (1984) is a philosopher whose stretching of poststructuralist insights about the nature of power as irremediably linked to local knowledge (see also Geertz, 1983; Cooke, 1983) has so provoked Jurgen Habermas (Bernstein, 1985) to defend the reformist inheritance of the Enlightenment project embodied in modernism that he equates postmodernism with neoconservatism and worse.

Thus, in Jameson's lexicon, Habermas the progressive finds himself bracketed with Hilton Kramer, founding editor of *The New Criterion*, who also wishes to eradicate the 1960s for its permissive liberalism but, unlike Wolfe, aims to create a conservative culture built on the best of the serious masterpieces of thought and action bequeathed by modernist culture. By contrast, Manfredo Tafuri (Tafuri and Dal Co, 1979), the Venetian architectural historian, is critical of postmodernism, which he considers to be a diversion from a task that he is also critical of modernism for shirking.

Modernism, argues Tafuri, with its protopolitical or utopian project of transforming society by transforming space was a failure, displacing the real task, the transformation of social relations, as a prerequisite for the transformation of culture. This double critique, stemming from an unreconstructed Marxism, leaves Jameson incapable of placing Tafuri on the spectrum of aesthetic politics.

This modernist pigeonholing and oppositionism took its most extreme form in what Hutcheon (1987) calls "the now infamous Lyotard-Habermas-Rorty argument" (see Lyotard, 1984; Bernstein, 1985). Lyotard had proposed that Habermas' work on universal pragmatics, as the means by which a rational society adjudicates the legitimacy of truth claims and makes decisions, was, as the poststructuralists such as Derrida (1978) and Foucault (1980) showed, based on the unquestioned foundations of European rationalism. Such *logocentrism* derived historically from European dominance of other cultures and associated assumptions of superiority, rather than some set of extra-discursive rules which might legitimize that logos.

Habermas' fury was directed at Derrida and Lyotard for undermining the foundations of Western metaphysics. He found this project to be anarchistic, rhetorical, incapable of enabling consensus to be achieved, boundlessly subjective and, in the case of Lyotard, neoconservative in its implications. Habermas also argued that the poststructuralist project was a failure in its own terms because it depended for its existence on precisely the structures of thought which were subject to critique. Habermas has moved closer to an American pragmatism in his recent social philosophy, arguing that knowledge is fallible and subject to reconsideration - in the light of contingency. This itself, as Rorty suggests (Bernstein, 1985), is something of a move away from certain of the grand narratives to which Lyotard and the poststructuralists object, notably Marxism.

Moreover, Habermas now accepts that a philosophical paradigm-change has occurred as the result of an exhaustion of European metaphysics, and that language is the source for a new theory of knowledge. This seems to bring the warring factions closer, yet as Hohendahl (1986) points out, while Habermas shares a stress on language with the poststructuralists, he cannot accept the idea that words may perform as a chain of signifiers for which what is signified can never be established with certainty. This, ultimately for Habermas, is what makes consensus impossible and lets in the Nietzchean "will to power" as the adjudicator, something which Habermas conceives in terms of certain distinctly baleful consequences in the German past.

However, it now seems that the postmodern urge towards combination or reconfirmation of thought is becoming prevalent over the modernist tendency to oppose thought. Lyotard's most recent work on the debate considers the imputed political reaction embodied in postmodernism:

Does what I say lead to an advocacy of neoliberalism? Not in the least. Neoliberalism is itself an illusion. The reality is concentration in industrial, social and financial empires served by the States and the political classes. It is becoming apparent...that these monopolitical monsters do not perform well in any case, and can cause blockages of the will...the ideal is no longer physical strength as it was for the man of antiquity; it is suppleness, speed, the ability to metamorphose... Svelteness, awakening, a Zen and Italian term" (Lyotard, 1987, 218-19).

I wish to explore aspects of the contradiction between this "svelteness" as a cultural motif of postmodernism and the "blockages" of the will which seem characteristic of the modernist tendencies towards, as Hassan would put it, *purpose, distance, centering, selection and determinacy*, in the economic and social forms of the "monopolitical monsters." Furthermore, I will undertake this discussion in a spatial context and with special attention to the effects of postmodernism as they may be observed in changes in the contemporary city. As a prelude, though, I will draw attention to another aspect of the modernity-postmodernity debate apposite to the focus on space and the city, which forms the basis of the remainder of the paper.

Berman, Jameson and Postmodernization

Rather in the manner of the founding fathers of modern social science, Marx, Weber and Durkheim, who each wrote extensively about the onset of modern capitalist society at a time when it was still possible to compare the new with its preceding cultural paradigm: feudalism-capitalism; modernity-premodernity; mechanical-organic solidarity, we see in the perceived demise of modernity an upsurge in writing about its lineaments and motifs in the face or from the perspective of another paradigm, that of postmodernity (Berman, 1983; Bernstein, 1985; Frisby, 1985; Said, 1984; Foster, 1985).

Marshall Berman's remarkable book is the best place to begin thinking about the nature of the modern transformation, since he correctly places great stress on the role of the city in forming the modern, experiential world. He conceives of its structure as consisting in three transformations. The first is the existential experience, by the subject, of *modernity*, something first observed by Baudelaire in the 1850s as a transitory, fugitive and contingent quality of life. The individualistic experience of modernity is set within two objective, societal transformations. The first of these is the unleashing of competitive capitalism with its mass migrations, disruptive social rhythms, urban explosions, industrial transformations and technical as well as political innovations. This process of sociospatial *modernization*, argues Berman, is what uproots the subject from the stability of pre-modern life, either by enveloping or magnetizing the person into its field of forces. But this uprooting from tradition challenges the subject by liberating but also disorientating cognition. The will to engage in cultural movements, which themselves cause upheaval to inherited aesthetic, academic and appreciative frameworks is what constitutes *modernism*. Hence Berman grounds the subjective individual and collective emancipation from tradition that is modernity in the objective processes of capitalist development. This is not achieved by resorting to a base-superstructure metaphor, but by conceiving the processes involved as being in dialectical relationships with each other.

In a very telling account of the early modern establishment of St. Petersburg (now Leningrad) in Imperial Russia, Berman shows how the decision was taken to establish the city at the mouth of the Neva to act as a window on the developing west which might help unblock the developmental backwardness of the czarist feudal empire. This political decision was sufficiently supple to embody recognition that development meant cultural innovation, so actors, musicians and writers as well as businessmen from the mercantile cities of the west were dragooned into joining the Czar in the Italianate urban scene. Their desire for luxury accommodation, clothing and other consumption goods stimulated economic demand and the emergence of a capitalist labor market. For native Russians drawn to St. Petersburg, the experience of modernity was such that some, such as Dostoevsky, Gorky and Pushkin, were among the first to give expression to the fleeting and contingent existentialism of modern life.

Berman has not been alone in seeking to ground modernity in the dialectics of modernization. Two other writers make this connection for the modern era; one is Russell Berman (Berman, 1987). He makes a different three-fold schema from his namesake in periodizing the inheritance and legacy of cultural modernism. He identifies three cultural programs: the premodernism of bourgeois realism; the modernism of avant-garde, twentieth century culture; and the postmodernism of the contemporary period. These programs "correspond" to three distinct phases in political economy: laissez-faire capitalism; modern, administered bureaucratic societies regulated by Keynesian and related instruments; and, contemporarily, the deregulated, privatizing, neo-market formations.

R. Berman makes these equations in the context of that made by Jameson (1984b) responding quite favorably to M. Berman's analysis of modernity and taking further the critical development of that analysis offered by Anderson (1984). Jameson conceives of modernism as the cultural correlate of the middle phase of capitalist development, usually referred to as Monopoly Capitalism, and postmodernism as the cultural equivalent of Mandel's (1975) Late Capitalism, or what has sometimes been dubbed Global Capitalism. In Anderson's (1984) appreciation of M. Berman's book, he questions the planar, undifferentiated nature of the concept of capitalism that it embodied, proposing a more parabola-like trajectory to the mode of production. Such transformations are created by crises inherent to the pursuit of profit under conditions of market competition, and such crises bring forth *spatially* uneven responses that are constituted ideologically and culturally, as well as politically and economically. In turn these give rise to counter-cultural movements, within both the aesthetic and the politico-economic spheres. On occasion there is *displacement* of political struggle into the cultural sphere. Anderson argues that such displacement may divert revolutionary tendencies into, for example, the overthrow of ruling elites in the Academy, their replacement by an avant-garde itself energized by technological revolution and an aesthetic interpretation of it, and the serious, though blocked, proximity of social revolution.

Jameson (1984b) chooses to focus on the architecture of the modern metropolis as a privileged terrain and strategic field of postmodern culture and in doing this he interweaves the dynamics of late capitalist development with the built form and aesthetic imagery of the contemporary city. Specifically, he focuses on a particularly American phenomenon of the 1980s, the downtown renaissance as the centerpiece of his iconography. The exemplar of this phenomenon is the Los Angeles Bonaventure Center, a classic of postmodernism's early detachment from High Modernism and of a piece with Atlanta's Peachtree Development, Detroit's Renaissance Center and the various Eaton malls in Canada, notably Toronto. Such *hyperspaces*, as Jameson terms them, are certainly to be found elsewhere, notably in the Hong Kong and Shanghai Bank in Hong Kong; the Lloyds Insurance building in London (and plans to extend the financial core eastward into the Docklands at Canary Wharf); Beaubourg in Paris, and some of James Stirling's museum buildings as at Stuttgart and recently at Harvard University.

The key to this architectural style is what Farrelly (1986) calls "giving the people what they want," something that in the context of the high elitism of the International Style (Corbusier, Mies van der Rohe, Philip Johnson) appears like an "all-too-rare architectural humility." However, as Jameson (1984b) notes, such *aesthetic populism,* predicated on the public outrage at deformed modernism's depredations toward neighborhood and local culture, is more a masking than an unmasking. Imbued with the ethics of pulp novels, "Dynasty," and Calvin Kleinism and apparently as depthless as Venturi's recommendation that architects start *Learning from Las Vegas,* it nevertheless is the cultural expression of the purer Global form of capitalism, with its planetary reach, that has succeeded modernism's Monopoly version.

It finds its way, stylistically, into the built environment rapidly and with particular clarity because of the intimate links between city planning and the real estate economy, metropolitan revenue generation which is largely dependent on stoking up property taxes, and the appetite of corporate capital for phallocentric emblematics. Jameson concludes that postmodernism's aesthetic stresses space over time, popular electronic culture over classicism and new technology over functionality. Moreover, the effect is particularly alienating. Where mirror-glass oppresses, hyperspace dominates, pedestrians get excluded or lost, elevators alarm as they transport subjects as though they wore jetpacks, it all seems metaphoric:

> [f]or the incapacity of our minds, at present, to map the great global multinational and decentered communicational network in which we find ourselves caught as "individual subjects" (Jameson, 1984b:84).

To get us out of this condition he calls for a postmodern equivalent to Kevin Lynch's (1960) decoding of modern city space, though the poststructuralist insight is a nonrepresentational one in which mapping the postmodern is impossible because of the world's fluidity in the face of our static theorisations (Huyssen, 1984; Dews, 1986).

Jameson takes a relatively uncomplicated base-superstructure reflection-theoretic position on the relation between culture and economy, with the former reflected in and governed by change in the latter. In this respect he is bolder than Russell Berman who notes ambiguously that such readings are inevitably more complex and multifold in reality. Neither is as subtle as Marshall Berman in his more dialectical analysis of the subject-object and culture-economy dichotomy, as modernism would express it. And in a sympathetically critical response to Jameson's (1984b) article, Davis (1985) comments on this. Davis' own rather interesting analysis stresses the centrality of Reaganomics to the real estate boom since high interest rates, set to cure inflation, simply sucked in enormous quantities of foreign dollars at a time when public stimulation of the construction industry was ideologically impossible due to the ending of urban reform ideals with the rise of neoconservative state policies. Some of that foreign windfall simply had to find an outlet in property development, given the perilous state of the industrial economy, and it did.

Hence postmodernism still lacks a well-grounded cultural correspondent in the political economy of late capitalism. Clearly, some of the pieces are in place. Jameson's stress on the new phase of Global capitalism is important as is Berman's (1987) attention to the privatistic, deregulated, welfare-phobic political formation that is monetarism's legacy. The question is, can we speak of post-modernization as relating to postmodernism in the same way that Berman's (1983) modernization relates to modernism, that is, dialectically rather than deterministically? I have argued elsewhere (Cooke, 1987a; 1987b, 1988) that it is reasonable to speak of a postmodernized political economy and that it consists in processes of flexible integration or flexible accumulation (Harvey, 1987) which link directly to Lyotard's (1987) request for a svelteness or suppleness that might counter the blockages caused by the monopolitical monsters.

Postmodernization, Flexibility and Space

There is some agreement that a break in the organization and effects of the accumulation process occurred in the mid-1970s, and that this transition became clearly visible in the 1980s, especially in the United Kingdom, but also in some industries and spaces in the United States and other OECD countries. Those who had adhered to a form of analysis of the modernist regime of accumulation and mode of regulation whereby mass production crises were resolved by state intervention to raise consumption (Fordism) began to speak of post-Fordism (Aglietta, 1978; Lipietz, 1982; Anderson, 1984; Davis, 1985; Albertsen, 1986) in light of the decay of mass-production economies and welfare capitalism. Fordist analysis was not as widely applied in the U.K. and U.S. social sciences as in continental European traditions. This may be, certainly in the U.K. case, because of a failure, not shared by the U.S., to engage in full-blooded mass-production industry until the second half of the twentieth century. By this time its inbuilt rigidities were already causing strains in those countries and cities where it had been established earlier.

In the U.K. case, it is more normal and more accurate to characterize the 1945-1975 period as one of more or less constant attempts by industrial capital and the state to modernize an economy which had been the first to modernize in the epochal sense but which for a century had been largely out-competed by late-comers to the competition such as the U.S., Germany and Japan. There was a considerable sharing of perspective on the nature of the modernization task that confronted governments of whatever stripe in the postwar U.K. There was acceptance of the ideal of full employment and state intervention not only to take the budgetary and fiscal measures to achieve this nationally but also to redistribute growth regionally by taking work to the workers. Old cities that arose with the first unleashing of competitive capitalism thus had their own and their satellite sub-economies protected and renewed by tariffs or replacement industry. It was also accepted that state intervention should aim to equalize housing conditions, hence housing renewal was understood as largely a state responsibility and morally superior to reliance on aspects of the privately-owned rented sector of the housing market. Moreover, to ensure that the mixed economy functioned in ways that enabled private capital to be competitive against foreign producers, the state expropriated inefficient private owners of utilities, transportation systems, steel and coal production and numerous other areas of economic life at various times.

I have argued (Cooke, 1987a; 1987b) that this interaction between the private and public sectors produced a new spatial paradigm in the U.K. into which diverse kinds of city and suburban environment were incorporated. I have mentioned the old industrial towns and cities that were assisted through the postwar era when major competitor countries were still devastated by war. Later, such cities as Liverpool, Glasgow, Manchester and Birmingham were massive recipients of public expenditure in collective consumption goods (Castells, 1977) such as new housing, schools, open space and health facilities, sometimes close,' sometimes not, to industrial complexes. Second, Britain developed a series of satellite New Towns beyond the metropolitan areas to which the population that could not be housed when inner city areas were renewed was dispersed. Such overspill localities and the enlarged or expanded towns that performed a similar function were to become important centers of modernized production in new factories, supplied with new, disorganized work forces, provided with good quality, suburban-style, publicly-owned and rented housing. Third, new suburbs were added, many of which were also state-provided and owned. This is not to say that private suburbanization was not also a feature of the metropolitan development process at this time. It was, but the emphasis was a broadly social democratic one with a major role for state provision in the spheres of production and reproduction.

Thus, it can be concluded that the modernization era in the U.K. was to produce a spatial paradigm conditioned by the following:

1. Political pressure from a large and dynamic skilled and semi-skilled working class for relatively widespread state intervention in the political economy;
2. Spatial equalization of modern development as between a prosperous core and more peripheral areas;
3. Relative, though slight, income equalization between the classes and a diminishing of unemployment levels between the regions;
4. Some linking of modern collective consumption provision and industrial modernization, especially in New Towns and Development Areas;
5. Manufacturing industry moving increasingly towards achieving economies of scale on an American "standardized product" model aimed at new mass-markets;
6. Labor markets characterized by high labor demand and relative job security for semi-skilled workers.

The U.K. space-economy was, for a time, enjoying boom conditions and the prosperity was being spread around. Once Britain's wartime enemies recovered, however, their later rounds of investment in more modernized production technology and labor relations meant they were in a strong position to out-compete the U.K. in foreign and, later, domestic markets. As a result the British economy suffered a severe profits squeeze and successive governments sought to restructure what was universally seen as an out-dated economy, but all were more or less unsuccessful. From being seen as the vital restructuring mechanism, the state came to be seen as the vital blockage to development that required removal. It became clear that the grand narrative of a purposive, centered, distanced and determining central power had proved contingently to be exhausted, for such was not the case in, for example, France or Japan. Much the same might be said for the Snowbelt cities from Detroit to Cleveland and Buffalo in the U.S.

It would be misleading to say that failure in the economic sphere triggered a crisis reflected in a cultural and political revolution, since the ideas which rushed in to fill the vacuum left by the exhaustion of modernization had been present throughout, though held by a political and cultural minority. However, the critique of the tinkering with institutions "best left alone" by the reforming, modernist state apparatus grew in strength and began to gain adherents from within the skilled working class seeing its privileges squeezed by the deskilling consequent on automation of production and the general erosion of real wages in an inflationary period during the 1970s. Simultaneously it became popular to criticize the quality of the collective consumption environments that had been delivered to the working class, especially when many proved to be defective and uninhabitable.

This hard evidence that the state could make mistakes on an enormous scale created space in the discourse of public policy for motifs based on the moral superiority of the market, private responsibility, value for money, a lesser role for the welfare state and a generally harsher tone towards collectivist solutions domestically and in countries possessing somewhat stultified command economies. Money-making suddenly became fashionable, not just for entrepreneurs, but for state and quasi-state agencies that began selling off assets such that today even museums follow the almighty cash nexus by auctioning off their unpopular exhibits and renting out masterpieces for display in department stores (Burger, 1986). A new sociospatial paradigm may be said to have emerged and to be characterized by the following:

1.   The rise of the service or professional class to political power and dynamism, demanding lower taxes and more freedom for private initiative. Such social forces are highly uneven in their spatial clustering;
2.   Uneven spread of postmodernized development in the form of high technology industry, downtown redevelopment, retail and entertainment complexes and aesthetic investments - a national North-South problem;
3.   Bifurcation in income distribution between classes and unemployment levels between regions;
4.   A tendency towards postmodernization processes occurring most rapidly and profoundly in privatized centers of consumption such as the suburbs and small, heritage towns;
5.   Industry inclining towards non-standardized products aimed at market segments in pursuit of economies of "scope" efficiencies (Teece, 1980);
6.   A growing casualization of employment due to labor market over-supply, in-migration from a debt-burdened Third World, short-term contract working, part-time employment and the growth of the urban informal sector.

In the U.K. context it is London's satellite towns that are the repositories of such postmodernization tendencies. They tend to be the localities possessing the svelte, supple or flexible workers unconcerned about the virtues of trade-unionism, the flexible new production technologies in factory and office, capable of achieving the joint-production economies of scope through flexible systems of advanced manufacturing or servicing technology. Often such localities constitute centers of microeconomic power strung out along major highway axes such as Britain's high-tech corridors M3, M4 and M11, linking London and Southampton, London and Bristol/Cardiff, and London to Cambridge respectively. Other booming localities are those ringing London at a distance of approximately sixty miles where producer services employment doubled in the 1970s and early 1980s, possibly because London finance houses were decentralizing back-office work rather as happened in some American global cities (Noyelle, 1986). London itself has benefited massively from the deregulation of its financial heart also.

In Britain, the professional class grew by exactly 25 percent during the 1971-1981 period while the blue-collar class declined by 13 percent and the unemployed grew in number by 93 percent. This, of course, was the period immediately prior to the greatest economic shakeout as state involvement in production and reproduction was rapidly withdrawn and companies began pursuing a "leaner but fitter" survival strategy. The professional class is largely a home-owning one (87 percent) with high levels of domestic comfort and appliance ownership and much higher private medical care consumption than the semi-skilled, only 35 percent of whom are owner-occupiers, and smaller proportions of whom own the full range of domestic comforts. Unemployment is 60 percent higher in Northern Britain than in the south, whereas at the beginning of the 1960s it was only just over 30 percent greater.

Hence, postmodernization means polarization on a macro space-economy scale. The professional service class is undoubtedly continuing to grow while those in secure non-professional work decline and those in the casualized, sub-employed and part-time segments of the labor market grow as the new "waged poor," competing for urban space with the unwaged poor and unemployed. It is an urban world of playful, postmodern architecture, theme parks, new sports stadia, plazas and malls; for the enterprising a world of overconsumption, and for the welfare-dependent exclusion and underconsumption. Moreover, as Davis (1985) points out, the overconsumption rests on neoconservative politics rooted in massive borrowing, protection at the expense of the rest of the world of the value of domestic currency, high levels of military spending funnelling into high technology and Star Wars efflorescences with the creation of an almost pre-modern sub-proletariat available to service the consumption economy as domestics, child minders, cleaners and machine repairers.

But the postmodernized cityscape is not only a site of overconsumption in the new hyperspaces. It is often also, within the interstices of the play areas of the professional class and the enclosures of the poor, a site of emergent progressive political forms. The postmodern insight into the importance of *local* power has reflected a new issue-based urban politics centered on opposition to the materialism of overconsumption. Rainbow coalitions of ethnic, gender-based, environmentally-concerned and peace-seeking political movements have taken power in some of the most advanced of the postmodern redoubts, such as London, San Francisco and Los Angeles. This too, as Jameson (1982), Arac (1986), Berman (1987) and Schulte-Sasse (1987) have noted, is postmodernism in action from a progressive rather than a mindlessly consuming perspective.

The Postmodern Cityscape: Los Angeles and London

Rather in the vein of Jameson's (1984a) schema of progressive and regressive postmodernists and modernists, this analysis has shown that postmodernism is a politically contested terrain, and that although the initiative is often perceived, to have been grasped earliest as "no more than the pretty plaything of rampant capitalism" (Farrelly, 1986) it chimes with a new non-monolithic politics of social movements (Castells, 1983).

Such coexistences in space as citadels of overconsumption and new social movements that seek to replenish or endow locality with local meaning, such that consumers of both *perspectival spaces* (Baudrillard, 1976) may partially overlap, are precisely motifs in the postmodern cityscape. Both express an awakening to the possibilities of exerting local power in the face of an increasingly dead power exerted by neoconservative governments bloated by excesses of accumulation in both the monetary and military spheres. Centralized power has begun to lose its aura when it professes to be apocalyptic but finds itself paralyzed.

Thus, urbanity as a site of consumption becomes an escape from the dinosaur stumblings of the monopolitical monsters. Global finance capital and its networks exercise control functions from an increasingly widespread range of cities, hence excessive accumulation and distribution of wealth and income are city-focused. The casualties from hypertrophic expansion of debt from such centers (New York's Citicorp recently in effect wrote off $3 billion in Latin American debt, and even minor-league Minneapolis' Norwest Banking Corporation wrote off $63 million to the same region) are sucked out of their failing domestic economies to meet the new labor demand in the global cities (Sassen-Koob, 1984). For the first time in decades the population of central global cities such as London and New York may have ceased declining as both the new poor and the new rich flock to downtown residential areas. Some of the new poor occupy the inner suburban housing of the middle-class of previous generations, while some of the new rich occupy for-mer factories and warehouses that used to sustain the departed working classes. The postmodern cityscape is in part a terrain of paradox where space has become hyperflexible, but it is also recharged with traditional meaning. Downtown con-tinues to convey the image of accumulation in its newly-risen postmodern towers, giving legitimacy to the specific interest in profit-taking as transcendental local knowledge.

Los Angeles

From being the suburbs in search of a city, Los Angeles has rapidly become a definitive world-regional center of accumulation and trade. In a recent account of the restructuring of the city's urban and social fabric (Soja, Morales and Wolff, 1983) the city is perceived as having combined four experiences, typical of urban trajectories found elsewhere. For all the iconography of Hollywood and Malibu, it contained an industrial base in oil, auto, electrical and aerospace engineering from which much of its working population derived an income. In the 1970s, Los Angeles experienced that Detroit feeling as plant after plant closed, so that now only the Van Nuys auto assembly plant remains, and steel mills, as well as tire and component plants, have been closed.

However, to compensate for the downside, Los Angeles has had three other experiences that Soja, Morales, and Wolff (1983) equate to the Houston, Manhattan and Hong Kong trajectories. Aerospace and electronics have boomed as military expenditure has increased and substantial contracts have been awarded to Los Angeles firms such as Lockheed and McDonnell-Douglas. Scott (1985) has shown that high technology, most of it defense-related in aerospace, missile systems, computers and electronics, employs 250,000, compared with the Silicon Valley's 160,000. This complex of activities takes spatial form in the Aerospace Alley, which curves from the coast at Santa Monica to Orange County.

The Manhattan trajectory is expressed in the growth of a discernible downtown financial hub to Los Angeles, centered on the Bonaventure complex. Much of the capital responsible for this growth is foreign, particularly Canadian, British and Japanese who, unlike Californians who continued to perceive San Francisco as the banking capital of the West, saw the potential of Los Angeles as banker to the Pacific Rim. Thus Los Angeles now has a downtown symbolism much of which, like the Bonaventure, is clad in mirror-glass and is rather hostile to its surroundings. This is a mixture of last-gasp late modernism and interior-decorator postmodernism, with little evidence of playfulness or pastiche except in the Egyptianstyle museum, complete with pyramids, now in place next door.

Last, Los Angeles' Hong Kong experience lies in the massive immigration from less-developed and newly industrializing countries to its south and west. From being 85 percent "Anglo" in 1950, Los Angeles is now 50 percent so. Migrant communities have settled in ethnic enclaves such as little Tokyo, little Korea, Chinatown and little Vietnam, joining still sharply-segregated Watts and east Los Angeles whose *barrio* is itself composed of Hispanics from many countries, not only Mexico.

Los Angeles has a tightly defined segregated residential system and finegrained class as well as ethnic sub-divisions, with corridors such as Wilshire Boulevard distorting and compartmentalizing the rent-gradients which sieve the population so precisely. However, for all its fragmented and exclusive social discourses, Los Angeles has had two progressively-run local administrations, one in West Hollywood where a coalition of gays and senior citizens took control of the council, instituting rent control and other progressive policies; the other in Santa Monica, a self-styled people's republic where rent control was only a base for more ambitious plans to collectivize some retailing and other service provision. Moreover, as Lipsitz (1987) has shown, Los Angeles' ethnic minority cultures are in the process of creating a new, postmodern synthesis in the world of popular culture. East Los Angeles' exclusion from political power has produced a remarkable cultural displacement ranging from low-riders to Los Lobos.

London

London has experienced the schizophrenia of progressive postmodernism in its politics and radical excess in its postmodern global economy during the 1980s. Although it began to sprout high-rise office buildings, especially in the early postwar years when bomb-site developers erected the modernist equivalent of high-rise tarpaper shacks, London failed to imprint its global, imperial functional dominance in the sphere of circulation on the sky as it did on the ground. From having been a somewhat pale imitation of Paris with its Portland stone and brick neoclassicism, and not unpleasant in its spatial scale, London made the unforgivable mistake of failing to focus its new highrises. The result was a mess of single stumps poking into the air. Rather as Los Angeles has developed its new downtown so, more recently, has metropolitan definition been given to the true power center of the U.K. economy, the financial core known as "the City." Here some new buildings, like the logoform Natwest Bank or the distinctly postmodern Lloyds Insurance building, soon to be joined by more in the Manhattanization of east-central London, now cluster to celebrate rather than, as previously, mask the business of accumulation.

This recent transformation is a product of neoconservative finance policy in Britain which, first, removed exchange controls, resulting in a flood outward (to places like Los Angeles) of U.K.-based banking capital; second, raised interest rates to cure inflation leading to a lesser influx of capital to the British finance system; and third, deregulated the financial institutions of the City of London to open it up as the most internationalized finance center in the world. In 1970 London had 163 foreign banks; in 1984 it had 403. New York, the nearest competitor, had 75 in 1970 and 307 in 1984 (Thrift, 1985).

This process of internationalization has substantially distorted the metropolitan housing market, giving advantage to those already in it or who may suddenly become rich on inheriting a family residence that may now be worth a million dollars. Such capital gains and the salaries of excess that are earned in finance and related industries have created new demands for private health, education and other luxury consumption, and the personnel to service it. Hence there is a revival of demand for domestic servants who, as Ascherson (1986) puts it are:

commuter servants, as in Johannesburg, who catch a 5 a.m. train in a distant suburb to wear maid's uniform or even butler's livery all day (Ascherson, 1986).

Such people might hitherto have been part of London's industrial work force, but that has in large measure been blown away by monetarism and world recession.

Nevertheless, some part of the 400,000 London unemployed resisted for five years by helping to keep in power Britain's possibly most radical progressive metropolitan council from 1981. The Greater London Council under Ken Livingstone was constituted in terms of what Arac (1986) and Jameson (1982) conceive as the postmodern politics of *difference* in which issue-based coalitions are stitched together to express spatially local and non-local political concerns. Policies towards furthering the interests of women, ethnic and other minorities, the disabled and the unemployed were backed by the establishment of new departments and committees with interests being bound together imaginatively and not without difficulty in strategic decision-making. The ethnic sub-motif of popular culture, diverse but dynamic in the manner that Lipsitz (1987) describes that of East Los Angeles, except that it is black and reggae in character rather than Hispanic, was a beneficiary of such policies. Indeed, progressive postmodernism in the political sphere presented sufficient of a symbolic threat to the legitimacy of the neoconservative project that, in an unprecedented act, local power was abolished for metropolitan areas by the Thatcher government in 1986. The postmodern condition is thus one of paradox and struggle sited in the perspectival space of the city as perhaps never before.

To summarize, the debate between the defenders of modernism and the protagonists of postmodernism, which has largely been ignored by contemporary urbanists, contains valuable conceptual instruments for analyzing change processes in late twentieth-century cities and society. It is important not to see this cultural, political and economic reformation in terms of simple oppositions, conflict and antagonism. Too much of the debate has taken that form in the social philosophical literature, as a result of which the emergent cultural form has been labeled too early as neoconservative and vilified or ignored as a result. There are changes taking place in urban society and in ways of perceiving it which link in complex ways the cultural and political-economic spheres. It is essential for progressive urbanists to recognize that although, in terms of the physical appearance of new developments in the built form of cities, it appears that the interests of capital have been furthered most in the appropriation of postmodern motifs, there are numerous progressive counter-currents operating on the contested terrain of postmodernism. That these often reject the inherited social and political forms of the modernist era is as significant as the rejection by capital of inherited, monolithic forms such as the Fordist productive structure and welfare capitalism.

References

Aglietta, M. (1978) *A Theory of Capitalist Regulation.* London: Verso.
Albertsen, N. (1986) "Towards post-fordist localities?" Mimeo available from the author, School of Architecture, 800 Aarhus, Denmark.
Anderson, P. (1984) Modernity and revolution, *New Left Review, 14* 96-113.
Arac, J. (1986) "Introduction," *Postmodernism and Politics.* Minneapolis: University of Minnesota Press.
Ascherson, N. (1986) London's new class: The great cash-in, *The Observer,* May 25, 9.
Baudrillard, J. (1976) *L'Exchange Symbolique et la Mort.* Paris: Gallimard.
Berman, M. (1983) *All That is Solid Melts Into Air.* London: Verso.
Berman, R. (1987) The routinization of charismatic modernism and the problem of post-modernity, *Cultural Critique, 5,* 49-68.
Bernstein, R. (Ed.) (1985) *Habermas and Modernity.* Cambridge: Polity.
Burger, C. (1986) The disappearance of art: The postmodernism debate in the U.S., *Telos, 68,* 93-106.
Castells, M. (1977) *The Urban Question.* London: Edward Arnold.
Castells, M. (1983) *The City and the Grassroots.* London: Edward Arnold.
Cooke, P. (1983) *Theories of Planning and Spatial Development.* London: Hutchinson.
Cooke, P. (1987a) Britain's new spatial paradigm: Technology, locality and society in transition, *Environment Planning A, 19,* 1-13.
Cooke, P. (1987b) Space, culture, and the paradigm of postmodernity. In P. Cooke and N. Thrift (Eds.), *Captive Britain.* Cambridge: Cambridge University Press.
Cooke, P. (1988) Modernity, postmodernity and the city, *Theory, Culture and Society, 5,* (forthcoming)
Davis, M. (1985) Urban renaissance and the spirit of postmodernism, *New Left Review, 151,* 106-114.
Derrida, J. (1978) *Writing and Difference.* London: Routledge & Kegan Paul.
Dews, P. (1986) Adorno, post-structuralism and the critique of identity, *New Left Review, 157,* 28-44.
Farrelly, E. (1986) The new spirit, *Architectural Review, 180,* 7-12.

Foster, H. (Ed.) (1985) *Postmodern Culture.* London: Pluto.

Foucault, M. (1980) *Power/Knowledge.* New York: Pantheon.

Frisby, D. (Ed.) (1985) *Fragments of Modernity.* Cambridge: Polity.

Geertz, C. (1983) *Local Knowledge.* New York: Basic Books.

Harvey, D. (1987) "Flexible accumulation through urbanization: Reflections on 'post-modernism' in the American City." Mimeo available from the Department of Geography, Oxford University.

Hassan, I. (1971) Postmodernism: A paracritical bibliography. *New Literary History, 3.*

Hassan, I. (1985) The culture of postmodernism, *Theory, Culture and Society, 2,* 119-131.

Hohendahl, R. (1986) Habermas' philosophical discourse of modernity, *Telos, 69,* 49-65.

Hutcheon, L. (1987) The politics of postmodernism: Parody and history, *Cultural Critique, 5,* 179-208.

Huyssen, A. (1984) Mapping the postmodern, *New German Critique, 33,* 5-52.

Jameson, F. (1982) Interview. In *Diacritics, 12,* 72-91.

Jameson, F. (1984a) The politics of theory: Ideological positions in the postmodernism debate, *New German Critique, 33,* 53-65.

Jameson, F. (1984b) Postmodernism, or the cultural logic of late capitalism, *New Left Review, 146,* 53-94.

Jencks, C. (1977) *The Language of Postmodern Architecture.* New York: Rizzoli.

Lipietz, A. (1982) Towards global Fordism? *New Left Review, 132,* 33-48.

Lipsitz, G. (1987) Cruising around the historical bloc: Postmodernism and popular music in East Los Angeles, *Cultural Critique, 5,* 157-178.

Lynch, K. (1960) *The Image of the City.* Cambridge: MIT Press.

Lyotard, J.F. (1984) *The Postmodern Condition: A Report on Knowledge.* Minneapolis: University of Minnesota Press.

Lyotard, J.F. (1987) Rules and paradoxes and svelte appendix, *Cultural Critique, 5,* 209-219.

Mandel, E. (1975) *Late Capitalism.* London: Verso.

Noyelle, T. (1986) "Services and the world economy: Towards a new international division of labour." Mimeo available from Conservation of Human Resources, Columbia University, New York.

Said, E. (1984) *The World, the Text and the Critic.* London: Faber and Faber.

Sassen-Koob, S. (1984) The new labor demand in global cities. In M.P. Smith (Ed.), *Cities in Transformation.* Beverly Hills: Sage.

Schulte-Sasse, J. (1987) Introduction - Modernity and modernism, postmodernity and postmodernism: Framing the issue, *Cultural Critique, 5,* 5-22.

Scott, A. (1985) High technology industry and territorial development: The rise of the Orange County Complex: 1955-1984. In *Working Paper 85,* Department of Geography, University of California, Los Angeles.

Soja, E., R. Morales, and E. Wolff (1983) Urban restructuring: An analysis of social and spatial change in Los Angeles, *Economic Geography, 59,* 195-230.

Tafuri, M., and F. Dal Co (1979) *Modern Architecture.* New York: Abrams.

Teece, D. (1980) Economies of scope and scope of the enterprise, *Journal of Economic Behavior and Organization, 1,* 198-223.

Thrift, N. (1985) "The urban geography of international commercial capital." Mimeo available from Department of Geography, Bristol University.

Wolfe, T. (1981) *From Bauhaus to Our House.* New York: Washington Square Press.

THE COMMUNITY QUESTION RE-EVALUATED[1]

Barry Wellman
University of Toronto

Given its importance to humankind and accessibility to public discourse, it is a safe guess that the community question in some form will remain open to the end of time. Since World II important transformations have taken place in scholarly approaches to the question. Systematic efforts to gather data have supplanted armchair theorizing. New ways of studying local social histories have demythologized notions of stable pastoral villages. Network analysis has freed the community question from its traditional preoccupation with solidarity and neighborhood. The broad shift towards structural analysis in the social sciences has created possibilities for the integration of the community question with studies of the family, household, and personal health. The development of political economic thought has made salient questions about how relations of power and dependency in large-scale social systems engender and reflect interpersonal relationships of cooperation and power.

Looking for Community

"Things ain't wot they used to be" the music hall song laments. Contemporary urbanites perversely flatter themselves by remarking how stressful are modern times. They fear that communities have fallen apart, with loneliness and alienation leading to a war of all against all. They are sure that their pre-industrial ancestors led charmed lives when they could bathe in the warmth of true solidary community.

A large part of the fear comes from a selective perception of the present. Many urbanites think they are witnessing loneliness when they observe people walking or driving by themselves. Mass media quickly and graphically circulate news about New York subway attacks and Parisian "terrorist" bombings. The public generalizes its fears -- the attack could take place next door tomorrow-- and ahistorically forgets to compare contemporary crime and political violence rates with the past.

Paradoxically, few urbanites will confess to living lives of lonely desperation. They know that they have supportive communities, and that their friends, neighbors, kin and coworkers have them as well. Yet each person believes that he or she is the exception: it is the vast hordes out there in the "mass society" who are lonely and isolated.

At the same time, nostalgia for the perfect pastoral past dims awareness of the powerful stresses and cleavages that have always pervaded human society. The inhabitants of almost all contemporary societies have less to worry about than their predecessors with respect to the basics of human life. Worldwide, people now are likely to eat better, be better housed and clothed, suffer less personal and property crime, live longer, and see their loved ones live longer. In their concern about current problems, people often forget about the ones that are no more. AIDS does not appear to rival the Black Death; automobile pollution is more benign than knee-deep horse manure.

The basic question -- *the community question* -- is how the large-scale structure of social systems reciprocally affects the small-scale structure and contents of interpersonal relations within them. Traditionally the public (as well as scholars) have called such ties "communities" when they have clustered in neighborhoods. But much the same issues pertain to the study of kinship groups, households and work groups.

It is likely that pundits have worried about the impact of social change on communities ever since human beings ventured beyond their caves. The community question clearly preoccupied biblical scholars concerned (then, as now) that the establishment of the Israeli state would lead to tribal disintegration (Zeidman and Wellman, forthcoming). It was a major issue to Renaissance intellectuals whose concerns ranged from Machiavelli's (1532) celebration of the liberation of communal patterns to Hobbes' (1651) fears that the absence of social structures would result in the interpersonal war of all against all. It was a key theme in the thinking of eighteenth century British social philosophers such as Locke and Hume (Wills, 1978), who sought to deduce the social basis of larger-scale societies from their understanding of primordial communal relations. Their student, Thomas Jefferson, gave the question an anti-urban cast. Communal bonds are not viable in industrial, commercial cities, he asserted. "The mobs of great cities add just so much to the support of pure government, as sores do to the strength of the human body" (1784, p. 86).

In the ensuing two centuries, many leading social commentators have been gainfully employed suggesting various ways in which large-scale social changes associated with the Industrial Revolution may have affected the structure and operations of communities. Their analyses have continued to reflect the ambivalence with which nineteenth century pundits faced the impacts of industrialization, bureaucratization, capitalism, imperialism and technological developments on interpersonal relations. Where religion, locality and kinship group had some integrative claims on interpersonal relations, the shift to mobile, market societies now had the potential to disconnect individuals from the strengths and constraints of traditional societies (White and White, 1962; Marx, 1964; Williams, 1973; Smith, 1979).

On the one hand, such analysts noted that the large-scale reorganization of production has created new opportunities for community relations. Thus Marx

(1859) acknowledged that industrialization had reduced poverty and Engels (1885) realized that working-class home ownership would heighten neighborhood communal bonds. Max Weber (1946, 1958) argued that bureaucracy and urbanization would liberate many from the traditional bases of community, and Émile Durkheim (1893) suggested that the new complex divisions of labor would bind urbanites together in networks of interdependencies. Georg Simmel (1902-1903, 1922) focused on the consequences for the individual of these urban divisions of labor. No longer bound up totally by one social circle, they would have greater personal freedom as they maneuvered through their partial social attachments.

On the other hand, these same analysts feared the negative consequences of the large-scale changes. Thus a centerpiece of Marx and Engels' analysis was the new types of interpersonal exploitation brought by industrial capitalism. Weber feared that bureaucratization and urbanization would weaken communal bonds as the liberated citizens escaped traditional authority, and Durkheim similarly feared that the loss of solidarity could foster social pathology. In the same essay in which he celebrated urban liberation, Simmel (1922) worried that the new individualism would lead to superficial relationships.[2]

This ambivalence about the consequences of large-scale changes has continued well into the twentieth century. Analysts have kept asking if things have, in fact, fallen apart. Are interpersonal ties likely to be few in number, short in duration and specialized in content? Have personal networks so withered away that the few remaining ties serve only as the basis for disconnected bilateral relationships rather than as the multilateral foundation for more extensive and integrated communities?

Indeed science-fiction authors promise continuing interest in the community question (see Wellman's 1987 review). Recent novels have provided scenarios ranging from alienation in densely-packed (Ballard, 1975), hyper-capitalistic (Brunner, 1968) mass societies, to post-atomic holocaust returns to tribal solidarities (Lessing, 1974; Atwood, 1985), to wired people in wired cities moving easily between interest groups (Delaney, 1976; Brunner, 1975; Gibson, 1986).

Given its importance to humankind and accessibility to public discourse, it is a safe guess that the community question in some form will remain open to the end of time. Yet since World II important transformations have taken place in scholarly approaches to the question. First, systematic efforts to gather data have supplanted armchair theorizing. Second, new ways of studying local social histories have demythologized notions of stable pastoral villages. Third, network analysis has freed the community question from its traditional preoccupation with solidarity and neighborhood. Moreover, the broad shift towards structural analysis in the social sciences has created possibilities for the integration of the community question with studies of the family, household, and personal health.

Fourth, the development of political economic thought has made salient questions about how relations of power and dependency in large-scale social systems engender and reflect interpersonal relationships of cooperation and power.

Rediscovering Community

One intellectual generation ago the watchwords of community sociologists were documentation and description. The profession preoccupied itself with demonstrations that community persisted -- dare they say "flourished." Scholars of the First (industrialized, non-socialist) World wanted to show that supportive communal bonds remained even in the supposedly most pernicious habitats: inner-city slums (e.g., Whyte, 1943; Young and Willmott, 1957; Gans, 1962; Liebow, 1967) and middle-class suburbs (e.g., Clark, 1966; Gans, 1967; Bell, 1968). Scholars of the Third (colonized) World battled fears that the migrants flooding into industrializing cities would form communally-disconnected, politically-dangerous hordes.[3]

With hindsight, postwar "loss of community" fears came from the same place as evil creatures from outer space and Joe McCarthy's search for Reds under the bed. Those holding such fears saw alien forces ripping apart the small-scale tried-and-true. They believed that the Frankensteinian "machine in the garden" (Marx, 1964) had run amok. Beneath the jingoistic celebration of small-town virtues lurked the fear that people were inherently evil: ready to rob, rape, pillage and turn atheistically communist as soon as communal bonds were loosened.

The rediscovery of community has been one of sociology's great post-World War II triumphs. By the 1960s urban scholars were able to show that community had survived the major transformations of the (post) Industrial Revolution. Rapidly developing ethnographic and survey research techniques demonstrated that neighborhood and kinship groups continue to be abundant and strong. Large institutions have neither smashed nor withered communal relations. On the contrary: the larger and more inflexible the institutions, the more people seem to depend on their informal communal ties to deal with them. Communities may well have changed in response to the pressures, opportunities and constraints of large-scale forces. However, they have not withered away. They buffer households against large-scale forces, provide mutual aid, and serve as secure bases to engage with the outside world (see the reviews in Keller, 1968; Fischer, 1976; Gordon, 1978; Warren, 1978; Wellman and Leighton, 1979; Smith, 1979; Choldin, 1985).

This scholarly rediscovery of community resonated strongly with the political developments of the 1960s. The civil rights movement encouraged more positive evaluations of urban black neighborhoods (e.g., Stack, 1974) and, by extension, of lumpenproletariat life everywhere. The neo-Rousseauian student movement preached the inherent goodness of humankind. Students and anthropologists boarded newly-cheap charter flights to spend $5 a day discovering that Europe and the Third World were full of nice people in interesting villages and cities. Planners turned away from urban renewal towards the preservation of dense, noisy downtown neighborhoods (as expressed most vividly in Jane Jacobs' 1961 anthem).

This transformation in thinking has become the current academic orthodoxy. Scholars no longer think of cities as evil, permeated with Original Sin. Their current Jacobsean cum Rousseauesque celebrations of community have the lingering aroma of the 1960s, seeing urbanites as permeated with Original Good and happily maintaining mutually supportive ties. The rest of the populace has been slower to catch on: policymakers, the media and the public at large are still quick to fear the urban and to yearn for the pastoral.

How Green were the Valleys?[4]

At the same time as urban sociologists were discovering the existence of contemporary communities, the more historically minded started using similar systematic empirical research techniques to study preindustrial villages, towns and cities. Until their work became known, analysts had contrasted the disorderly urban present with the pastoral ideal of bucolic, solidary villages (Poggioli, 1975). They assumed that such communities were socially cohesive and stable, with little movement in or out. Yet the supposed communalism of society's preindustrial has turned out to be an artifact of how earlier scholars studied the problem. By looking for community in localities and not in networks, they had focused on local phenomena and stability rather than on long distances and mobility.

Social scientists have recently analyzed local histories in preindustrial and newly-industrializing European and North American societies. They have concentrated on the period between 1600 and 1900 when emerging national governments began to keep more careful records. By using such sources as parish registers and early censuses, historical demographers have enumerated the gender, marital status and occupations of all persons living in a household. Record linkage techniques help trace the social and spatial movement of persons and households (Laslett, 1971; Anderson, 1971; Aminzade and Hodson, 1982; Thernstrom, 1969; Katz, 1975; Darroch, and Ornstein, 1983).

The data indicate that the average preindustrial household was quite small, and that many families were socially and spatially mobile. People were not very local. When young, they often worked in the city but kept ties back to their rural villages. Artisans and soldiers were frequently on the road. Women married and moved, geographically and socially. Servants' ties to their distant families concurrently linked masters' families to the servants' rural homes. And, as all readers of Jane Austen know, these complex connections linked far-flung networks of community ties.

Indeed, LeRoy Ladurie's (1975) rich account of medieval village life in southern France reveals a good deal of geographical mobility as early as the 1300s. In order to trace networks of Albigensian heretics, Catholic investigators asked all residents to report who their friends were, who had influence, and how they spent their days. They used this information to build up detailed accounts of the village community.

Many villagers travelled widely. Some were shepherds following their flocks over the Pyrenees, some were itinerant soldiers, while others travelled south to the Spanish coast or west along the Mediterranean to northern Italy. The people of Montaillou had frequent contact with other villages, and passing travellers often gave them news of the outside world. With such contact came the acquisition of new ideas, intermarriage, and the formation of new alliances.

Montaillou was by no means a solidary village. Various factions competed within it for wealth and status. Each faction used their ties outside the village to enhance their local standing, and each used their local support to build external alliances. Like preindustrial villages everywhere, their local life was very much a part of the larger world (see also Davis, 1975, 1983; Hufton, 1974; Tilly, 1964).

Community as Network

The discovery of the complexities of past and present communities led analysts to move beyond seeking to prove or disprove that communities continued to exist. They began to realize that to demonstrate that community remains in neighborhoods is not to show that community is confined to neighborhoods. By the early 1970s several analysts had expanded the definition of community to take into account far-flung, sparsely-knit ties stretching beyond the boundaries of neighborhood or kinship solidarities. They argued that the essence of community was its *social* structure and not its *spatial* structure. They suggested that only through such a revision in the ways in which scholars thought about community could they fully understand how urbanites supported each other. This, they contended, is because large-scale changes in the division and control of labor and resources had transformed the nature of community. Rather than being full members of one solidary local or kinship group, contemporary urbanites now juggled limited memberships in multiple, specialized, interest-based communities.

These analysts started treating "community" as "personal community": a network of significant, informal "community ties" defined from the standpoint of a "focal person".[5] Their research has relied on large-scale surveys, with investigators relying on respondents' accounts of their networks for reasons of economy. Investigators usually gather information about the networks' structure (e.g., links between network members), composition (e.g., the percentage who are kin), and contents (e.g., social support). They have been centrally concerned with questions of social structural form originally raised by Georg Simmel (e.g., 1922): how do patterns of relations in networks affect the ways in which resources flow to their members?[6]

This transmutation of "community" into "social network" has been more than the repackaging of old intellectual goods. It has helped document the strong persistence of communities even when their neighborhood traces are faint. It has left open the extent to which such personal communities are socially homogeneous, spatially local, tightly bounded or densely knit. It has encouraged analysts to evaluate different types of ties -- kin or friend, intimate or acquaintance, local or distant -- in terms of the access to resources which they provide. It has shown how the structural location of individuals and households in large-scale divisions of labor -- such as their involvement in domestic and paid work-- affects the kinds of networks of which they are members and the kinds of resources which flow to and from them through these networks (e.g. Pahl, 1984; Wellman, 1985). It has provided a basis for understanding if kinship and friendship are substitutable, complementary or dispensable in contemporary social systems (Pitt-Rivers, 1973; Fischer, 1982).

On the debit side, the concentration of the network approach on personal connections has separated the study of public communities from that of private (network) communities. The focus on strong ties has meant the analytic neglect of neighborhoods and other public places as real ecological entities in which all inhabitants must rub shoulders and come to terms with each another. Yet the network approach can contribute to studying the mutual observing and regulating endemic in public communities (Lofland, 1973, 1983). Thus, disconnected strangers are rarely involved in collective political disorders, be they mass meetings, riots or rebellions. Strong and weak ties underlie and structure such seemingly massified public activity (Feagin, 1973; Feagin and Hahn, 1973; Tilly, 1964, 1975, 1978, 1979, 1988; Brym, 1978).

Starting in the 1970s, many studies have documented the existence, scope and importance of personal communities in a variety of social systems: *Toronto* (Wellman et al., 1973; Wellman, 1979; Wellman, Carrington and Hall, 1988; Shulman, 1976; Leighton, 1986); *London* (Willmott, 1987); *France* (Ferrand, 1981; Reichmann, 1987); *Hong Kong* (Wong, 1987); *India* (Howard, 1974,1988; Bandyopadhyay and van Eschen, 1981); *Mexico* (Lomnitz, 1977, 1985); *Northern California* (Fischer, 1982; Campbell, Marsden and Hurlburt, 1986);

Detroit (Laumann, 1973; Fischer, et al., 1977; Verbrugge, 1977; Warren, 1981; Connerly, 1985); *Kansas City* (Greenbaum and Greenbaum, 1981; Greenbaum, 1982); Black American areas of *Los Angeles* (Oliver, 1984, 1986); and, abandoning local areas entirely as a sampling frame with a U.S. national General Social Survey sample (Burt, 1984, 1986a, 1986b; Marsden, 1986, 1987).

The similarities are striking in the basic parameters of these samples, holding between cities and countries. Wherever studied, personal communities usually:

-- contain about a half-dozen intimate ties and perhaps a dozen active, if not quite intimate, ties out of the total of about 1,500 relationships that tentative evidence suggests people maintain (Boissevain, 1974; Pool and Kochen, 1978).

-- contain a mixture of both kin and non-kin. Many samples contain about half kin and half friends, neighbors and workmates. Few people maintain active ties with all or most of their kinfolk.

-- have only one or two intimate neighboring or workmate relationships, but a half-dozen to a dozen weaker community ties with neighbors and workmates. For example, our current East York (Toronto) research finds that the average active tie stretches nine miles between residences (Wellman, Carrington and Hall, 1988).

-- are moderately knit, with less than half of the members of a person's network being actively linked with each other. The East Yorkers' active networks typically comprise one core cluster of densely-knit relations, one or two small social circles, and one or two isolates who know no one in the network other than the East Yorker. Because these relationships are rarely tightly bounded in a single network, they act as "local bridges" indirectly connecting members of one community with another. The interweaving of these ties connects networks and integrates social systems (Granovetter, 1973, 1982).

-- provide a variety of socially supportive resources crucial to the household and the operation of larger social systems. Such support is efficient, low-cost, flexible and more controllable than aid from bureaucracies. While urbanites gain a wide range of support from their networks, most ties specialize in the kinds of aid they provide. For example, some relationships provide emotional support while others help with household needs. This means that individuals and households must work to maintain an array of potentially supportive relationships. When they have problems, they must shop for assistance at specialized boutiques of relationships, rather than being able to count on finding help at relational general stores.

Researchers have gone beyond just demonstrating the sheer existence of communities to analyzing differences in the composition, structure and operations of these communities:

Weighing the Balance between Local and Distant Relations: The fact that most ties are nonlocal does not mean that neighborly relations have disappeared. The characteristics of neighborhoods -- such as their homogeneity -- affects the extent to which people stay on their own block or neighbor more widely. Most people engage in selective neighboring, maintaining friendly relations with a few local residents. In addition to serving as handy sources of domestic goods and services, neighboring ties increase residents' senses of security and belonging (Gates, Stevens and Wellman, 1973; Warren, 1981; Greenbaum and Greenbaum, 1981; Connerly, 1985).

Investigating Urban/Suburban/Rural Differences in the Composition of Personal Communities: Fischer's (1982) study draws upon a northern California sample using sites from central San Francisco to the Sierra Nevada foothills. When compared with those living in smaller places, urban dwellers are less involved with people drawn from the traditional complex of kin, neighborhood and church. Although maintaining some kin and neighborhood ties, they are more involved with persons drawn from the worlds of friendship, work and secular associations. To be sure, urbanites have more "modern" communities but the essential similarity of most networks in all locales is quite striking.

Investigating the Health Consequences of Socially Supportive Ties: High levels of support appear to make individuals healthier, feel better, cope better with chronic and acute difficulties, and live longer. Thus one massive longitudinal study found that Alameda County, California residents "who lacked social and community ties were more likely to die in the follow-up period than those with more extensive contacts" (Berkman and Syme, 1979, p. 186). At the same time, the means by which support works is still open to debate. Analysts have variously argued that support prevents people from encountering stress, "buffers" them from experiencing the full brunt of stress when it is encountered, or steers them to useful caregivers.[7]

Identifying the Social Causes of "Social Support": Several scholars have shown that rather than being a broad, unidimensional characteristic of relationships, different types of relationships specialize in the kinds of support they provide. While no standard typology currently exists, researchers often distinguish between empathetic understanding, emotional support, material aid (goods, money and services), and providing information (Wellman with Hiscott, 1985; Barrera and Ainlay, 1983; Hammer, 1983; Tardy, 1985; Wellman, Carrington and Hall, 1988; Israel and Rounds in press). Parents and adult children provide a broad spectrum of aid, women are especially likely to exchange emotional aid, while neighbors (and other frequently seen network members) exchange many services (Rosenthal, 1987; Wellman, et al., 1987a; Wellman, 1985). The nature of networks also matters: Large networks are more supportive than small, sparsely-knit networks are more companionate, and heterogeneous networks -- with their access to the resources of many social worlds -- are better providers of goods and services (Wellman, et al., 1987b).

Discovering the Differences between Social Support in First and Third World Communities: In (post) industrial social systems, informal social support is egalitarian, reciprocally exchanged and specialized, with different relationships tending to provide companionship, emotional aid, goods and services. It contributes primarily to the household's domestic needs (Hall and Wellman, 1985; Wellman, Carrington and Hall, 1988). In Third World systems, there is more of a tendency for such aid to flow through inegalitarian parent-client relationships. Ties are sometimes more broadly based, providing assistance with paid work as well as for domestic needs (Roberts, 1973; Lomnitz, 1977, 1985; Bodemann, 1988).

The main difference is the insecurity each household wishes to diminish. In turn this involves differences in the types of resources mobilized through the network. Because Torontonians have no urgent need for survival they can manage with resources with less apprehension than Latin Americans living on the margins. The Torontonians' life strategy is not close to a survival edge, and their insecurity comes from spheres other than the economy. It is associated more with personal disequilibria, emergencies, and a wide range of crises. They obtain three main types of support: they enjoy companionship, avoiding isolation; reduce insecurity facing crises or emotional stress; upgrade living conditions through home improvement. Unlike the Third World, economic support from community members is usually limited to upgrading homes, such as obtaining mortgages for better houses or improving current residences.

'Support' remains 'social' for Torontonians insofar as economic survival is not their most urgent demand. Their supportive relationships tend to reproductive, domestic and community concerns. Other relationships of exchange, support and control help them to accomplish paid work. The absence of the economic aspect of social support is one of the main differences with those Third World social contexts where economic motivation is stronger. Consider, for instance, those countries where employment is unstable and there are no retirement funds. In these countries, security of survival is an urgent demand. For marginal groups, this involves the development of survival strategies. Middle-class groups develop informal networks and formal relationships to support upward mobility. Traditional oligarchies combine property accumulation with the expansion of kinship relationships.[8]

Seeing How Involvement in Paid and Domestic Work affects the Communities of Men and Women: There is no reason to posit a discontinuity between relations in the community and relations in the household. Such a tendency to treat the household as special reflects a particularly American tendency to idolize the household as haven (Sennett, 1970; Lasch, 1977). Several scholars have argued that the sacralization of the household masks unequal divisions of labor within it, with women bearing the major share. They suggest that social relations of reproduction in the household should be studied as domestic work rather than as family psychodrama. Domestic ties often are neither egalitarian nor broadly reciprocal, and many ties may not be integrated into densely-knit, supportive networks. For example, not only does the independent access to resources of Hong Kong "working daughters" profoundly weaken their dependency on their parents, the kinship networks of their families significantly affect the degree to which these women are drawn into the industrial labor force (Salaff, 1981).

Such a conception of the household opens matters up to deal with asymmetric exchanges of resources inside the household and alliances made by women in order to deal with reproductive burdens. Thus Luxton (1980) shows in fine ethnographic detail the ways in which working class Canadian housewives operate to gain access to necessary material and emotional resources. An important thrust of this line of research has been to show how household members' positions in large-scale and small-scale social systems greatly affect domestic relations. Women, for example, maintain personal community networks for their families. When they are overwhelmed by the double load of paid and domestic work, their families cut back on their friendship ties rather than have the husbands pick up the slack. Indeed, such analyses have argued that gender itself is as much a relationally defined variable as an inherent sexual attribute: what men and women do is greatly determined by the resources, claims and opportunities that their ties bring them (e.g., Bott, 1971; Tilly and Scott, 1978; Fox, 1980; Luxton, 1980; Peattie and Rein, 1983; Eichler, 1985; Wellman, 1985; Peattie, 1986).

Studying the Extent to which Networks Integrate and Decouple Urban Social Systems: While most personal network studies concentrate on the ties and small-scale networks themselves, several analysts have wondered how such networks integrate larger-scale social systems (see Granovetter's seminal discussions, 1973, 1982). For example, the social map of relationships in Northern Ireland almost perfectly reproduces its Protestant/Catholic cleavage (Boal, 1972) while religious, ethnic and socioeconomic groups overlap in Detroit (Laumann, 1973) and Kansas City (Greenbaum and Greenbaum, 1981; Greenbaum, 1982).

Indian research shows much complexity beneath the veneer of caste differences. A comparative study of networks in rural Bengal shows that the social organization of villages varies from patron-clientism to egalitarianism. Caste, class and family relationships intersect and cleave as villagers manipulate alliances and exchanges to gain resources from each other and state authorities (Bandyopadhyay and van Eschen, 1981).

Villagers often manipulate their opportunities for relationships by migrating to cities. In the Indian industrial city of Ranchi, workers in large factories are more likely to have egalitarian relationships with coworkers than workers in small artisanal shops. Factory workers, facing a bureaucratic structure jointly, co-operate across caste, tribal and neighborhood boundaries to deal with their work and domestic situations. In contrast, artisanal workers compete among themselves for their patrons' favors in securing and retaining jobs (Howard, 1974, 1988). The situation is the direct opposite of romantic notions of communally integrated artisanal workshops and alienated, disconnected factories. Although artisanal workers rarely form supportive, densely-knit communities, the factory workers-- jointly subject to standardized bureaucratic rules and less dependent on competitive patronage -- readily maintain supportive, densely-knit communities.

Mating Network Analysis with Political Economy

Now that we have community, what are we going to do about it? For the "community question" (Wellman, 1979) is more than just a suggestion that network analysis provides useful tools to move community studies out of their neighborhood cul-de-sac. It is the question of specifying the ways in which large-scale divisions of labor affect the composition, organization and content of interpersonal ties.

How can we address this question without getting continually diverted into the apocalyptic rhetoric about whether "community" still exists? One way is to avoid throwing out the baby with the bath-water. Just because we have refuted the notion that large-scale social transformations can destroy community, we still must investigate the ways in which they can affect community. Early discussions of the impact of large-scale phenomena on community were heavily abstract and reified. Yet social forces do not work in the abstract. They work through con-crete relationships between groups and individuals which specify opportunities and constraints, and which channel scarce resources to those in different locations in social systems.

Network analysis provides concepts and tools to see how such flows of resources operate (see Burt, 1980; Berkowitz, 1982; Rogers and Kincaid, 1981; Knoke and Kuklinski, 1983; Wellman, 1983). Network analysis is more than a set of techniques to gather and handle data. It is a paradigmatic approach which argues that the main business of social scientists is to study social structure and its consequences. Rather than working toward an indirect understanding of "social structures" in the abstract, network analysts try to study concrete social structures directly. They map these structures, describe their patterns, and seek to uncover the effects of these patterns on the behavior of the individual members of these social structures -- whether people, groups or organizations. Reversing the traditional logic of inquiry in sociology, network analysts argue that social categories (e.g., classes, races) and bounded groups (e.g., traditional communities) are best analyzed by examining relations between social actors. Rather than beginning with an *a priori* classification of the observable world into a discrete set of categories, they begin with a set of relations. Thus they draw inferences from wholes to parts, from structures and relations to categories, from behaviors to attitudes (these points are further developed in Wellman and Berkowitz, 1988).

The network approach enables analysts to get beyond broadly vague arguments about whether community has fallen apart held together at the core or is really a heterogeneous, sparsely-knit set of friends (Wellman and Leighton, 1979). At the interpersonal level, network analysis provides a vocabulary to see how differential location in social structures affects to whom persons link in communities, how these links are organized, and what community members get out of their relationships. Analysts can take the bird's-eye view of the outside observer to see the overall shape of community in a social system. They can adopt the Ptolemaic viewpoint of individuals to examine their communal relationships as these individuals see them. They can even zoom in to take a microscopic look at the nature of ties and clusters within an individual's personal community.

Nor are investigators limited to one analytic level. By seeing clusters of community relations as supernodes, the "network of networks approach," analysts have a means of moving up and down the scales to trace the reciprocal impacts of large-scale and interpersonal processes (Craven and Wellman, 1973). They can treat a cluster of friends or kin as a node in a larger social structure just as analysts of intercorporate relations do when they trace the linkages of the directors of these corporations (Mintz and Schwartz, 1985; Stokman, Ziegler and Scott, 1985).

Like network analysis, political economic analyses are also inherently relational in their epistemology (Marchak, 1985), be they looking at how control over the means of production defines classes (Wright, 1979, 1980) or how linked international relations of dependency affects national development (Frank, 1969). To a great extent, the relational conceptualization of the political economists has remained at the metaphorical level, but it does provide the basis for a fruitful linkage with network analysis, the relational approach par excellence.

Network analysis, in practice if not in principle, has tended to treat community networks in isolation from larger social phenomena and to assume that most relationships of companionship and support are egalitarian. In contrast, political economy insists that all relationships are potentially uneven in the resources to which each party has access and in the power which they have over each other. Rather than nice relationships of companionable supportiveness, the political economic world is an arena of potential dominance and dependency. This is true on the scale of the world-system (Wallerstein, 1974) or small towns in large societies (Peattie, 1968; Roberts, 1973).

Political economists have also provided the lead in placing community relationships in larger context. Thus Luxton (1980) has shown how the everyday lives of Canadian housewives are conditioned by the ways in which their husbands' jobs fit into world divisions of labor, Bodemann (1988) has shown how changes in the nature of capitalism -- from regional to national to trans-national -- have concretely affected the social, economic and political relations of an isolated Sardic village, and Zukin (1982) has shown how political and economic relations shape upper Bohemian life in New York's Soho.

Tackling Some Big Questions Structurally

The potential linkage of network analysis and political economy provides exciting possibilities for studying important questions about how large-scale social arrangements are affecting communities:

National governments and multinational corporations now run many activities previously run by local governments and small enterprises. Charles Tilly (1988) has argued that such an increase in national scale in nineteenth century France may have caused a decline in local communal solidarity. Instead of hanging together to decide their common fate, each interest group tried to make separate deals with these external agencies. What are the factors which make for commitment to the village, neighborhood, kinship group, work group, or other potential solidarities?

Is capitalism more than a praise-word or a curse-word in its implications for the everyday lives of people? Both Karl Polanyi (1944) and Richard Titmuss (1970) have suggested that capitalist modes of behavior have affected how people deal with each other in everyday life. Recall how Ayn Rand (1957) looked forward to the time when people would transform their communal exchanges into bargains for goods, services and love. Yet the calculation of exchanges is a phenomenon more broadly-based than capitalism. Ethnographies of socialist and pre-industrial countries show similar wheeling and dealing (e.g., Mandelstam, 1970; Sahlins, 1965; Roberts, 1973). Has capitalism really reduced commitment to the common good?

Paid work is increasingly done in large bureaucracies, socially and spatially separate. What are the consequences of divorcing paid work from domestic work? Torontonians' community lives are almost completely preoccupied with domestic needs (Wellman, 1985; Wellman, Carrington and Hall, 1988). They want help in renovating the house and soothing the upset, not in manning a fishing boat or getting in the harvest. Yet the informal organization of work flourishes in large bureaucracies. Indeed Leslie Howard's work in India (1974, 1988) suggests that workmates' community suffers the most in small artisanal shops -- where supervision is close and personal and happiness depends on the boss' grace and favor.

The large size and diversity of cities nourishes the growth of many different interest groups. Urbanites easily maintain partial commitments to subcultures of like-minded individuals (Kadushin, 1966, forthcoming; Fischer, 1975; Erickson and Nosanchuk, 1986). While there are many small circles of friends, it is important to avoid confusing absolute numbers with percentages. Interest groups seem to play a small part in most urbanites' lives. When we shift attention from all the ties urbanites have, and concentrate only on those they see often, we find that their worlds are constricted to neighborhood and workplace during the week, and kinfolk on weekends. Indeed the more women get liberated through going off to paid work, the more their subsequent double load means that they do not have the time to see their friends and reduce their social lives to occasional visits with kin.

While assistance obtained through relationships has largely been used to meet domestic needs in industrialized social systems, the scope of these needs may be changing. Large bureaucratic institutions now do many of the reproductive things which families and communities used to do for themselves. In the Second and Third Worlds as well as the First, people often purchase clothing, food and emotional comfort, and hire large institutions to care for the young and infirm. This "McDonaldization" of life may have reduced the number and scope of things which community members do for each other. Have community members expanded their activities into what is left? Has the combination of increased bureaucratic centralization and specialization reduced interdependence between individuals? Is the "informal economy" a distorting sideshow or, as Ray Pahl (1984) suggests, the cheap and flexible infrastructure which keeps households and societies going?

Low-cost, efficient and widespread transportation and communication facilities have made it easier to sustain long-distance ties, but at a possibly large social cost. If cars, telephones and modems may have liberated community, they may also have fragmented it. Individuals often maintain and manipulate a disconnected set of discrete dyads. Yet users of computerized conferencing need the broad-banded interactions of in-person meetings as much as they value the easy connectivity of electronic mail (Hiltz and Turoff, 1979; Johnson-Lenz, 1978; Rice, 1984). What are the consequences for the maintenance of the public community of such potentially privatized communities has directed attention. Will the freeway drivers and keyboard strokers be able to ignore the loud music from the strangers next door or the race riots around the corner?

Where To?

Now that we are certain communities still exist, we can move on. Community analysis has the potential to be the queen of the social sciences. (I use the term "queen" advisedly, as it is clear that women hold community networks together in North America, just as they hold together households.) The keys are:

-- To realize that "community" is the basic metaphor for that most important class of relationships: the primary ties extending outside of our households which articulate people with larger social systems and provide them with imaginative, flexible means for gaining access to the resources of these social systems. The concepts and procedures we have devised are as applicable to the study of kinship, social support and informal work relationships as they are to the traditional milieux of community studies. They enable community analysts to do some of the key intellectual linkages of sociology.

-- To show how the composition and structure of community relations affect their contents: the kinds of things that happen within them.

-- To show how the structural location of individuals and households in large-scale divisions of labor -- such as the nature of their involvement in paid or domestic work -- affects the kinds of communities of which they are members and the kinds of resources which flow to and from them through their community ties.

-- To show how the structure and composition of these community networks concatenate to organize larger-scale social systems.

In helping individuals and households to maintain themselves, community networks are both passive reactions to the pressures of large-scale social systems and active attempts to gain access to, claim, and control resources. I doubt that people are inherently evil, suffering from the Original Sin of Community Lost, and it is clear twenty years later that the children of the sixties have not been permanently steeped in the inherent goodness underlying the Community Saved model.

That leaves the Community Liberated model with its implicit view that people are entrepreneurial operators. In this view communities are not merely demure recipients of dominant production relations struggling to survive in a heartless, changing world. They are active arrangements by which members of that world reproduce themselves. Such thoughts date back to both Durkheim (1893), with his emphasis on organic solidarity as interdependence among network members, and Marx (1852), with his discussion of a class in itself and for itself. Each saw a key to large-scale social integration in the formation of specialized links between interdependent clusters of network members--in short, communities.

To conclude, treating large-scale social structure as a web of networks provides a way of linking small-scale to large-scale phenomena without imposing a radical discontinuity in analysis. The network model suggests a means for going beyond capitalism and urbanization as abstract forces, acting and being acted upon only in transcendentally diffuse ways. It offers ways of studying these phenomena as patterns of concrete social relations between individuals and groups interconnected through complex communal bonds. Thus it provides a useful tool for those macroscopic studies which current leave out interpersonal relations and those interpersonal analyses which assume that relationships operate in a social-structural vacuum.

Notes

1. A preliminary version of this paper was originally the keynote presentation at the "Community Question Re-evaluated" session of the Annual Meetings of American Sociological, New York, September, 1986. The other panelists, Albert Hunter, Charles Kadushin, Melvin Oliver and Lisa Peattie, made many useful comments at that time. My thanks also to Vicente Espinoza, William Michelson, Patricia Parisi-Smith, Cyndi Rottenberg and Bev Wellman for their advice and assistance with this paper. Support for this work has been provided by the National Welfare Grants Program of Health and Welfare Canada, the Social Science Council of Canada, the (U.S.) Center for Studies of Metropolitan Problems (NIMH), and the University of Toronto's Centre for Urban and Community Studies, Department of Sociology, Programme in Gerontology, and Joint Program in Transportation Studies.

2. These points are adapted from Berkowitz (1982:55-56).

3. For a summary of mass society fears, see Kornhauser (1968). Mayer (India, 1966), Cohen (Nigeria, 1969), Mayer with Mayer (South Africa, 1974), Mitchell (Rhodesia, 1956) and Peattie (Venezuela, 1968) are some key Third World community studies from this period. Community sociologists were not able to tackle similar questions in the Second (socialist) World even when their argument that capitalism had shaped urban communities called for comparative approaches (e.g. Castells, 1972; see also Fischer's 1978 discussion).

4. This section has been revised from Wellman (1984).

5. See Webber, 1964; Kadushin, 1966; Tilly, 1970; Wellman, 1972; Craven and Wellman, 1973; Shulman, 1976; Fischer, 1975; Fischer et al., 1977; Wellman and Leighton, 1979; Wellman, Carrington and Hall, 1988.

6. For discussions of concepts and procedures see Craven and Wellman, 1973; Wellman, 1982; Burt, 1984. For discussions of reliability see Bernard, Killworth and Sailer, 1981; Hammer, 1980; Romney and Weller, 1984. See also Laumann, Marsden and Prensky's 1983 discussion on realism and nominalism in such studies.

7. See the reviews and compilations in Thoits, 1982; Hammer, 1983; Brownell and Shumaker, 1984; Bronfenbrenner, Moen and Garabino, 1984; Cohen and Syme, 1985; Gottlieb, 1981, 1985; Hall and Wellman, 1985; Kessler and McLeod, 1985; House, 1985; Sarason and Sarason, 1985; Shumaker and Brownell, 1985; Lin, Dean and Ensel, 1986; Pilisuk and Park, 1986; Israel and Rounds, in press.

8. The preceding two paragraphs based on writing by Vicente Espinoza for Wellman, et al., 1987a.

References

Aminzade, Ronald and Randy Hodson (1982) Social mobility in a mid-Nineteenth Century French city. *American Sociological Review 47* (Aug), 441-457.

Anderson, Michael (1971) *Family Structure in Nineteenth Century Lancashire.* Cambridge: Cambridge University Press.

Atwood, Margaret (1985) *The Handmaid's Tale.* Toronto: McClelland and Stewart.

Bell, Colin (1968) *Middle-Class Families.* London: Routledge and Kegan Paul.

Ballard, J.G (1975) *High-Rise.* London: Jonathan Cape.

Bandyopadhyay, Suraj and Donald van Eschen (1981) *An Extended Summary of the Conditions of Rural Progress in India.* Calcutta: Indian Statistical Institute.

Barrera, Manuel Jr. and Sheila Ainlay (1983) The structure of social support. *Journal of Community Psychology 2*, 133-141.

Berkman, Lisa and S. Leonard Syme (1979) Social networks, host resistance, and mortality. *American Journal of Epidemiology, 109*, 186-204.

Berkowitz, S.D (1982) *An Introduction to Structural Analysis.* Toronto: Butterworths.

Bernard, H. Russell, Peter D. Killworth and Lee Sailer (1981) Summary of research on informant accuracy in network data and the reverse small world problem. *Connections 4*(2): 11-25.

Boal, Fred W (1972) Close together and far apart: Religious and class divisions in Belfast, *Community Forum 3*(2), 3-11.

Bodemann, Y. Michal (1988) Relations of production and class rule: The hidden basis of patron clientage. In Barry Wellman and S.D. Berkowitz (Eds.), *Social Structures: A Network Approach*. Cambridge: Cambridge University Press.

Boissevain, Jeremy (1974) *Friends of Friends*. Oxford: Basil Blackwell.

Bott, Elizabeth (1971) *Family and Social Network*. 2nd edition. London: Tavistock.

Bronfenbrenner, Uri, Phyllis Moen and James Garbarino (1984) Child, family, and community, *Review of Child Development Research 7*:283-328.

Brownell, Arlene and Sally Shumaker (Eds.) (1984) Social support: New perspectives on theory, research and intervention, I, theory and research. Special Issue of the *Journal of Social Issues 40*:4.

Brunner, John (1968) *Stand on Zanzibar*. Garden City NY: Doubleday.

Brunner, John (1975) *The Shockwave Rider*. New York: Harper & Row.

Brym, Robert J (1978) *The Jewish Intelligentsia and Russian Marxism*. London: Macmillan.

Burt, Ronald (1980) Models of network structure, *Annual Review of Sociology 6*, 79-141.

Burt, Ronald (1984) Network items and the general social survey, *Social Networks 6*, 293-339.

Burt, Ronald (1986a) A note on sociometric order in the general social survey network data, *Social Networks 8*, 149-74.

Burt, Ronald (1986b) Strangers, friends and happiness. New York: Center for the Social Sciences, Columbia University. Preprint P110.

Campbell, Karen, Peter Marsden and Jeanne Hurlbert (1986) Social resources and socioeconomic status, *Social Networks 8*, 97-117.

Castells, Manuel (1972) [1977] *The Urban Question*. 2nd edition. Translated by Alan Sheridan. London: Edward Arnold.

Choldin, Harvey (1985) *Cities and Suburbs*. New York: McGraw-Hill.

Clark, S.D (1966) *The Suburban Society*. Toronto: University of Toronto Press.

Cohen, Abner (1969) *Custom and Politics in Urban Africa*. Berkeley: University of California Press.

Cohen, Sheldon and S. Leonard Syme (Eds.) (1985) *Social Support and Health*. New York: Academic Press.

Connerly, Charles (1985) The community question: An extension of Wellman and Leighton, *Urban Affairs Quarterly 20*, 537-56.

Craven, Paul and Barry Wellman (1973) The network city, *sociological inquiry* 43:57-88.

Darroch, A. Gordon and Michael Ornstein (1983) Family coresidence in Canada in 1871: Family life cycles, occupations and networks of mutual aid. Working paper. Toronto: Institute for Behavioural Research, York University.

Davis, Natalie Zemon (1975) *Society and Culture in Early Modern France.* Stanford, CA: Stanford University Press.

Davis, Natalie Zemon (1983) *The Return of Martin Guerre.* Cambride, MA: Harvard University Press.

Delaney, Samuel (1976) *Triton.* New York: Bantam Books.

Durkheim, Emile (1893) [1933] *The Division of Labor in Society.* New York: Macmillan.

Eichler, Margaret (1985) Feminist approaches to anglophone sociology, *Canadian Review of Sociology and Anthropology 22,* 619-44.

Engels, Frederick (1885) [1970] *The Housing Question,* Second Ed. Moscow: Progress Publishers.

Erickson, Bonnie and T.A. Nosanchuk (1986) *Making Contacts: Status and Weak Ties in a Voluntary Association.* Toronto: Centre for Urban and Community Studies, University of Toronto.

Feagin, Joe (1973) Community disorganization, *Sociological Inquiry, 43* (Winter), 123-46.

Feagin, Joe and Harlan Hahn (1973) *Ghetto Revolt: The Politics of Violence in American Cities.* New York: Macmillan.

Feld, Scott (1981) The focused organization of social ties, *American Journal of Sociology 86* (March), 1015-1035.

Ferrand, Alexis (1981) *Manieres Meylanaises.* Grenoble: Equipe de Sociologie, Universite des Sciences Sociales II.

Fischer, Claude (1975) Toward a subcultural theory of urbanism, *American Journal of Sociology 80,* 1319-41.

Fischer, Claude (1976) *The Urban Experience.* New York: Harcourt Brace Jovanovich.

Fischer, Claude (1978) On the Marxian challenge to urban sociology, *Comparative Urban Research 6*(2-3), 10-19.

Fischer, Claude (1982) *To Dwell Among Friends.* Berkeley: University of California Press.

Fischer, Claude, Robert Max Jackson, C. Anne Steuve, Kathleen Gerson, Lynne McCallister Jones with Mark Baldassare (1977) *Networks and Places.* New York: Free Press.

Fox, Bonnie (1980) *Hidden in the Household.* Toronto: Women's Press.

Frank, André Gunder (1969) *Capitalism and Underdevelopment in Latin America*, revised ed. New York: Monthly Review Press.

Gans, Herbert (1962) *The Urban Villagers*. New York: Free Press.

Gans, Herbert (1967) *The Levittowners*. New York: Pantheon.

Gates, Albert S., Harvey Stevens and Barry Wellman (1973) What makes a good neighbor? Paper presented to the annual meeting of the American Sociological Association, New York, August.

Gibson, William (1986) *Count Zero*. New York: Arbor House.

Gordon, Michael (1978) *The American Family*. New York: Random House.

Gottlieb, Benjamin (Ed.) (1981) *Social Networks and Social Support*. Beverly Hills: Sage.

Gottlieb, Benjamin (1985) *Social Support Strategies*. Beverly Hills: Sage.

Granovetter, Mark (1973) The strength of weak ties, *American Journal of Sociology 78*, 1360-80.

Granovetter, Mark (1982) The strength of weak ties: A network theory revisited. In Peter Marsden and Nan Lin (Eds.), *Social Structure and Network Analysis*, 105-130. Beverly Hills: Sage.

Greenbaum, Paul and Susan Greenbaum (1981) Territorial personalization: group identity and social interaction in a Slavic-American neighborhood, *Environment and Behavior 13*, 574-89.

Greenbaum, Susan (1982) Bridging ties at the neighborhood level, in *Social Networks 4* (December), 367-84.

Hall, Alan and Barry Wellman (1985) Social networks and social support. In Sheldon Cohen and S. Leonard Syme (Eds.), *Social Support and Health*, 23-41. New York: Academic Press.

Hammer, Muriel (1980) Reply to Killworth and Bernard, *Connections 3* (Winter): 14-15.

Hammer, Muriel (1983) 'Core' and 'extended' social networks in relation to health and illness, *Social Science and Medicine 17*, 405-11.

Hiltz, S. Roxanne and Murray Turoff (1979) *The Network Nation*. Reading, MA: Addison-Wesley.

Hobbes, Thomas (1651) [1982] *Leviathan*. C.B. MacPherson, editor New York: Penguin Books.

House, James (1985) Structures and sentiments of social support. Paper presented at the annual meeting of the American Sociological Association, Washington.

Howard, Leslie (1974) Industrialization and community in Chotanagapur. Doctoral dissertation, Department of Sociology, Harvard University.

Howard, Leslie (1988, in press) Work and community in Industrializing India. In Barry Wellman and S.D. Berkowitz (Eds.), *Social Structures: A Network Approach*. Cambridge University Press.

Hufton, Olwen H (1974) *The Poor of Eighteenth-Century France: 1750-1789.* Oxford: Clarendon Press.

Israel, Barbara and Kathleen Rounds (In press) Social networks and social support: A synthesis for health educators. *Advances in Health Education and Promotion.* Greenwich CT: JAI Press.

Jacobs, Jane (1961) *The Death and Life of Great American Cities.* New York: Random House.

Jefferson, Thomas (1784) [1972] *Notes on the State of Virginia.* Edited by William Peden. New York: Norton.

Johnson-Lenz, Peter & Trudy Johnson-Lenz (1978) On facilitating networks for social change, *Connections 1* (Winter), 5-11.

Kadushin, Charles (1966) The friends and supporters of psychotherapy: On social circles in urban life, *American Sociological Review 31,* 786-802.

Kadushin, Charles (forthcoming) The community question re-evaluated: Multiple layers of connectedness, *Connections.*

Katz, Michael (1975) *The People of Hamilton, Canada West.* Cambridge, MA: Harvard University Press.

Keller, Suzanne (1968) *The Urban Neighborhood.* New York: Random House.

Kessler, Ronald and Jane McLeod (1984) Sex differences in vulnerability to undesirable life events, *American Sociological Review, 49:*620-31.

Knoke, David and James Kuklinski (1983) *Network Analysis.* Beverly Hills: Sage.

Kornhauser, William (1968) Mass society, *International Encyclopedia of the Social Sciences 10,* 58-64.

Lasch, Christopher (1977) *Haven in a Heartless World.* New York: Basic Books.

Laslett, Peter (1971) *The World We Have Lost.* 2nd Ed. London: Methuen.

Laumann, Edward O. (1973) *Bonds of Pluralism.* New York: Wiley.

Laumann, Edward, Peter Marsden and David Prensky (1983) The boundary specification problem in network analysis. In Ronald Burt and Michael Minor (Eds.), *Applied Network Analysis,* 18-34. Beverly Hills: Sage.

Leighton, Barry (1986) The myth of the demise of community: Experiencing personal community networks. Ph.D. Thesis, Department of Sociology, University of Toronto.

LeRoy Ladurie, Emmanuel (1975) [1978] *Montaillou.* Translated by Barbara Bray. New York: Braziller.

Lessing, Doris (1974) *Memoirs of a Survivor.* New York: Octagon Press.

Liebow, Elliot (1967) *Tally's Corner.* Boston: Little, Brown.

Lin, Nan, Alfred Dean, and Walter Ensel (Eds.) (1986) *Social Support, Life Events and Depression.* Orlando: Academic Press.

Lofland, Lyn (1973) *A World of Strangers*. New York: Basic.

Lofland, Lyn (1983) Understanding urban life, *Urban Life 2*, 491-511.

Lomnitz, Larissa Adler (1977) *Networks and Marginality: Life in a Mexican Shantytown*. Translated by Cinna Lomnitz. New York: Academic Press.

Lomnitz, Larissa Adler (1985) Order generates disorder: Informal exchange networks in formal systems. Working Paper, Universidad Nacional Autonoma de Mexico.

Luxton, Meg (1980) *More Than a Labour of Love*. Toronto: Women's Press.

Machiavelli, Niccolo (1532) [1961] *The Prince*. Edited and translated by George Bull. New York: Penguin.

Mandelstam, Nadezdha (1970) *Hope Against Hope*. New York: Atheneum.

Marchak, Patricia (1985) Canadian political economy, *Canadian Review of Sociology and Anthropology 22* (December), 673-709.

Marsden, Peter (1986) Heterogeneity in discussion relations. Paper presented at the annual meeting of the Sunbelt Social Networks Conference, Santa Barbara, CA (February).

Marsden, Peter (1987) Core discussions networks of Americans, *American Sociological Review 52* (February), 122-131.

Marx, Karl (1859) [1913] *A Contribution to the Critique of Political Economy*. Chicago: Kerr.

Marx, Karl (1852) [1950]. The eighteenth brumaire of Louis Bonaparte. In *Karl Marx and Frederick Engels: Selected Works I*, 223-311. Moscow: Foreign Language Publishing House.

Marx, Leo (1964) *The Machine in the Garden*. New York: Oxford University Press.

Mayer, Adrian (1966) The significance of quasi-groups in the study of complex societies. In Michael Banton (Ed.), *The Social Anthropology of Complex Societies*, Pp. 97-122. London: Tavistock.

Mayer, Philip with Iona Mayer (1974) *Townsmen or Tribesmen*. 2d ed. Capetown: Oxford University Press.

Mintz, Beth and Michael Schwartz (1985) *The Power Structure of American Business*. Chicago: University of Chicago Press.

Mitchell, J. Clyde (1956) The Kalela Dance. Manchester: Manchester University Press.

Oliver, Melvin (1984) The urban black community as network. Unpublished paper. Department of Sociology. University of California, Los Angeles.

Oliver, Melvin (1986) Beyond the neighborhood: The spatial distribution of social ties in three urban black communities. Paper presented at the Minorities in the Post-Industrial City Conference, University of California, Los Angeles, May.

Pahl, R.E (1984) *Divisions of Labour*. Oxford: Basil Blackwell.

Peattie, Lisa Redfield (1968) *The View From the Barrio*. Ann Arbor: University of Michigan Press.

Peattie, Lisa Redfield (1986) Family and social network. Paper presented at the annual meeting of the American Sociological Association, September, New York.

Peattie, Lisa Redfield and Martin Rein (1983) *Women's Claims*. New York: Oxford University Press.

Pilisuk, Marc and Susan Hillier Parks. 1986. *The Healing Web*. Hanover, NH: University Press of New England.

Pitt-Rivers, Julian (1973) The kith and the kin. In Jack Goody (Ed.), *The Character of Kinship*, 89-105. Cambridge: Cambridge University Press.

Poggioli, Renato (1975) The oaten flute. In *The Oaten Flute: Essays on Poetry and the Pastoral Ideal*, Pp. 1-41. Cambridge MA: Harvard University Press.

Pool, Ithiel de Sola and Manfred Kochen (1978) Contacts and influence, *Social Networks 1*, 5-51.

Polanyi, Karl (1944) [1957] *The Great Transformation*. Boston: Beacon Press.

Rand, Ayn (1957) *Atlas Shrugged*. New York: Random House.

Reichmann, Sebastien (1987) De la menace du chômage à sa réalité: Structure de réseau et perception du support social, *Connections 10*(2), in press.

Rice, Ronald E. and Associates (1984) *The New Media: Communication, Research and Technology*. Beverly Hills: Sage Publications.

Roberts, Bryan (1973) *Organizing Strangers: Poor Families in Guatemala City*. Austin: University of Texas Press.

Roberts, Bryan (1978) *Cities of Peasants*. London: Edward Arnold.

Rogers, Everett and D. Lawrence Kincaid (1981) *Communication Networks*. New York: Free Press.

Romney, A. Kimball and Susan Weller (1984) Predicting informant accuracy from patterns of recall among individuals, *Social Networks, 6*, 59-77.

Rosenthal, Carolyn (1987) Aging and intergenerational relations in Canada. In Victor Marshall (Ed.), *Aging in Canada*, 2nd edition, 311-342. Markham, Ontario: Fitzhenry and Whiteside.

Sahlins, Marshall D. (1965) On the sociology of primitive exchange. In Michael Banton (Ed.), *The Relevance of Models for Social Anthropology*. London: Tavistock.

Salaff, Janet W. (1981) *Working Daughters of Hong Kong*. Cambridge: Cambridge University Press.

Sarason, Irwin and Barbara Sarason (1985) *Social Support: Theory, Research and Applications*. The Hague: Martinus Nijhoff.

Sennett, Richard (1970) *Families Against the City*. Cambridge, MA: Harvard University Press.

Shulman, Norman (1976) Network analysis: A new addition to an old bag of tricks, *Acta Sociologica 19*, 307-23.

Shumaker, Sally and Arlene Brownell (Eds.) (1985) Social support: New perspectives in theory, research and intervention, II, Interventions and Policy. Special issue of the *Journal of Social Issues 41*, 1.

Simmel, Georg (1902-1903) [1950] The metropolis and mental life. In Kurt Wolff (Ed. and trans.), *The Sociology of Georg Simmel.* Glencoe IL: Free Press.

Simmel, George (1922) [1955] The web of group affiliations. In *Conflict and the Web of Group Affiliations*, 125-195. Glencoe, IL: Free Press.

Smith, Michael P. (1979) *The City and Social Theory.* New York: St. Martin's Press.

Stack, Carol B. (1974) *All Our Kin.* New York: Harper & Row.

Stockman, Frans, Rolf Ziegler and John Scott (1985) *Networks of Corporate Power.* Cambridge: Polity Press.

Tardy, Charles (1985) Social support measurement, *American Journal of Community Psychology 13*, 187-202.

Thernstrom, Stephan (1969) *Poverty and Progress: Social Mobility in a Nineteenth Century City.* New York: Atheneum.

Thoits, Peggy (1982) Conceptual, methodological and theoretical problems in studying social support as a buffer against life stress, *Journal of Health and Social Behavior 23*:145-59.

Tilly, Charles (1964) *The Vendée: A Sociological Analysis of the Counter-revolution of 1793.* Cambridge, MA: Harvard University Press.

Tilly, Charles (1970) *Community: City: Urbanization.* Ann Arbor: Department of Sociology, University of Michigan.

Tilly, Charles (1975) Food supply and public order in modern Europe. In Charles Tilly (Ed.), *The Formation of National States in Western Europe*, 380-455. Princeton, NJ: Princeton University Press.

Tilly, Charles (1978) *From Mobilization to Revolution.* Reading, MA: Addison-Wesley.

Tilly, Charles (1979) Collective violence in European perspective, revised version. In Hugh Davis Graham and Ted Robert Gurr (Eds.), *Violence in America: Historical and Comparative Perspective*, revised ed., 83-118. Beverly Hills: Sage.

Tilly, Charles (1988, in press) Misreading, then rereading, nineteenth-century social change. In Barry Wellman and S.D. Berkowitz (Eds.), *Social Structures: A Network Approach.* Cambridge: Cambridge University Press.

Tilly, Louise, and Joan W. Scott (1978) *Women, Work and Family.* New York: Holt, Rinehart and Winston.

Titmuss, Richard (1970) *The Gift Relationship.* London: Allen and Unwin.

Verbrugge, Lois (1977) The structure of adult friendship choices, *Social Forces* 56, 576-97.

Wallerstein, Immanuel (1974) *The Modern World-System*, vol. I. New York: Academic Press.

Warren, Donald (1981) *Helping Networks*. Notre Dame IN: University of Notre Dame Press.

Warren, Roland (1978) *The Community in America*. Chicago: Rand McNally.

Webber, Melvin (1964) The urban place and the nonplace urban realm. In Melvin Webber et. al. (Eds.), *Explorations into Urban Structure*. Philadelphia: University of Pennsylvania Press.

Weber, Max (1946) *From Max Weber: Essays in Sociology*, Translated and edited by Hans Gerth and C. Wright Mills. New York: Oxford University Press.

Weber, Max (1958) *The City*. Translated and edited by Don Martindale and Gertrud Neuwirth. Glencoe IL: Free Press.

Wellman, Barry (1972) Who needs neighborhoods? In Alan Powell (Ed.), *The City: Attacking Modern Myths*, 94-100. Toronto: McClleland and Stewart.

Wellman, Barry (1979) The community question, *American Journal of Sociology 84*, 1201-1231.

Wellman, Barry (1983) Network analysis: Some basic principles. In Randall Collins (Ed.), *Sociological Theory 1983*, 155-200. San Francisco: Jossey-Bass.

Wellman, Barry (1984) Looking for community, *Environments 16* (2):59-63.

Wellman, Barry (1985) Domestic work, paid work and net work. In Steve Duck and Daniel Perlman (Eds.), *Understanding Personal Relationships*, vol. I., 159-191. London: Sage.

Wellman, Barry (1987) Condos, communes and compuserv: Science-fiction looks at community. Paper presented to the Futures Forum, Spaced-Out Research Library, Toronto, July.

Wellman, Barry and S.D. Berkowitz (Eds.) (1988) *Social Structures*. Cambridge: Cambridge University Press.

Wellman, Barry, Peter Carrington and Alan Hall (1988) Networks as personal communities. In Barry Wellman and S.D. Berkowitz, *Social Structures*. Cambridge: Cambridge University Press.

Wellman, Barry with Paul Craven, Marilyn Whitaker, Sheila du Toit, Harvey Stevens and Hans Bakker (1973) Community ties and support systems. In Larry S. Bourne, Ross D. MacKinnon and James W. Simmons (Eds.), *The Form of Cities in Central Canada*, 152-67. Toronto: University of Toronto Press.

Wellman, Barry with Robert Hiscot (1985) From social support to social network. In Irwin Sarason and Barbara Sarason (Eds.), *Social Support*, 205-222. The Hague: Martinus Nijhoff.

Wellman, Barry and Barry Leighton (1979) Networks, neighborhoods and communities, *Urban Affairs Quarterly 14*, 363-90.

Wellman, Barry, Clayton Mosher, Cyndi Rottenberg and Vicente Espinoza (1987) Different strokes from different folks: Which ties give what support? Working Paper. Berkeley: Institute for Urban and Regional Development, University of California.

Wellman, Barry, Clayton Mosher, Cyndi Rottenberg and Vicente Espinoza (1987) The network basis of support. Paper presented at the annual meeting of the American Sociological Association, Chicago, June.

White, Morton and Lucia White (1962) *The Intellectual Versus the City*. Cambridge MA: Harvard University Press.

Whyte, William Foote (1943) *Street Corner Society*. Chicago: University of Chicago Press.

Williams, Raymond (1973) *The Country and the City*. London: Chatto & Windus.

Willmott, Peter (1987) *Friendship Networks and Social Support*. London: Policy Studies Institute.

Wills, Garry (1978) *Inventing America: Jefferson's Declaration of Independence*. Garden City, NY: Doubleday.

Wong Yuk Lin, Renita (1987) Personal network and local community attachment: illustrations from two public housing estates in Shatin. M.Phil. thesis, Department of Sociology, Chinese University of Hong Kong.

Wright, Erik Olin (1979) *Class Structure and Income Determination*. New York: Academic Press.

Wright, Erik Olin (1980) Varieties of Marxist conceptions of class structure, *Politics and Society, 9*, 323-370.

Young, Michael and Peter Willmott (1957) *Family and Kinship in East London*. London: Routledge and Kegan Paul.

Zeidman, Reena and Barry Wellman (forthcoming) Integration or alienation? A study of the twelve tribes, *Connections*.

Zukin, Sharon (1982) *Loft Living*. Baltimore: Johns Hopkins University Press.

THE CITY IN BLACK KINSHIP:
A COMPARISON OF RURAL PAST
AND URBAN PRESENT

Barbara Frankel
Lehigh University

Using four common indices of familial "disorganization" as proposed by Moynihan, a comparison of old rural and more recent urban data on black families is undertaken to assess the effects of urbanization. The tentative conclusion is that change has been less than profound and is more notable at the formal than at the psychocultural level. More important, the study raises questions as to the relevance of the indices used, and seeks more meaningful dimensions of analysis, pointing to the necessity of drawing a distinction between the terms "disorganization" and "instability." It is suggested that the latter may, in fact, be a principle of organization if pejorative connotations of the term are dropped.

Inspired by Leeds' pointed observation that anthropologists have, while purporting to do urban studies, more often studied "kinship in the city... (than) the city in kinship," I will take up his challenge that we address ourselves to the problem of determining "the effect of cityness in the operation of kinship" (Leeds, 1968:31). The data examined in this article were gathered in the course of a larger folklore study conducted in 1968-69 at Temple University Hospital in the North Philadelphia ghetto area. As part of the larger study I gathered household data on the family and kinship relations of low income black families in North Philadelphia. The recent resurgence of public and scholarly concern with poor families, especially black families (Engram, 1982; Murray, 1984; Norton, 1985) has caused me to reanalyze that data.

In this paper I will examine kinship data from that early study, comparing the patterns governing urban ghetto household composition and kin relationships of the late 1960s with those which existed in the rural South in the 1930s and 1940s. I chose this strategy because my informants, if they were not born there themselves, were, with few exceptions, children of parents born and raised in the rural South. Thus it should be possible, by examining the kinship system from which they or their immediate forbears came, to discern changes in that system which may be attributed to migration into the urban North.

In this setting I interviewed 50 women who were confined for childbirth in the hospital's obstetrical ward. All were receiving some form of public assistance or were otherwise certifiable as "poor" according to straight economic standards set by the federal, state or city authorities. All were American black females of childbearing age. The youngest and oldest informants were 27 years apart in age.

These informants represented 50 separate households containing a total of at least 297 individuals. All resided within the heart of the ghetto save two, who had recently moved to its fringes, where some neighborhoods were in transition from white to black occupancy.[1]

Kinship, family and household are not interchangeable terms in U.S. society and certainly not among the ghetto poor. **Kinship** in this discussion will refer to that relationship existing between persons who consider themselves related either by blood or marriage; i.e., in anthropological jargon, consanguines and affines. David Schneider (1969:26-29) sees these two sorts of relationships within American culture as falling within two more general symbolic domains; the domain of *nature* and that of *law*, which are opposed to one another. Natural relations are material and substantial, while in-law relations are based entirely on code-for-conduct, or custom. One's kindred consists of all those persons to whom a particular individual is related by blood or marriage. It is not a "group" as is a clan, but an ego-centered network not identical for any two persons except siblings.

A **family** is here used to mean that portion of the group of persons related to one another by kinship who either reside together or maintain a close and cooperative relationship. They, unlike kindred, are a "group" in the solidary sense, functioning together for certain specific purposes. In the present context the purpose to be emphasized is the care of children in several senses -- economic, succoring and socializing. In this sense the family is a "corporate" unit.

A **household** is a residential unit consisting primarily, but not always, of family members. It is therefore closely related to but not identical with the family unit. Some writers have called such a unit the "hearth group," meaning all the people who cook and eat together under one roof. Households may be built up in a variety of ways, and fall into many "types" -- nuclear, augmented, joint, extended, matrifocal, and so on, depending on the specific people composing them. The nuclear, of course, is the most common in the U.S. Others occur, though they are culturally classified as more or less "deviant" by the mainstream of U.S. society.

"Disorganization" or "Instability?"

Daniel Patrick Moynihan's controversial report, *The Negro Family: The Case for National Action*, not only raised a tremendous political furor which has yet to end, it also raised some important questions concerning kinship (Cf. Rainwater and Yancey, 1967 for the report itself and for an able and comprehensive review of both these dimensions).[2] One aspect of the controversy bears on issues having to do with the urbanization of the Negro family, and with its effects on kinship.

Not only Moynihan, but other sociologists before him (notably Wirth, 1938; and Frazier, 1948) viewed the city as a milieu with a strong tendency to produce "anomie" as that term is used by present-day sociologists (e.g. Berger, 1969), though not exactly as Durkheim originally used it. Anomie refers to a sense of estrangement from others, existential meaninglessness, and loss or lack of personal identity which is said to have a disorganizing effect on family life, as well as other dire effects. These theorists reason that anomie stems from the conditions of urban life, which feature large scale industrialism, "rationalized" production, impersonal standards of value, marked social heterogeneity, and the predominance of secondary over primary relationships. Others have argued that this is not true of all cities in all times and places, but there does seem to be substantial agreement that it accurately describes the state of affairs in the modern Western industrial city.

The family, both in nature and in law, is seen by Berger and Kellner as a "nomos producing instrumentality," the setting in which the "real self," so easily lost or starved in the impersonality of the industrial system of production, is located and nourished. It acts, then, as a kind of antidote to the anomie-producing urban milieu, and since anomie is a major source of social pathology the strength of the familial relationship is a matter of some importance (Cf. Berger and Kellner, 1964, and also Luckmann and Berger, 1964). According to this reasoning, the "self," since it cannot be developed in the public sphere of the working world, is necessarily located in the private sphere of home and family, where primary relationships still exist. Many viewers-with-alarm maintain that the black family in the urban milieu has become so unstable and disorganized that it cannot adequately perform the functions that Berger and Kellner subsume under the heading of "nomos production." The consequence is what Moynihan termed the "tangle of pathology" which afflicts ghetto families and the society around them.

The terms "disorganization" and "instability" have seldom been clearly defined, and in fact have been used almost interchangeably in the literature on poor urban families, and especially that on black families. These words do, however, have fundamentally different meanings. Whereas "disorganized" implies some standard or yardstick of organization against which black families are being measured and found wanting, "unstable" means merely fluid or changeable, a quality which is not the antithesis of "organized." In fact, "instability" may be a principle of organization in that if we strip the word of its pejorative connotations, it may be used to refer to the capacity of black families to retain flexibility and to adapt rapidly to changing conditions.[3]

In discussing the matter of family disorganization and instability among blacks, Moynihan's 1965 report used four basic indices of that unwelcome state of affairs: 1) the brittleness of marriage, as indicated by rising divorce rates and the number of absent husbands; 2) the illegitimacy rate, measured in the number per thousand live births; 3) the proportion of female-headed households, which he sees as a consequence of the first two facts; and 4) the proportion of families that ever become socially dependent, as measured by the number of recipients of A.D.C. (Aid to Dependent Children, the standard program for support of indigent families through the welfare system). Based on significant increases, over the previous thirty-odd years, of all four of these indicators, Moynihan concluded that the black family is "disintegrating," producing the "tangle of pathology" which he discerned at its worst in urban ghettos (Rainwater and Yancey, 1967:51-60, 63).

I will address the following questions regarding the effects of urbanization on the lower class black family:

1. What was the picture regarding the brittleness of marriage, rates of illegitimacy, matrifocality and welfare dependency in the rural South from which my informants or their immediate forbears came?
2. What is the picture along these same dimensions for my Philadelphia ghetto informants?
3. What changes can be noted through comparing the above?
4. What are the possible reasons for and/or effects of these changes?
5. What, in fact, are the patterns of black kinship in the city?
6. Did the situation among the ghetto families studied indicate family disorganization, or were there organizing principles missed in Moynihan's analysis?

Although so-called matrifocality is among his indicators of family pathology, Moynihan was not entirely consistent in his 1965 analysis. For example, it is notable that, having branded female-headed families "pathological" he later acknowledges that "there is, presumably, no special reason why a society in which males are dominant in family relationships is to be preferred to a matriarchal arrangement." In fact, among black families he perceived a "matriarchal structure," but asserted that such a structure "seriously retards the progress of the group as a whole" because it is "so out of line with the rest of American society" where male leadership is the norm (Rainwater and Yancey, 1967:75). In 1986, Moynihan's tone is somewhat tempered in its male chauvinism, but he continues to take a similar tack regarding single-parent families which are, of course, overwhelmingly female-headed.

Since the idea of "structure" (matriarchal or patriarchal) is hardly consonant with the notion of "disorganization," there is some obvious conceptual confusion here. Indeed, the matter of whether the American norm is indeed "patriarchal" is contestable. Phillip Wylie, in the 40s, enthusiastically harangued Americans about their affliction of "momism," and he was not addressing blacks, but the white middle class. In fact, a case can be made for the dominance of mothers in the lives of most American children, not to mention their dominance in the consumer economy, where they spend most of the money. Indeed, comparisons of white and black families can be strongly criticized. Engram (1982), for example, reviewed several decades of research on sex roles in both black and white families, finding most of it to be in a sorry state; flawed by unjustified assumptions about mainstream U.S. norms, full of inconsistencies, and rife with methodological deficiencies. It was such studies, however, that Moynihan relied upon for his facts.

The Rural Southern Past

The indices of family "disorganization" used by Moynihan have already been enumerated. Older studies, many by black investigators, have used similar measures and made similar assumptions regarding the adequacy of these criteria for making such judgments. What, then, was the status of lower-class Southern black families with respect to these four factors? What was the general structure of families in the South during the 30s and 40s,[4] and what functions did they fulfill for their members in the Southern rural economy and society?

Marriage

Powdermaker (1939), whose study was done in the early 30s in a small Mississippi market town serving a rural hinterland, reported that "a licensed marriage in the lower or lower-middle class is extremely rare." Most black marriages were of the "common law" variety then legally valid in the state, and most of the remainder were temporary unions rather than licensed marriages. Since legal marriage was generally associated with the behavior of people of high status, the few couples who possessed wedding licenses displayed them as "ornaments of rare glamour." Consensual unions, however, were not necessarily unstable, and where they continued over many years developed the "same internal balances and cohesions found in licensed associations." In this class of blacks there was no stigma or sense of sin attached to living together without formal marriage, and Powdermaker considered such people, for purposes of her cultural analysis, "married" (1939:149-53).

Authorities on rural Southern blacks of this period generally agree that though an affectional element was important in stable consensual or formal unions, they seemed to be as much economic partnerships as anything else (Frazier, 1948:105; Johnson, 1941:409-411; Davis, 1941:412; Powdermaker,

1939:154). If the couple did not work well together, or if either partner shirked their share of the work, the union was not likely to last. The overt reasons for marital dissolution, however, were more often linked to the affectional tie between mates. Powdermaker's portrait of marriage among the rural and small-town poor of Cottonville is a summary for much of the rural South.

> A few of the middle-class Negroes have been married only once, and they are extremely proud of it. Most of them have had several mates, from whom they have separated for one reason or another. Permanence in marriage ties and legalized divorce have barely penetrated below the upper class. In others the marriage bond is broken as unceremoniously as it is tied...The frequency with which infidelity is cited as the cause for the breaking up of a marriage is interesting in view of the fact that it seems to be very much the rule among Negroes among all except the upper class...Broken marriages are perhaps to be considered as much a part of the pattern as is infidelity. Many women accept both as of the natural order (Powdermaker, 1939:157-58).

There is general agreement that whatever the situation in an earlier day, by the 1930s among the poorer classes in the rural black communities of the South marriages were relatively "brittle," though no precise figures are given in the older studies.[5]

Illegitimacy

If most black marriages in the South were informal or consensual then, of course, most babies were being born "out of wedlock" according to the legal standards used by keepers of vital statistics. But even if one grants that stable, unstigmatized "common-law" marriages may be considered legitimizing for any offspring, the patterns of pre-marital sexual activity in the rural South for lower-class Negroes were such as to practically assure a high rate of illegitimacy. Again there is consensus among several investigators that pre-marital intercourse was nearly universal among young people, so that "a large number of the women have children before they have husbands. Unless they marry very young indeed, they are seldom virgins at the time of marriage" (Powdermaker, 1939:153). She also reports that attitudes toward illegitimacy varied among different age and class segments of the black community, but among older people of the lower strata "there was fairly complete acceptance of illegitimate children, with no feeling that they are branded or disgraced." She adds that shame attached to illegitimacy was in general "a white attitude, and the degree to which a class or age group has adopted it is an indication of the degree to which they are assimilated to white patterns" (Powdermaker, 1939:204-5).

Frazier describes the situation more precisely, telling us that although there were wide variations between Southern states regarding illegitimacy rates in rural areas, the most reliable estimate seemed to be that from 10 to 20% of Negro children were born out of wedlock, and that although illegitimacy rates were generally higher for urban than for rural areas, there were rural areas in which illegitimacy was more common than in urban ones (1948:90-91). His statistics, however, are based on a legal rather than a folk definition of marriage and thus are not strictly comparable to Powdermaker's findings. Further, he was aware that rural blacks were culturally isolated from the U.S. mainstream (1948:92-95).

Female-headed households

All writing on the rural black family between about 1930-45 contains substantially the same information regarding female-headed households. Frazier reported that in 1940 the number of such households in rural non-farm areas was 22.5%, in farm areas 11.7% and in urban areas of the South 31.1%. Davis (1941:412), reporting on "Old County," a cotton plantation area, tells us that one in seven autonomous cotton farmers were women heading "matriarchal" households (Cf. also Johnson, 1941:80).

Although such households were less common in rural than in urban areas, Frazier's opinion was that it was nevertheless in the rural areas of the South "that we find the maternal family functioning in its most primitive form as a natural organization" (1948:103-4). The picture Frazier paints is one in which the usual conjugal relations were not only informal, but also fragile and contingent. Mother-child relations, on the other hand, were "generally recognized as the most fundamental of all relationships" (1948:112). Because this bond continued inviolable throughout life, grown children (especially daughters) whose own marriages had dissolved often returned with their children to the maternal home, and daughters who had babies out of wedlock often remained there rather than marry. Indeed, they were sometimes discouraged from marrying by a mother who did not wish to see them leave. In either case the frequent consequence in kinship terms was a consanguineous family supported through the cooperation of several adult females of different generations, and headed by the eldest of these, i.e., the structure often called the "grandmother family."

Partly because of the importance of females (even in families where the father was present) children tended, in the South, to reckon descent through the female line, and often did not even know the occupations of their fathers or grandfathers (Frazier, 1948:120-22). This seems to contrast with the earlier periods reported on by Gutman (1976, Ch. 3), which were clearly characterized by bilateral kinship reckoning throughout slavery times, even where a father had been "sold away."

The female-headed household was very elastic in its composition, often containing children who had been "given away" and other non-kin. Indeed, the elasticity of households was not confined only to the poor. Even upper-middle and upper-class Negro households often contained orphaned or abandoned children, boarders, and transient visitors who would stay for a season and move on. Powdermaker remarks that this elasticity worked

...in two directions. Children drifted out of the home almost as easily as they drift into it, and it often happens that they also drift out of communication with their parents. It is not unusual for a mother in the middle class to say that the last time she heard from her son was eight years ago... (1939:209).

Most of the investigators of this period saw the Southern rural female-based household as "weak" and "disorganized," even though they also detected definite structural principles governing its formation and perpetuation. Both Johnson (1941:78) and Dollard (1937:414-15) were focally concerned with the effects on children of being reared in female-headed households. Like Moynihan some 25 years later, they felt that there were deleterious effects on adjustment and success within the larger society. Both emphasized the insecurity which may afflict individuals who have grown up in "irregularly organized or broken families," although Dollard (1937:390-433) also devoted a good bit of attention to the compensatory freedoms allowed to black people by the superordinate white caste. Whites seem to have tolerated sexual license and irregular families, even encouraged them, perhaps.

Although the female-based household is widely viewed by sociologists as a natural and adaptive unit in rural Southern black life, stemming largely from the history of slavery and subordination, it should be emphasized that at no time or place did this type of unit constitute a majority of households. The highest percentage estimated is given by Johnson for non-farm rural families at between 20 and 30% (1941:80). Where it did occur it was, like the male-headed household, generally of greater than nuclear dimensions, a pyramid-like corporate unit consisting of three or more generations cooperating in economic production and the care of children.

Welfare dependency

Social welfare on any large scale for indigent U.S. families really dates from the early 30s, when the first Roosevelt administration made efforts to provide relief for the millions of unemployed during the Depression. It is no secret, however, that in the South the "welfare state" hardly benefitted the black poor. There is evidence that the administration of such programs in the South was, like all else, highly discriminatory during this period. Nevertheless, it did begin to supplant an older system of dependence on the charity of patrician white land-owners, who stood in a paternalistic relation to their black tenants and workers (Cf. Dollard, 1937:386; Powdermaker, 1939:136-39). In any case, the traditional system was beginning to break down by the 1930s as middle-class whites more and more took over the ownership of the land and other places where blacks found employment. This new class of employers generally lacked the attitude of *noblesse oblige* which had been a part of the South's aristocratic ethic.

The receipt of donated goods, food and small sums of money from white people was, however, an unstigmatized part of the traditional black-white relationship in the South. As Powdermaker shrewdly observes,

Such donations are so much the pattern that they are not regarded as charity by most Negroes, but are accepted as part of an order which accords them wages insufficient for self-maintenance, and a tradition in which support from white people has played so large a part (1939:136).

There is no way to determine to what degree either formal-bureaucratic or informal-personalistic forms of economic dependency occurred among the rural black families of this period. It is probably safe to say, however, that few lower-class black families were able to dispense permanently with all forms of assistance if they were to survive the Great Depression.

The Urban Ghetto Present

Having reviewed the literature on the rural past, we now turn to an analysis and interpretation of the data collected in my folklore study at Temple University.[6] I shall deal with the same four variables outlined earlier. While presenting these data I shall also draw comparisons with what has gone before where appropriate. To facilitate such comparisons it is convenient to use the "ethnographic present" in my description.

Marriage

Legal marriage is by far the most common form of union among the informants, 31 of them having undertaken this bond at some time in their lives. Only six persons were living in consensual union, two of these having been legally married and, not being divorced, unable to contract another marriage. A third woman of the six was widowed, receiving social security, and not inclined to sacrifice that vital income for the sake of legalizing her union with the father of her three offspring. In Table 1 the marital statuses of the 50 informants at the time of the study are summarized:

Table 1

Marital Statuses of Fifty North
Philadelphia Mothers

	No.	%
Single	16	32
Separated	5	10
Married	23	46
Consensual	6	12
Total	50	100

These figures indicate that almost one-sixth of "marriages" take the consensual form, and half of the women whose marriages are consensual were once legally married. Taking consensual unions as equivalent to legal marriage, 68 percent of the informants are or have been married in one form or another, though about 20% of these later separated from their husbands. Nevertheless, since divorce is almost unknown among poor families in the ghetto (because of the expense, if for no other reason) the women who are listed as "married" (legally) are almost always married only once. Those currently in the "husband absent" category as defined in the Moynihan Report number about one in six of the ever-married women, a figure rather lower than the one in four reported for the Northeastern section of the country by Moynihan, and much lower than the implicit majority of Powdermaker's low-income Cottonville women who were or had been separated from their first husbands.

This relatively low "husband-absent" figure may be merely accidental, since with so small a number of cases the figures are easily skewed. It may also be because as a group these women were very young (only five were over thirty) and still busy with the care of small children. In any case marriage here does not seem so inordinately "unstable" or "brittle" as one might expect, although certainly the 16.5% rate with husbands absent is higher than for whites, whose rate for the same period in urban places is 7.9% (Rainwater and Yancey, 1967:52). However, since Moynihan's figures include *all* whites (most of them middle class), whereas my sample is entirely lower-class, the comparison has little meaning. This is because we have no figures for the comparable class of whites living in similar conditions at that time. (Of course, Moynihan in 1986 views white families in low-income groups with a dismay almost equal to that with which he viewed black families in 1965.)

Looking at the data in another way, so that the age of the informants is taken into account, all but six of the informants who are out of their teens either are or have been married, legally or otherwise. Three of the teenagers are married as well. Consensual union may or may not be higher than in other segments of the population. It is difficult to say that among my informants the proportion of unmarried couples living together was much higher than in the youthful white population of the late 1960s; it may merely have led more often to pregnancy and childbirth. It may also have met with greater traditional tolerance in the black community than in the white one.

If the norm in the rural South two generations ago was for women to have several husbands in the course of a lifetime and if this group is typical, a major change may be in progress among the urban descendants of those rural poor. Its direction, if this is true, is somewhat unexpected. What may have been occurring since the late 1960s is a fairly high degree of assimilation into mainstream norms of U.S. marriage. In this population legal marriage is the rule among those who marry at all, and the rate of marital breakup may not be very different than that for lower-class populations elsewhere in the society. I cannot explain this rather surprising bit of data, though it is possible that legalization of marriage does, in fact, promote marital stability. And legalization of a union is more likely to occur in the urban North than in the rural South, where poverty and cultural isolation appear to be greater for blacks than even in the ghettos of the North.

Illegitimacy

Sixteen of my informants have never been married, either legally or consensually. Five more are separated from their husbands, and he is not the father of the latest child. At a minimum, then, 42% of the babies being born to my informants during the course of the study were, by mainstream U.S. standards, clearly "illegitimate." If one adds to these the children of women whose unions are consensual (common-law marriage is not legal in Pennsylvania) the figure goes up to 54%. In addition, several informants had borne one or more children prior to their marriages. Thirteen of my fifty informants had given birth to their first child before age 16, and only one of them was married at the time. Several of the women who did not marry until rather late had borne two or more children prior to marriage, and at least one of these left her two daughters (by a previous union with a different man) with her mother when she married and established a home of her own.

The rate of illegitimacy, regardless of how it is defined, is obviously extremely high for these ghetto families. It is, indeed, much higher than the Moynihan statistics, which show a rate of 23.6 per cent for all U.S. Negroes and about 38 per cent for the lowest income category in Washington, D.C. as of 1963 (Rainwater and Yancey, 1967:54, 70). Again, despite small sample size it does seem safe to say that the incidence of illegitimacy among the North Philadelphia black poor is at least as high as any in the urban North and a good deal higher than it was in any area of the rural South a couple of generations ago.

Accounts of pre-marital sexual behavior in the rural South, however, indicate that the lower rate of "illegitimacy" there may have been more a function of a high infant mortality rate than of a low rate of out-of-wedlock pregnancy. Illegitimacy rates are routinely counted in terms of live births per 1,000, meaning that pregnancies which do not produce living issue are ignored. What may really account for the steep rise in illegitimate births that has accompanied black urbanization may not be an increased incidence of pre-marital intercourse, but rather the increased availability of modern medical care, with a consequent rise in female fertility. The infant mortality rate in the ghetto is still higher than for the general population,[7] but so is the number of pregnancies, and the result was an initial increase in family size for lower-class Negroes such that for the first time it surpassed white family size in 1960 (Rainwater and Yancey, 1967:73). Though this trend has since been reversed by a dramatic drop in black birth rates, the proportion of illegitimate births has risen steeply in both black and white populations. Norton (1985) informs us, in fact, that "two out of every three black women having a first child are single, compared to one out of every six white women."

What is significant here, behaviorally and culturally, is not the *number* of illegitimate babies born in the ghetto. That is, of course, a matter of concern to policy-makers and child welfare workers, since female-headed black households are the poorest in the nation, but it is not particularly important for considering the "effects of cityness on kinship" except insofar as there may be an increase in the mean size of black households. If this reached sufficient magnitude, it might create pressures that could force wholly new adaptive arrangements. However, for examining the effects we are interested in here the most significant datum is pre-marital or extra-marital sexual behavior and whether it has, indeed, undergone a change in the course of transition from rural South to urban North. Another factor of significance is the black sub-cultural attitude toward what white society defines as "illegitimacy."

The data suggest that the values and norms governing pre-marital and extra-marital intercourse have not really changed under the impact of urbanization, and that behavior is still much the same as in the rural South, past and present. This behavior and these norms are supported, then, by long tradition, and are hardly discouraged by customary white attitudes toward illegitimate births.

In a very real sense, there are no "illegitimate children" in the ghetto. That term was not once used by any of my informants, married or not, and babies appeared to be equally welcome (or unwelcome) in a family, whether born in or out of wedlock. Children are in no way stigmatized for being illegitimate, and most of them are acknowledged by and acquainted with their fathers, who pay them particular attention while they are small. Women are sometimes subject to malicious gossip if they have a great many such children, or if they are otherwise unpopular, but a young woman's "first mistake" is not harshly judged or treated. This is not to say that an unwelcome pregnancy doesn't create real anxiety for a poor family who lack resources for feeding another mouth. Still, a woman is clearly not ostracized for bearing children out of wedlock if she is otherwise on good terms with her neighbors, nor are illegitimate children a barrier to later marriage.

Because of this, placing a baby for adoption is extremely rare -- indeed it is considered both unnatural and immoral. Informal "giving away" of babies is another matter, and a good deal of this takes place, usually when the mother is under severe economic and/or emotional stress. However, because the mother may theoretically reclaim her child when she wishes, this is not viewed as abandoning one's child, whereas legal placement of a child for adoption is.

Having babies out of wedlock, while not negatively sanctioned, is often seen to be a practical disadvantage, however. There is evidence that even among teen-age girls some positive valuation may be placed on having a baby, and that older girls (around age 16 or 17) regard childbirth as a rite of passage into adult womanhood in much the same way a marriage ceremony serves this purpose for most whites and all middle-class girls.[8] Frazier has remarked that this was the situation in the rural South as well (1948:95), so that one could conclude that neither sexual behavior nor the values supporting it have greatly changed in the process of urbanization. This is entirely plausible. Like food habits, sexual attitudes are probably conditioned very early and rooted deeply. Tied to one of the basic human drives, it is likely that such patterns are highly resistant to change, whereas merely formal arrangements (such as legalization of marriage vs. consensual union) may be more malleable.

Female-headed Households and Household Reproduction

Table 2 showing the composition of informants' households appears below. From this it can be seen that 16 of the 50 households are headed by females, six of these being three-generation or "grandmother" households. In the female-headed households, as would be expected, teenage girls tend to live with their mothers or grandmothers, whereas most women past 20 have left their mothers' homes, whether or not they are married, to establish households of their own.

Table 2

Composition of Informants' Households
by Age Groups and Type of Head

Age	Informant	Older Female	Husband or Consort	Older Male
15-19	1	6	3	3
20-24	4	0	14	1
25-29	3	0	8	0
30-34	1	0	4	0
35-42	1	0	1	0
Total	10	6	30	4

Total Female-headed households	16
Total Male-headed households	34

Since estimates of the statistical frequency of families in which women head households vary widely for the South (Frazier, 1948:103 estimates 22.5% for non-farm and 11.7% for farm areas, while Johnson, 1941:59 gives figures for three plantation areas in the deep South ranging from 18.3% to 32.3%), it is difficult to say whether urbanization actually correlates with an increase in the incidence of "matrifocality."[9] Frazier believed that urbanization tended to produce more such families, at least in the South (1948:103). Moynihan's statistics imply the same thing (Rainwater and Yancey, 1967:52-57). Certainly the proportion of such arrangements in my sample is, at 32 per cent, very high, though it is not a majority. If matrifocality *is* truly an index of family disorganization and/or instability, and if children *are* handicapped through the relative insecurity engendered by such units, the matter is certainly serious. The question is whether either inference is warranted by these data.

Note that the proportion of families which at some time went through a phase during which a female was the head of household may be much higher than the present figure, which is only a "snapshot," that is, a synchronic rather than a diachronic picture. Many of my informants have had babies out of wedlock prior to marrying, and many of these lived with their mothers in matrifocal households during their childhood and teen years. Indeed, it is possible that most female life cycles in the ghetto include a period when they are either residing with *their* mothers in such households, or are themselves heading them. Only four of the 16 never-married female informants were living in homes where their fathers were present. The rest either lived with their mothers or were heads of matrifocal households in their own right.

None of the statistics for the South or the North indicate any longitudinal pattern, or what really happens to household composition when black families migrate to the cities. Thus it is difficult to judge whether or not urbanization intensifies the matrifocal pattern, regardless of whether this pattern survives from African tradition (Engram, 1982) or comes from the historic succession of slavery and caste in the South (Dollard, 1937). The most that can be said is that there seem to be no fewer, and possibly there are many more female-headed households among my informants than there were in the Southern areas from which they or their parents migrated.

Table 3 is designed to help detect any differences that might be discernible between people born and raised in the Northern ghetto and those more recently arrived from the South. The women in the first column are either lifelong urban ghetto residents or were brought to Philadelphia as infants. Those in the second column came from the rural farm and non-farm South. In the third column are those belonging to neither category, having been socialized in small Northern towns or large Southern cities. Nuclear families, or those which are augmented but have a nuclear core and a male head, as well as extended three-generation families headed by a male, are above the dashed line. Three-generation and two-generation matrifocal households are below that line.

These results do indicate that the ratio of female-headed to male-headed households may be somewhat higher among ghetto "natives" than among migrants from the rural South. The ratio is about 1:2.2 in the first case and about 1:2.66 in the second. The length of urban residence for the second group of informants ranges from one woman who had arrived only a year earlier, to a 34-year-old woman who had been here for 17 years. All, however, had spent their early years in the South. This tends to support the findings of earlier investigators that urbanization intensifies the matrifocal pattern, though the differences shown in these data are not statistically significant.

Table 3

Male-Headed and Female-Headed Households of
Northern-Born and Southern-Born Women

	Northern Urban	Southern Rural	Neither
Male Head	22	8	4
Female Head	10	3	3
Total	32	11	7

The next question, of course, is why this might be the case. Safa (1968) has suggested that both the welfare system and public housing administration are factors that "reinforce the matrifocal emphasis found in lower-class families generally." However, she sees as the most important factor the marginal economic position of black urban males. Because they are unable to find steady or adequate-paying employment and cannot support wives and children for a long period of time, they tend to drop out (or to be thrown out) of the household.

The centrality of the breadwinner role for males in U.S. society, and the lack of other meaningful functions for males within the family and household would, according to this line of reasoning, intensify this tendency. Both Engram (1982) and Norton (1985) substantially agree with Safa on this issue.

In the rural South, where the family was primarily a productive unit working on the land or in other endeavors requiring the strength of males, the father was still important. As a productive unit a family without a male head was adaptively disadvantaged to some extent, so that despite the heritage of a slavery and broken families there was a tendency for most families to have real need of a man in the household. In Northern cities, by contrast, the family is not a productive unit; it is primarily a unit for the care and socialization of children. If the father cannot contribute regularly and adequately to the support of his children he is superfluous except as the sexual partner of the mother. Since there is no shortage of sexual partners,[10] a man who does not earn steadily is, by this reasoning, all the more likely to drop out of the household, especially since it is then so much easier for his family to obtain support from public welfare.

There remains the question of whether there is a system of values that positively reinforces the matrifocal tendency. Safa has maintained that "the supremacy of the female in the Negro American household is not an inherent aspect of the subculture. It is not based on a value system which dictates that men are inferior and women are superior. Rather, it is based on years of cultural conditioning...in which Negro women were forced to take over" (Safa, 1968:18). A more recent study by a black female sociologist agrees: "Black women long have worked out of necessity and have combined family with labor market roles...while some researchers have suggested this role has been internalized culturally, there is as much evidence to suggest that this continuous labor force activity has been structurally maintained intergenerationally" (Engram, 1982:74).

While not denying structural forces, I submit that acknowledging them does not exclude cultural explanations of matrifocal tendencies. Indeed, if these were fully accounted for by material pressures for women to seek gainful employment, such tendencies would be much more widespread than they are in the world at large. It is hardly necessary for a cultural value system to assert that women are superior in order for it to support and validate the female-based household. Other values may easily come into play here, such as the strong bond between female consanguineal kin.

In a stratum of society where adult roles (for lower-class whites as well as for blacks) are rather strictly segregated, so that men and women have few joint interests or activities outside of sex and parenthood, bonds between same-sex consanguines are often strong. Newman (1965) interviewed several young pregnant black women in a California city who avowed their preference for living with their mothers and sisters rather than marrying and leaving home. Johnson (1941:238) found that rural Southern girls often disliked the idea of getting married because they had witnessed so many unhappy marriages within their own kindred. One or two even said that their mothers did not wish them to marry. Frazier (1948:113) reported that some Negro mothers were against their daughters' marrying the fathers of their illegitimate children because they were "unwilling to part with their daughters." Among my informants were several unmarried girls whose mothers would not consent to their marrying the fathers of their children because the boys were "no good." Such bits of evidence hint that in this subculture the emphasis is on the mother-child bond rather than the conjugal one, and in the case of mothers and daughters this seems to be especially strong.

There are, of course, valid historic and economic reasons to explain this development. Nevertheless, once established for adaptational reasons, cultural patterns tend to acquire a life of their own and persist even where they are no longer so clearly adaptive. The overwhelming symbolic importance of the mother-child bond is at least one major reason for the apparent ease with which ghetto families become matrifocal.

Welfare Dependency

All of the women interviewed in this study were selected specifically because they had low incomes. It is thus no surprise that three-fifths of these families were supported mainly or entirely by public welfare (29 of the 50, including 11 whose husbands were living with them). Only six of my informants received no form of public aid. The remainder received medical aid with eligibility based on a means test. The few non-assistance families belonged to the "working poor" and were hardly better off than those receiving public assistance. Several were, indeed, eligible for it but for various reasons had not applied.

While it is not possible to generalize from such a group about rates of dependency, speculation about the attitudes toward such dependency is possible. I earlier suggested that dependency attitudes described by Powdermaker and Dollard for the pre-World War II South may have become a feature of Southern black culture. Is it possible that this attitude was carried from South to North? It is possible that the Southern black's deep-seated conditioning to dependent status was not eradicated by the move to the Northern city. Any change, then, would have been not in the *fact*, but in the *form* of such dependency, e.g., a shift from reliance on the paternalism of individuals to reliance on the paternalism of a state bureaucracy.

If there is a major change regarding the acceptance of economic aid, it seems to be at the formal level. Unlike their rural Southern forbears, the needy black families of the ghetto receive what help they can rely on not from a patronizing employer but from a rigidly bureaucratic and impersonal arm of the state. It would be difficult to decide which may be the more distasteful for the recipient. It likely is not the proportion of families needing some form of charity that has altered drastically, but the source, the reliability and the amount of it that has changed as families made the transition to the ghetto.

Another View: The Role of Kin Networks

This discussion has centered on the Moynihan indices of "disorganization and instability" which, he argued, pointed to the rapid dissolution of the urbanizing black family. These indices are implicitly based on white norms defining "family" and "household," i.e., on the idea of a group of related people occupying a single dwelling and composing a single "hearth group."

It is possible, however, that Moynihan looked at the wrong things in the first place. Kinship in modern, urban industrial societies has usually been seen as consisting of isolated nuclear family units, mobile and independent of one another. There are indications, however, that this picture has been greatly exaggerated and that urban kinship, in or out of the ghetto, has never really been that atomistic. In a monograph on urban kinship among blue- and white-collar urban whites, Adams (1968) has documented that nuclear families in urban settings are not isolated units, but in fact are nearly always part of wider kin networks within which various degrees of interaction and cooperation regularly take place. Members of the married couple's families of orientation (parents and siblings) are the elements of this network with whom regular contact is generally felt to be obligatory, with some bias toward the wife's side, since the wife usually maintains the ties most actively. More remote or "secondary" kin (cousins, uncles, grand-parents, etc.) are contacted less frequently and such contact is more optional than obligatory.

When Bott (1955) investigated the kin relations of some London families she found a similar picture. Perhaps more important, she developed the idea that the "connectedness" of kin networks is correlated with the nature of the husband-wife relationship. In families where male and female roles are more "segregated" people tend to belong to more connected kin networks, while couples with "joint" or unsegrated conjugal roles tend to belong to more dispersed kin networks. This means that a couple sharing many activities depend less on kin contacts for affection, social life and assistance. Conversely, couples with highly differen-tiated sex roles and few shared activities tend to depend more on the companionship and aid of same-sex kin, and thus interact more with them. Other studies of both British and American kinship contain data which tend to support Bott's analysis (Cf. Young and Wilmott, 1957; Firth, Hubert and Forge, 1970; Schneider, 1969).

It is possible that in the rural South, where relatives were widely dispersed on farms or moved about frequently as tenants, the household was the effective boundary of the actively functioning kin unit. Large extended families with both male and female heads were especially common in farm areas, and the size of the agricultural work force was an important factor in farm productivity. Even in the non-farm small towns such as Powdermaker's "Cottonville" there were few Negro households that did not include a wider-than-nuclear kin group. It is therefore impossible to estimate the dimensions of the household in which Murdock's (1949) "universal functions of the family" were carried out. It apparently included a variety of relatives, but frequently contained three generations cooperating in economic and child-care functions. Most such households appear to have been pyramidal in structure and were dominated by the "oldest head," whether male or female.

In the urban ghetto, however, a transformation seems to have occurred. Carol B. Stack (1970; 1974) finds that not only can the "universal functions of the family" be carried out by units other than the nuclear or matrifocal family," but that urbanizing black families have also evolved a whole repertoire of such units for coping with stressful daily demands of ghetto life. Stack argues that "matrifocal thinking" has been misleading, and has provided us with little insight into the way units of domestic cooperation are organized. She found that such units are frequently based on alignments of siblings, both male and female, some of whom may reside together, while others are spread over several households. The most crucial function of these cooperative units is the care of children, arrangements for this purpose being highly flexible and variable. She further emphasizes that the history of the formation of a given domestic group is vital to understanding its organizing principles.

Among my own informants a wide range of residential arrangements was represented. Indeed, there were times when I believed that there were as many household "types" as there were households. There *is* a pattern, however, though it involves many alternatives and is therefore rather complex. The composition of households at the time of my study clustered into four general types, one of which has two subtypes (see Table 4).

Table 4 establishes the great variability of household composition, yet the data tell nothing of the relations *between* households. Bryce-Laporte (1967) outlines a similar notion in a study of the nature of cooperation between dwelling-units in a Puerto Rican housing project.

Table 4

Household Types for Fifty
North Philadelphia Families

Family Type	N	%
Nuclear	21	42
Augmented Nuclear[a]	9	18
Extended (3-generation)		
Male Head	4	8
Female Head	5	10
Matrifocal[b]	11	22
Total	50	100

a   "Augmented nuclear" here refers to households containing either non-kin or non-nuclear kin living in a home where the core unit is a married couple and their children, headed by a male. Often, such households contain an aging relative or an extra (related or unrelated) child, sometimes a sibling of one of the married pair, or some combination of these. Occasionally they contain a roomer or boarder as well.

b   "Matrifocal here designates a two-generation female-headed household, whereas the three-generation "grandmother household" is a subtype of the "extended" household containing three generations.

Since my data were not collected with such analysis in mind there is little systematic evidence on the extent of cooperation between the households of my informants and others. Two other kinds of data, however, provide hints as to the actual state of affairs. One is the name of the person listed as next-of-kin in the hospital records, to be notified in case of emergency. The large majority of women, of course, listed someone who lived with them -- most often a husband, sometimes a mother or father. A significant minority, however, numbering more than the number of women who headed matrifocal households (15, as opposed to 11 in the latter category) listed persons who lived at another address. Eight listed parents, three sisters, and four more distant kin or a friend who was also a near neighbor. Most of the other addresses were very near the informant's home, sometimes in the same block. This leads me to infer that many women who lacked other adults in the household had close cooperative ties with persons outside the household, and they could depend on them for help in a crisis. (Only three people in the sample of 50 were, for one reason or another, so isolated that they listed no one but "self" in the next-of-kin box on the admission form.)

Another perhaps more meaningful index of extra-residential cooperation is the data concerning baby-sitting arrangements for older children while mothers were confined for childbirth. Thirty-seven of the women had older children. In ten cases, they were cared for in the mother's absence by people who regularly resided in the home -- a mother or mother-in-law, teenage daughters and, in two cases, husbands. In 26 of the remaining 27 cases, the children were taken to the sitter's home, and there was a single case in which a neighbor moved in to take care of ten children because her home could not accommodate so many. Seven of the out-of-household baby sitters were parents of the informant, five were sisters, two were daughters, seven were affinal or more distant kin such as mothers-in-law, sisters-in-law or cousins, and five were non-kin. In only one case was the sitter paid for her services. Here again, the picture that emerges is one in which important ties of affection and mutual aid reach outside the residential unit, with most of them based on kinship.

Added to this are numerous random remarks and impressions from the interviews. One woman was moving as soon as she returned home in order to be near her husband's large and cooperative kin group in another neighborhood, and anticipated being "helped to death." No less than six informants lived only a block or two from a mother and/or sisters with whom they regularly cooperated. Several mentioned close relationships with a sister-in-law with whom they maintained an important alliance involving baby-sitting, house-cleaning and food shopping. Even women who were separated from their husbands sometimes kept up cooperative relationships with affines. Most of the women expected a sister, mother or other female relative to come daily for a few weeks after they returned home in order to help with housework and the care of the new baby. Some also had close neighbors, a few regarded as fictive kin,[11] whom they helped regularly and who also helped them. In short, the picture was not one of isolated households, whatever the composition of the household in question, but rather of extensive networks of mutual aid, with alliances extending across household lines.

Conclusion: Black Urban Survival Strategies

By comparing data on rural Southern families of a generation or two past with my own data on families in a Northern ghetto, I have tried to determine whether, as Moynihan and others have so glibly hypothesized, there is evidence of increasing "disorganization" of black families as they became more urbanized. Although it is impossible to reach any firm conclusions, further study may reveal that the following more aptly summarizes the changes that have and have not occurred in the transition from rural to urban environments, and from South to North, for large numbers of lower-class black families.

On a formal level there has been, first, a tendency to legalize marriage more often than before and (perhaps as a concomitant of this trend) the development of somewhat greater marital stability. Second, there is a tendency for economic dependency to take new forms, with a switch from reliance on personal patronage to reliance on impersonal public agencies.

Change is much less apparent on a more fundamental psychocultural level. The rise in illegitimacy rates in the urban setting seems to be more a function of lowered infant mortality than of changed sexual behavior patterns. Matrifocality among lower-class blacks, also a traditional adaptation with a long historic rationale, seems to have risen with urbanization, though somewhat less sharply than the rate of illegitimate births. This is probably not due to any fundamental cultural change, for such arrangements had considerable cultural sanction in the South. More likely, it is due to the increased economic marginality of males who lack occupational skills and suffer from the "last-hired-first-fired" syndrome that has always afflicted black men in U.S. society. The easier availability of welfare payments for fatherless households probably also plays a role in intensifying matrifocal tendencies, as does public-housing policy, since both institutions are available to present-day urban families, whereas they were not to rural Southern black families, even in the recent past.

Beyond this, however, the four indices used by Moynihan and others as evidence that the black family is "disintegrating" under the impact of migration to Northern ghettos may not, in fact, be the most salient dimensions of inquiry. Having concluded, at least provisionally, that along these four dimensions the Negro family is neither disintegrating nor becoming more disorganized, but merely doing more of most of the same things they did in the Old South, I have sought more meaningful dimensions for understanding ghetto kinship.

Following lines of conceptualization laid down by both Stack (1970 and 1974) and Bryce-Laporte (1967) as well as a variety of other network theorists (Barnes, 1954, 1960; Bott, 1955; Srinivas, 1964; Jay, 1964; Eames, 1967; Goode, 1968; Firth, Hubert and Forge, 1970), the examination of my own data indicates that kinship organization has indeed undergone changes with lower-class black urbanization, and that these are structural in nature. There appears to be a trend away from the pyramidal, self-contained extended family household (whether male- or female-headed) that dominated the Southern scene, and toward another kind of organization that has evolved out of the older one but differs from it substantially. There are relatively "connected" networks of affiliated households in the new structure, focused largely on the care of children.

In the rural South the head of household acted as the organizer of a family work-force in which male strength was an important asset, and in which children, too, played an active and essential role. In the urban industrial system, on the other hand, the wage earner does not take an administrative role, but merely brings home cash wages. Children, furthermore, lack the economic function they once had in the rural South. They must instead be supported through the labor of relatively youthful adults, the only employable family members, and women are often more readily employable than men. This is not wholly without Southern precedent, however, since in non-farm rural areas the same situation is often found. The transfer to an urban environment, then, did involve major changes in economic subsistence patterns and in the arrangements necessary for the care of children, a primary function of the family.

In ways that are not clear from so limited a study, other factors seem to have influenced kin relations in the city as well. The *kinds* of households found in the ghetto do not differ from the kinds found in the South, but their *distribution* does appear to have changed, with a paradoxical increase in the proportion that are female-headed at the same time that there also appears to be an increase in legalized marriages. This may result from the differential impact on individual families of a variety of systems which are either unique to the city or more fully developed there, such as welfare, public housing, urban labor markets, and mass communications. These all provide different pressures and opportunities, and only their cumulative effects can be measured. Such factors cannot really be sorted out without further study, but it does appear that polar structural tendencies among poor black families may be intensified by urbanization.

Flexibility is hardly a new quality in the black family; it is a long tradition developed under the harshest of conditions and for sheer survival.[12] In the city that flexibility is expressed through what might be phrased as a combination of assimilation, exploitation and decentralization. In the trend toward legal marriage, and an apparent concomitant stability of marriage, there are signs of *assimilation,* possibly a function of mass communications, reduced cultural isolation, and increased economic opportunity. In the increases in illegitimacy, matrifocality and social dependency there are signs of *exploitation* of resources never before extensively available to blacks, such as hospitals, welfare agencies and public housing. In the trend toward spreading the unit of domestic cooperation over several households there are signs of *decentralization*. Such flexible, kin-based networks of affiliation permit each individual family and household to be "unstable," to change its form and personnel as circumstances require. But even though each node in the network may become destabilized from time to time, the structure as a whole remains, a network of multiple connected nodes, each of which is a household. This sort of kinship arrangement is a sociological invention neither disorganized nor close to dissolution. Instead, it enables people to survive who might not, if they were rigidly committed to maintaining a "normal" family structure.

Moynihan and others (now including a sizeable segment of the black elite) condemn this sort of flexible (hence unconventional) arrangement as a barrier to blacks' partaking of the American Dream. If the realistic hope of all Americans is something we call "upward mobility," they might be right. But without the luxury of that particular option, the lower-class black family survives as it can-- and as it does -- in a wide variety of forms.

Notes

1. Informants were selected, within the parameters already set forth, only on the basis that both they and I would be available for at least two long interviews before they were to leave the hospital. Those women whose date of admission indicated this would not be possible were rejected. The essential randomness of selection should not have been affected by this (babies, after all, can be born at almost any time), therefore, I make the assumption that the 50 informants represent a fair cross-section of poor black mothers of the North Philadelphia ghetto in the late 1960s and that kinship data on them reflects a general pattern of some sort. Of course, not all ghetto women are mothers, and not all mothers give birth in hospitals. However, since my definition of the family includes only units in which there are children, and since hospitalization for childbirth was by then the norm for nearly all ghetto women, I believe it is possible to generalize from these examples.

2. Throughout this essay, references to page numbers 47-124 in Rainwater and Yancey (1967) actually refer to the famous -- or infamous -- document known as "The Moynihan Report," published in Washington, D.C. in 1965. The actual title was *The Negro Family: The Case for National Action*. Daniel Patrick Moynihan's name was never officially attached to this

publication, which came out of the U.S. Department of Labor. Where I refer to it in the text I use the popular title and the Rainwater and Yancey page numbers.

3. Lifton (1968) has argued that a new personality type has arisen in adaptation to rapidly changing social conditions of our modern age. He calls this type "Protean Man," and it is characterized by low levels of commitment to any single value system or personal style, along with a capacity to act and evaluate action in those ways that facilitate successful survival. A similar thesis might hold true for families as well as individuals, producing something like a "Protean Household."

4. I do not propose here to deal with the entire history of the black family in the rural South. That task has been admirably taken on by Herbert Gutman (1976) in his monumental history of the black family, which covers a period of some 200 years before and after the Civil War. His finding that a durable two-parent family survived, even in slavery, in a high percentage of cases casts considerable doubt on earlier assumptions, often of black researchers, that slavery destroyed the traditional male-headed family that had been normative in Africa. Indeed, if "disintegration" is symptomatized by matrifocality, it is a recent phenomenon which even now is not statistically normative, much less culturally supported.

5. This may have been less true of farm than of non-farm rural families, past and present, probably because the black tenant family is a "productive unit, and every effort is made to keep it intact by both tenant and landlord" (Johnson, 1941:411). This might explain statistics cited by Rainwater and Yancey (1967:52) which show considerable differences between rural non-farm and rural farm families with respect to the number of absent husbands. (The figures are for blacks: urban, 22.9 percent; rural non-farm, 14.7 percent; and rural farm, 9.6 percent in 1960.)

6. In this section I rely mainly on data collected from female residents of a typical northern ghetto area in the late 1960s, not long after the publication of the Moynihan report. The conditions of its collection were described earlier. The sample size represents only fifty families, so conclusions are tentative.

7. According to doctors at Temple University Health Sciences Center, where the study was done, most infant mortality is attributable to premature births in

the black ghetto population. The reasons for this are little understood, but may have some relation to the extreme youth of so many mothers who are still growing girls themselves. It is probably also related to the poorer general health of mothers whose incomes are very low, and whose diets and education may both be substandard. There are indications, too, that some very young mothers tire of being pregnant, do not really want their babies anyway, and "do things" (their term) to bring on labor early.

8.   In line with the evidence that at a certain age having a baby may be the "thing to do" is an interesting linguistic usage among black high school-age boys and girls in North Philadelphia. Here the word "virgin" is applied not to a girl who has never had intercourse, but to one who has never had a child.

9.   Because I had no opportunity to observe informants in their own homes or to assess the power relationships within families, I employ here the Solien definition of matrifocality, which simply uses the lack of an adult male in the husband-father role as the criterion for classification (Cf. Kunstadter, 1963).

10.   Statistics cited by Engram (1982, p. 62) and others indicate a startling surplus of females in the black population, and some reason that this demo-graphic imbalance causes women to compete with one another for the avail-able men. Others have claimed, however, that this phenomenon is merely an artifact of inaccurate census-taking due to: a) the unstable residence pattern of jobless men and; b) the "statistically absent father" whose family is receiving public assistance that his official presence would jeopardize. Whether the imbalance is real and factual, real but exaggerated, or not real at all is not settled at this time, so far as I know. It seems reasonable, therefore, to assume that the sex ratio in the black population is not markedly different from that of other groups.

11.   Cf. Liebow (1967) for an extended discussion of fictive kin relationships and the nature of kinship terminology as used between unmarried couples. My own findings were similar to his. Women who did not call their partner "husband" nevertheless referred to the mothers and sisters, etc. as "in-laws." There were also women, otherwise without relatives, who called a close friend a "play mother" or "play sister." These practices possibly emphasize the important functions filled by kinfolk in the ghetto; if one has none they need to be invented.

12. Clearly, adaptation for survival is not the same as adaptation for upward mobility in the urban setting. The functional requirements for the two kinds of adaptation are undoubtedly different and this may account for the apparent sharpening of differences between families, with the upwardly mobile tending to adopt "respectable" patterns of behavior while the "survivors" intensify those strategies which best enable them to survive.

References

Adams, B. (1968) *Kinship in an Urban Setting*. Chicago: Markam.

Barnes, J.A. (1954) Class and committees in a Norwegian island parish. *Human Relations, 7,* 39-58.

Barnes, J.A. (1960) Marriage and residential continuity, *American Anthropologist, 62,* 850-866.

Berger, P.L. and H. Kellner (1964) Marriage and the construction of reality, *Diogenes, 46*(1), 24.

Berger, P.L. (1969) *The Sacred Canopy*. New York: Doubleday.

Bott, E. (1955) Conjugal roles and social networks, *Human Relations, 8,* 345-384.

Bryce-Laporte, R.S. (1967) Family adaptation of relocated slum dwellers in a Puerto Rican housing project: Some academic and applied implications. Paper presented at the 1967 meeting of the Society of Applied Anthropology, Washington, D.C.

Davis, A. (1941) *Deep South*. Chicago: University of Chicago Press.

Davis, A. and J. Dollard (1940) *Children of Bondage*. Washington, D.C.: American Council on Education.

Dollard, J. (1957) *Caste and Class in a Southern Town*. New York: Doubleday. (Originally published 1937)

Eames, E. (1967) Urban migration and the joint family in a north Indian village, *Journal of Developing Areas, 1*(3).

Engram, E. (1982) *Science, Myth, Reality: The Black Family in One-Half Century of Research*. Westport, CT: Greenwood Press.

Firth, R., J. Hubert, and A. Forge (1970) *Families and their Relatives*. London: Routledge, Kegan and Paul.

Frankel, B. (1977) *Childbirth in the Ghetto: Folk Beliefs of Negro Women in a North Philadelphia Hospital Ward*. San Francisco: R & E Research Assoc.

Frazier, E.F. (1951) The Negro Family in the United States. New York: Dryden Press. (Originally published 1948)

Goode, W.J. (1968) World revolution and family patterns. In Fava (Ed.), *Urbanism in World Perspective*. New York: Crowell.

136   *Comparative Urban and Community Research*

Gutman, H.G. (1976) *The Black Family in Slavery and Freedom.* New York: Pantheon.

Jay, E. (1964) The concepts of "field" and "network" in anthropological research, *Man, 64,* 137-139.

Johnson, C.S. (1967) *Growing up in the Black Belt: Negro Youth in the Rural South.* Washington, D.C.: American Council on Education. (Originally published 1941)

Kunstadter, P. (1963) A survey of the consanguine of matrifocal family, *American Anthropologist, 65,* 56-66.

Leeds, A. (1968) The anthropology of cities: Some methodological issues. In Eddy (Ed.), *Urban Anthropology.* Athens: University of Georgia Press.

Liebow, E. (1967) *Tally's Corner: A Study of Negro Streetcorner Men.* Boston: Little, Brown.

Lifton, R.J. (1968) Protean Man, *Partisan Review, 35,* 13-27.

Luckmann, T. and P. Berger (1964) Social mobility and personal identity, *European Journal of Sociology, 5,* 331-344.

Moynihan, D.P. (1986) *Family and Nation: The Godkin Lectures at Harvard University.* San Diego: Harcourt, Brace, Jovanovich.

Murdock. G.P. (1965) *Social Structures.* New York: Free Press. (Originally published 1949).

Murray, C. (1984) *Losing Ground: American Social Policy 1950-1980.* New York: Basic Books.

Newman, L.F. (1965) *Culture and Perinatal Development in American Society.* Unpublished Ph.D. dissertation, University of California, Berkeley.

Norton, E.H. (1985) Restoring the traditional black family, *New York Times Magazine,* June 12, 43-ff.

Powdermaker, H. (1939) *After Freedom.* New York: Atheneum.

Rainwater, L. and W.L. Yancey (1967) *The Negro Family: The Case for National Action,* 47-124. Washington, D.C.: U.S. Department of Labor.

Rainwater, L. and W.L. Yancey (1967) *The Moynihan Report and the Politics of Controversy.* Cambridge: M.I.T. Press.

Safa, H.I. (1968) The negro matrifocal family: A product of class or culture? Mimeo.

Schneider, D. (1969) Middle class and lower class American Kinship, Chicago. Seen in draft.

Srinivas, M.N. and A. Beteille (1964) Networks in Indian school structure. *Man, 64,* 165-168.

Stack, C.B. (1970) The kindred of Viola Jackson: Residence and family organization of an urban black American family. In Whitten and Szwed (Eds.), *Afro-American Anthropology.*

Stack, C.B. (1974) *All Our Kin: Strategies for Survival in a Black Community.* New York: Harper and Row.

Wirth, L. (1938) Urbanism as a way of life, *American Journal of Sociology, (44),* 1-23.

Wylie, P. (1942) *A Generation of Vipers.* New York: Farrar & Rinehart.

Young, M. and P. Wilmott (1957) *Family and Kinship in East London.* London: Routledge, Kegan and Paul.

THE BLACK URBAN REGIME:
STRUCTURAL ORIGINS & CONSTRAINTS[1]

Adolph Reed, Jr.
Yale University

Black urban regimes often are seen as representing a significant advance for democratic interests in urban politics, at least to the extent that their empowerment implies that blacks can begin to ascend the American upward mobility queue. Yet several scholars have cautioned restraint of this optimism, citing the institutional limitations that beset those regimes as well as the fact that once in office they often opt for "corporate center" policy agendas that subordinate the interests of their black electoral constituency to those of private developers. Comprehending how this occurs requires situating the black urban regime structurally and historically, which in turn requires an examination of both the forces that allow black regimes to come to power and the pressures that constrain them once in power.

By the end of 1986 black regimes -- black-led and black-dominated adminis-trations backed by solid council majorities -- governed thirteen U.S. cities with populations over 100,000, several of them among the nation's largest (JCPS, 1986:1).[2] Popular accounts often herald accession of those regimes as fulfillment of grand democratic ideals. A more sophisticated, and more modest, view sees the black regime as a current point in an unfolding saga of urban ethnic succession. That view also entails an inference that black municipal governance signifies something more than office-holding. Black "succession" implies that the semi-Hobbesian democracy of "street-fighting" pluralism works now even for blacks, who therefore will finally join the long march of upward mobility along with other, allegedly earlier, "immigrant" groups. The first view is simply naive in its civics text-like exuberance. The second suffers from an ahistoricism that 1) glosses profound structural and institutional changes that have reshaped the urban context over the last two generations, and 2) forgets that the strength of the racial element in American politics short-circuits neat comparisons with earlier instances of "ethnoracial transition" (Eisinger, 1980). Both take the rise of black regimes as reason to indulge a self-satisfied celebration of American political institutions and racial democracy. To be sure, black officials contribute to the perception that they represent larger purposes by presenting themselves as legatees of the civil rights movement (see contributions by Hatcher and Gibson in Baraka, 1972).

Certain other viewpoints counsel restraint of such celebrations. While genu-flecting perfunctorily toward the rhetorical elan attending the first wave of black mayoral successes, Holden (1971) and Preston (1976) stressed the limitations placed on mayoral capacities by political institutions and entrenched patterns of political behavior. More recent scholarship has examined consequences of those limitations by assessing black mayors' impact on budgetary allocations, including service delivery patterns and composition of public employment. Although the specific findings of that research have been mixed, the general conclusion seems to be that presence of a black mayor or regime has some, but less than dramatic, racially redistributive effect on allocation of public resources (Watson, 1980; Karnig and Welch, 1980; Eisinger, 1982, 1983, 1984; Keller, 1978). However, black mayors have been unable to affect the high levels of poverty and unemployment that characterize the cities over which they preside. Benefits of racial redistribution have been concentrated among middle class blacks, in part because the regimes adopt "corporate center" development strategies that generally contradict the reform platforms on which they are elected (Nelson, 1987). The key to apprehending the real significance of black urban governance lies in examining how and why regimes adhere to development strategies so much at odds with their "electoral platforms."

To what complex of pressures does the black regime respond in choosing corporate centered strategy? What is the nature of the tension expressed in Nelson's juxtaposition of the corporate and popular racial constituencies? What alternative courses, if any, might be pursued? These questions seldom have been addressed systematically in relation to black municipal governance. In what follows I shall respond to them by proposing a structurally and historically situated account of the black urban regime as a distinctive phenomenon. This account has two elements: 1) reconstruction of the demographic, socio-economic and ideological/political pressures that created the conditions for ascendancy of the black regime; and 2) examination of major structural constraints and issues that confront those regimes as they attempt to govern. In the latter connection I shall assess ways in which black regimes generally have reacted to those constraints and issues. In a concluding section I shall discuss possibilities for enhancing democratic interests -- apropos of both practical politics and the discourse of political scientists -- in the context of black urban governance.

Structural Origins of the Black Regime

Although individual perspicacity and organizational talent are probably the most pertinent factors determining election of a given regime, we can hardly believe that electoral political wisdom and aptitude came to urban black communities only in the late 1960s. Black control of the official institutions of municipal governance has been made possible by elaboration of a particular set of demographic, socio-economic and ideological pressures operative in the post-World War II urban arena.

Demographic Pressure

Most simply put, throughout the two decades following the war, the non-white share of big city populations rose steadily. This increase was fed by three factors: 1) absolute increase of non-white population, largely by in-migration; 2) relative, and sometimes absolute, white decrease, mainly by out-migration; and 3) comparative fixity of municipal boundaries (Tilly, 1968; Bradbury, et al., 1982: 133-138). New migrants, largely black and Hispanic, flocked to the nation's major cities in quest of a better way of life. At the same time, spurred by federal housing policies that subsidized single-family, low-density housing, middle class and stable working class whites increasingly began relocating beyond municipal boundaries into the suburban SMSA. Consequently, by the latter 1960s, the prospect of black majority cities had become an issue for national policy concern.

While the pull factors drawing non-whites to the central city are straight-forward and familiar, the push factors nudging whites out are somewhat more complex. Moreover, the latter suggest a material as well as an attitudinal basis for the "white flight" syndrome. White exodus from central cities has been a response first of all to the ideology of upward mobility, buttressed by federal transportation and housing policies that stimulated suburban development in the post-war era (Ashton, 1978:73-74). For many, leaving the old in-city enclaves for modern, disconnected tract houses has been a symbol -- albeit one largely articulated and propagated by private real estate development ideology -- of arrival, a statement of self-improvement. For many as well, the mortgage subsidies provided by federal programs brought the relatively new "American dream" of home ownership within reach of a substantial portion of the population who would not otherwise have been able to afford it (Ashton, 1978; Solomon, 1980:10-12; Judd, 1979:171-174). Moreover, white departure has been stimulated by non-white in-migration, in part for reasons that, although ultimately bigoted, are instrumentally rational. The cliched fear of loss of property value has a factual basis. Property values do tend to fall when blacks enter a neighborhood because one element of property value in residential real estate markets is white exclusivity (Downs, 1981:51; Orfield, 1985; Darden, 1986).[3]

Therefore whites who want to avoid living near blacks "pay more for other-wise similar housing in white neighborhoods than in integrated neighborhoods, pushing prices higher in the white interior than in the transition zone." More-over, "white expectations about the future of neighborhoods in the transition zone depress prices for housing there" (Downs, 1981:91-93; O'Brien & Lange, 1986). We can thus see the tragic cycle. Whites flee with black encroachment. Real estate "values" fall, accelerating flight. As "values" fall, housing stock begins to deteriorate, prompting stable and middle income blacks to follow fleeing whites, whose new neighborhoods lose their relative attractiveness once blacks move in. Moreover, federal housing policy played an active role in reinforcing this dynamic, often by building segregation into program priorities (Pettigrew, 1980).

This ironic situation has obvious revenue implications for the municipalities that anchor SMSAs. Suburban sprawl has meant relative and in some cases absolute reductions in municipal tax bases. In addition, the city finds itself in the position of providing services daily to hordes of suburban freeloaders. Nor is that the only harmful consequence of suburbanization for central municipalities. Orfield provides a useful summary:

> Suburbanization not only redistributes taxable wealth, but also redistributes jobs and educational opportunities in ways that make them virtually inaccessible to minorities confined by residential segregation to parts of the central city and declining segments of the suburban ring. It greatly increases the physical scale of racial separation, particularly for children, since middle-class white families with children become rarities in many central cities. It overlaps the system of racial separation and inequality with a system of political and legal separation. Thus the best services, education, and access to new jobs are made available to affluent, virtually all-white communities that openly employ a full range of municipal powers to attract desirable jobs from the city while preventing low- and moderate-income families, or renters of any kind, from moving into the communities. As a consequence, black and Hispanic political aspirations are concentrated very largely on municipal and educational institutions that lack the tax base to maintain existing levels of services, to say nothing of mounting vast new responses to the critical problems of these expanding minority communities (pp. 163-4; also see Newton, 1975; Shlay & Rossi, 1981; R.S. Harrison, 1982; Babcock, 1973; and Judd, 1979:171-88).

A simple solution to this problem would be for central municipalities to adopt programs of aggressive annexation. However, that response is impractical for a number of reasons. For one thing, given patterns of racial voting, elected officials and aspirants to officialdom in black majority or near-majority cities are understandably loath to annex pockets of potentially antagonistic white voters. The latter can, in any event, expect sufficient support in state legislatures to ward off unilateral annexations. Successful annexation appears to be strongly associated with both relatively low status differentiation between central city and suburbs and a relatively brief period of urban settlement (Dye, 1964; Black, 1980:97-98; Bradbury, et al., 1982:51-55; Oakland, 1979:325). Black regimes, as shown below, tend to hold power in older cities and in cities substantially differentiated from their SMSAs.

This means, of course, that the kind of city most likely to be governed by a black regime is also the kind of city most likely to suffer the regressive effects of suburbanization and least likely to have the option of mitigating them by means of expanding municipal boundaries.[4] However, while the proximate cause of this situation is, to paraphrase Orfield, the dialectic of suburbanization and ghettoization, its ultimate sources lie deeper, in the dynamics of changing urban and metropolitan economic function.

Socio-Economic Pressure

The modern American city has its roots in the logic of industrial production; so, in large measure, does the impetus of suburbanization. The heyday of urban growth coincided with the burst of industrial growth between the last quarter of the 19th century and the first quarter of the 20th. By the 1920s, however, the processes of suburbanization had taken hold. Individuals had been moving farther away from the inner city for some time and for a variety of reasons (Warner, 1978), but theretofore cities simply responded with periodic, often imperialistic annexations (Ashton, 1978:67). What was different after 1920 was that industry, particularly manufacturing, had begun to leave the city (Gordon, 1977:74-75). Two related developments made relocation outside the central city attractive. New mass production technologies increasingly required production processes -- and therefore plants -- to be laid out horizontally over larger parcels of land; this development favored location in suburban rings where land was cheaper than in central cities (Kain, 1968). However, movement to the suburban ring was underway even before the proliferation of such mass production techniques. What especially made suburban relocation desirable was the search for more isolable, and thus more tractable, labor (and along the way perhaps reduced taxes) (Gordon, 1977; 75-77; Walker, 1981:399-401). This was an early manifestation of one of the corporation's most powerful assets in its relations with labor and government: the relative mobility of capital. It is not unusual in the history of capitalist development for labor's assertiveness to stimulate the forces of technical innovation as an instrument of managerial control (Braverman, 1974).

The defection of manufacturing production was the central event in launching the suburbanization dynamic in two respects. As Walker maintains, "Only with the dispersal of employment -- of production and circulation activities as a whole" -- was mass suburbanization possible even though residential decentralization had begun earlier; the location of industry grounded and accelerated the process (Walker, 1981:399). More mundanely, but no less consequentially, newly suburbanized industrial elites gave the necessary muscle to well-off residents and other advocates of suburban independence to boost the home rule movement and thereby curtail central cities' powers to annex (Markusen, 1978:100-101; Ashton, 1978:71). At the same time, downtown came to be recast as the locus for concentrating administrative business activity. "Downtown office space in the ten largest cities increased between 1920 and 1930 by 3,000 percent. Tall skyscrapers suddenly sprouted; by 1929 there were 295 buildings 21 stories or taller in the five largest cities alone" (Gordon, 1978:51). Decentralization of plants to the suburbs, thanks to new communications technology, had made possible separation of productive and administrative functions. The latter clustered downtown, creating the new central business district and completing what Gordon describes as the transition from the "Industrial City" to the "Corporate City," which is built around several dispersive tendencies: 1) dispersion of manufacturing from the inner-city through the metropolitan area and eventually beyond; 2) dispersion and segmentation of working-class housing; 3) dispersion of shopping centers from downtown, to be replaced by corporate institutions; and 4) intensified dispersion of middle and upper class housing (Gordon, 1978:54-55).

Reproduction of the corporate city, and thus of its centrifugal tendencies, became a principal project around which political entrepreneurs, corporate elites of other major interest configurations converged -- growing from the New Deal experience -- to improvise the distinctive American form of political-economic management that Wolfe (1981:49 ff) has called "counter-Keynesianism." As Wolfe puts it succinctly: "If Keynesianism implies the use of government to influence and direct decisions made in the private sector, then postwar macroeconomic planning could only be defined as counter-Keynesian: the use of the private sector to influence the scope and activities of government" (p. 54).

Reproduction of the corporate city entailed reproduction of the principle of dispersion, by definition on a widening scale. This dynamic -- aided and encouraged by federal and local government policy -- not only created and exacerbated the now familiar problem of metropolitan fragmentation which, of course, has contributed significantly to central city deterioration; also, spurred by the tremendous postwar advances in communications technology (themselves often by-products of the federally-sponsored, "private" defense industry), the tendency toward decentralization of production has proceeded even beyond the suburban fringe. By the end of the 1960s the corporate sector of the U.S. economy had begun, for a variety of reasons, systematically to deindustrialize, as investment in industrial production increasingly left the United States altogether in favor of more congenial climes where wage-scales often fall in the sub-50 cent/hour range

144   *Comparative Urban and Community Research*

(Bluestone and Harrison, 1981; Bowles, et al., 1982; and Miller and Tomaskovic-Devey, 1983).[5]

This economic dynamic combines with the demographic one discussed in the previous section to create a pattern of central cities that have become increasingly black and have offered rapidly declining opportunities for the kind of labor-intensive employment that supported earlier urban populations. Blacks in metropolitan areas are twice as likely as whites to live in central cities; they are more likely as well to reside in the largest metropolitan areas (Pettigrew, 1980:62). These tend also to be the oldest SMSAs and, in part because the processes of decentralization are more advanced in them, the most depressed (Kasarda, 1985:46). Bradbury, et al. found that while the black share of the population declined by .4 percent in growing cities in growing SMSAs between 1960-70, it increased by 7.8 percent in severely declining cities in declining SMSAs (Bradbury et al., 1982:75).

At the same time that the central city's non-white population was growing and becoming ever more marginalized economically, the scope and character of urban politics were changing. The counter-Keynesian framework for local politics that developed in most cities after World War II, with its new concatenations of stakes and constituencies joined by a progrowth imperative, eventually -- but only after the appearance of mass uprisings and "defiant" black political activity-- articulated mechanisms to incorporate and channel forms of black systemic representation. That arrangement became the immediate context out of which black municipal governance emerged.

Ideological/Political Pressure

Three currents in the postwar urban political scene came together to set the stage for the rise of the black regime: 1) consolidation of a "progrowth" framework as the driving imperative of and basis for allegiance in urban politics; 2) expansion of public service bureaucracies and their entry into the local political arena as interest configurations and constituencies; and 3) the development and spread of black activism. Of the three the first is central in that the progrowth agenda both increased public sector functions and employment *and* generated the specific issues in relation to which black activism was articulated.

John Mollenkopf (1983) has provided a cogent account of the sources and composition of progrowth politics at the local level, and there is no need to rehearse all of its elements here. The guiding principle of the progrowth framework has been aggregation of local interests to effect federally authorized local development projects. Toward that end, Mollenkopf observes:

These progrowth coalitions brought together a variety of constituencies into what Robert Salisbury has called "a new convergence of power." Among them were downtown business elites, ambitious political leaders seeking to modernize urban politics, middle class, good government reform groups, the professional city planners to whom they turned for advice, a powerful new stratum of public administrators, and private development interests, including developers, lenders, builders, and the construction trades (Mollenkopf, 1983:141).

While each of the participating groups brought its particular interest (i.e., developers and building trades unions wanted construction to occur, planners and reformers wanted modernized, scientific government, politicians wanted identification with visible symbols of progress), the broader project of the agenda they served was completion of the functional transition from industrial to post-industrial or corporate city.

In addition to offering clear incentives for local participants the progrowth framework held out at least two attractions at the national level. First, it provided the national Democratic party with a way to bring together its "disparate urban constituencies" and to unite them organizationally around a program of publicly underwritten local growth and development (Mollenkopf, 1983). Second, the progrowth agenda became a significant part of national economic policy and provided a useful context for counter-Keynesian economic strategy in the postwar period. Mollenkopf estimates that "metropolitan physical development accounts for perhaps one-fifth of the GNP and perhaps one-fourth of its growth since World War II" and notes that government spending has contributed substantially to the magnitude and direction of those expenditures. Those considerable public expenditures have been directed toward reconstructing physical and institutional infrastructures along lines compatible with the functional requirements of the new corporate city. In the process the expanded governmental role naturally entailed an expansion of municipal functions and employment, a development which reinforced tendencies already operative in public bureaucracies (Mollenkopf, 1983:42-44).

On the one hand, the growth of public employment, both absolutely and relatively, increased the significance of public employee unions as interest configurations in the local polity. This tendency was relatively more pronounced in older, larger cities which had larger critical masses of public employees and experienced declines in non-public sector employment (Shefter, 1985:118-119; Mollenkopf, 1983:33-34). On the other hand, the expanded public role also contributed to the spread of professionalistic interests and ideologies in local politics. Professionalization has been driven by endemic forces in municipal service delivery, as in other spheres in American society, over most of this century (Yates 1977:54-73; Bledstein, 1976; Larson, 1977; Luke, 1986). With elaboration of the progrowth framework professional and technical interests became embedded institutionally in local politics by virtue of the centrality of planning, engineering and administrative functions in forming and realizing the growth agenda (Sayre & Kaufman, 1960; Lowi, 1967:83-92; Salisbury, 1964:775-797; Greer, 1979). However, professionalization, as technique and as ideology, extended as well into the human service bureaucracies, which also grew in the post-war years.

At the same time, the general expansion of local public sector activity was tied in three ways to development of what Piven and Cloward have called "defiant" urban black activism in the 1960s. First, urban renewal, which was a main programmatic vehicle for realizing the progrowth agenda, became a focal point for black oppositional activity. The racial effects of urban renewal through the early 1960s are well known and best summarized in the phrase of the day, "Negro removal" (Anderson, 1964:7-8 f; Fainstein & Fainstein, 1983; Stone, 1976; Swanstrom, 1985:37-55; Mollenkopf, 1983; Sanders, 1980; Friedland, 1983:78-124). By the middle of the decade blacks had begun to react politically against the displacement and ghettoization that characterized the program. Second, growth of the local public sector increased the stakes of patronage politics, especially because of the relative success that blacks have had, along with women and other minorities, in governmental employment with respect to stability and upward mobility (Carnoy, et al., 1983:122-149; Hout, 1984). Finally, extension and professionalization of the local public sector added a new epicycle to urban politics (i.e., the relationship between public agencies and their constituents/clients). As agencies professionalized, they sought greater autonomy in defining the terms and standards for their operations, especially in the human services. A result was increased tension between service providers and recipients (Lipsky, 1980; Piven and Cloward, 1974; Stone, 1983; Crenson, 1982). As cities were simultaneously becoming blacker than the agencies, race was built into the texture of that politicized relationship.

Blacks were the one major urban constituency of the national Democratic party that had benefitted least from the progrowth framework. In fact several factors, including the racial component of real estate value, combined to make blacks victims rather than beneficiaries of progrowth politics. The urban uprisings not only signalled discontent with the general quality of black life in cities and the insensitivity of institutions of social administration, they also indicated a need for additional mechanisms to cement black political loyalty. Both a sense of urgency produced by the uprisings (as well as by the energy recently set in motion through the civil rights movement) and the obdurateness of local governing coalitions that excluded black interests led to establishment of parallel linkages to create channels for black systemic representation. The federal program administration apparatus provided a linkage that by-passed entrenched local coalitions without destabilizing them (Button, 1978; Shefter, 1985; Piven and Cloward, 1974).

Successful incorporation of blacks into the progrowth framework entailed two adjustments, one ideological and one programmatic. Ideologically, as Peterson argues (1981:178-181), municipal governments, because of their fundamental commitments to economic growth and revenue enhancement, naturally tend to reformulate potentially redistributive demands so that they articulate symbolic rather than redistributive goals. Thus, official black representation in decision-making processes became an alternative to alteration of growth-oriented patterns of resource allocation. Programmatically, however, while the demand for black representation was an alternative to broad-scale redistribution, accommodation of that more limited demand nonetheless required expanding the public sector pie to provide niches for minority functionaries in the social management apparatus (Shefter, 1985; Brown and Erie, 1981; Reed, 1986b; Button, 1978:169). Moreover, this strategy had longer term implications.

Once black assertiveness was channeled into auxiliary linkage mechanisms of progrowth politics, i.e., what Brown and Erie (1981:301) call the public "social welfare economy," black political activity increasingly assimilated to familiar forms of urban ethnic pluralism. To that extent, as increasing black population in one city after another made it possible, in Carl Stokes' (1973; Katznelson, 1981:177-178) phrase, to "take City Hall," the process of "ethnoracial transition" was smoothed by the presence of a black leadership cohort that already was incorporated into the broader progrowth coalition and accepted its imperatives. Eisinger found in a study of black elected officials, for example, that especially in larger cities the Community Action Program "provided an avenue to public service for a particular generation of young and relatively well-educated activists" (Eisinger, 1979:133; Woody, 1982, 81-83), and Karnig & Welch (1980:50-78) found black success in mayoral and city council aspirations to be associated with prior Model Cities experience. Sometimes the auxiliary linkages were more directly and immediately meaningful, as in the Ford Foundation's underwriting of a CORE voter registration project that enabled Stokes to win the Cleveland mayoral election on his second attempt (Hadden, et al., 1969).

As I have argued elsewhere (Reed, 1986b:62-67), the interests of a growing professional-managerial stratum within the black community converged with those of progrowth white elites to produce a new framework for black political activity in the post-civil rights movement era. That framework is largely a product of the several structural dynamics discussed here. Some scholars have seen this development as a natural progression from protest to mainstream political participation, which in that view had been the real or proper political objective all along (Smith, 1980; Kilson, 1980, 1971). From that vantage point, election of a black regime realizes an element of a "modernizing" tendency in Afro-American politics.

That interpretation is more or less true in general (particularly if its teleological connotations are discounted), and more or less laudable in given instances, and it discloses an important aspect of black political development. However, it does not account for three rather disturbing points. First, the dynamics that make possible the empowerment of black regimes are the same as those that produce the deepening marginalization and dispossession of a substantial segment of the urban black population. Second, the logic of progrowth politics, in which black officialdom is incorporated, denies broad progressive redistribution as a policy option and thereby prohibits direct confrontation of the problem of dispossession among the black constituency. Third, the nature of the polities that black regimes govern is such that the relation between the main components of their electoral and governing coalitions often is zero-sum. These conditions limit and shape the black regime's behavior in ways that will be explained in the following sections.

Structural Constraints and Issues
Facing the Black Regime

Clearly, the black regime does not inherit a *tabula rasa*. Indeed, for a regime that comes to power at the nodal point of long-term currents of ghetto-ization and deindustrialization and a collateral alignment of "systemic power" (Stone, 1980:981),[6] the environment for making policy decisions must appear nearly as confining as the geographical environment. The preceding discussion has identified dynamics that have structured the operating context of municipal regimes in cities of the general type most likely to experience transition to black rule. Now we will examine some of the more important ways that those dynamics constrain the behavior and optional field of the black regime in power. These constraints stem from three main sources: 1) the city's changing economic base and functions; 2) fiscal and revenue limitations; and 3) competition and conflict --both latent and overt -- among the regime's constituencies.

Changing Economic Base

The black regime assumes power typically in a context of rapidly diminishing private sector employment opportunities for inner city residents. Private economic activity continues to favor suburbs at the expense of anchoring municipalities; in fact, the processes of deconcentration are such that exurban areas beyond SMSAs have become increasingly attractive as production locations. Sternlieb and Hughes (1977), after noting that through the 1970s non-metropolitan areas grew at a faster aggregate rate than SMSAs, observe that manufacturing firms, long the staple of the urban labor force, now show a locational preference for the rural South. There is, moreover, a portentous racial dimension to this preference; manufacturers seek the upcountry, "white South" where workers are more docile (blacks are seen as being less anti-union) and where problems of managing racial tension do not exist. Because residential and industrial movements are mutually reinforcing, the result is a general population shift toward exurbs as well (Sternlieb and Hughes, 1977; Squires, 1984; Bradbury, et al., 1982:182; Goodman, 1979:44 ff).

Not surprisingly, therefore, cities led by black regimes are among the most likely to have suffered both population and functional decline. Of the 11 of the 13 black-governed cities included in a ranking by population change, two scored as "stagnant," and nine were "severely declining;" moreover, six of the nine were located in growing SMSAs (Bradbury, et al., 1982:6-7).[7] On a City-SMSA disparity index, all 13 cities had negative scores (indicating an unfavorable comparative position for the central city), and all but two scored toward the extreme end of the disparity scale. On the City-SMSA divergence index, 10 of the 13 received negative scores, indicating a worsening trend (Bradbury, et al., 1982:52-55).[8] Of the 11 listed, 10 had experienced worsening City-SMSA per capita income ratios between 1960-1973, with the worst losses occurring in Sunbelt cities (Birmingham, Atlanta and New Orleans) (Oakland, 1979:323-325). Thus, by the time the black regimes came to power the cities they were to govern already were among the most depressed.

Perhaps the most striking indication can be seen on the Nathan and Adams "Index of Central City Hardship." Not only did all ten of the cities listed that are currently black-led show disadvantage (as did 43 of the 55 central cities examined), eight of the cities which have black regimes were among the 14 most disadvantaged (1976:51-52). In a different, later ranking, Bradbury, et al. counted six of the black-led cities among the 14 most "troubled" (1982:9). Twelve of the 13 had unfavorable "city distress" ratings (the 13th, Portsmouth, was at parity with its SMSA), and eight of them fell into the worst categories of distress (Bradbury, et al., 1982:51-55).

The components of both the "Central City Hardship" index and those reflecting City-SMSA "distress," "decline," "disparity," and "divergence" have much to do with employment opportunity. The six elements of the Nathan and Adams index, for example, include three that directly concern employment: unemployment, income level and poverty. The "City distress" index constructed by

Bradbury, et al. has five components, of which two are unemployment rate in 1975 and percent of population poor in 1969. (Several of the other measures are arguably indirectly related to employment opportunity, e.g. crowded housing, education, violent crime rate.) I have noted already that black-led cities are among the most likely to have lost manufacturing, wholesale and retail jobs. However, even such employment as remains is not likely to do much for central city residents.

Several of the black-led cities have realized increases in service sector employment and, consistent with the progrowth scenario, have experienced expanding office economies (Black, 1980: esp. 104 and 109). However, neither development holds out particularly optimistic prospects for residents of depressed central cities. The "service sector" rubric actually conceals a dual labor market composed of a high-wage, professional component specializing in what have been called "advanced corporate services," and a low-wage, low-status and dead-end consumer service component; the latter is filled largely by women and minorities (Cohen, 1981; Miller and Tomaskovic-Devey, 1980:30-31).

Of course, the increases in the advanced corporate services component are not likely to create much of a direct employment benefit for city residents, in part because they are not likely to have had the specialized training that much of that activity requires. Although central city residents do gain some lower level technical jobs in both private and public service sectors, the employment effects of expansion in that component, especially for better paying jobs, generally cluster in the suburbs. Growth in the office economy does stimulate some growth in the low-wage service industries, in restaurants, hotels and other facilities catering to the non-resident labor force and consumers of urban culture. The output from this activity is tied to the specific locale of its "production" and therefore accommodates a very small market. For that reason and because the typical service firm has relatively few employees this segment of the dual labor system cannot begin to compensate numerically -- not to mention in wages and benefits -- for employment possibilities lost to dispersion, deindustrialization and capital flight (Black, 1980:104 and 106; Birch, 1981).[9] Moreover, even low-wage service sector jobs are growing faster in the suburbs than in central cities (Black, 1980; Friedland, 1983:73-75).

Friedland observes that the low wages paid in the consumer service sector make traveling from central cities for such jobs uneconomic, and he notes that they usually are filled by "a secondary labor market of wives and children of employed suburban males, who [are] willing to accept low wages and [are] closer to work" (Friedland, 1983:73; Kasarda, 1985:55-57). However, more complex market forces also may operate to limit reverse commutation for consumer service sector employment. For one thing, such jobs often are filled through word-of-mouth networks, especially during periods of slack labor supply; this amounts to a guild-like advantage for living in suburban communities. For another, inner-city residents are likely to be penalized by what has been called "statistical discrimination" along racial lines (Thurow, 1975; Jencks, 1985). Because inner-city non-whites are assumed generally to have inferior skill levels and work habits, employers may prefer, when labor supply permits, to hire suburban whites for jobs which technically could be performed by either group. Operation of some such principle would explain the circumstance that when white suburban youth have access to more attractive sources of disposable income and eschew consumer service sector jobs, blacks and Hispanics with adequate "skills" and work habits materialize to replace them. Suspicion in this regard is strengthened by instances, as could be seen in many areas beginning in the summer of 1986, when changes in the white suburban opportunity structure have resulted in shifts from nearly all-white to nearly all-minority crews in metropolitan fast-food restaurants and similar establishments. However, it is also possible that expansion of white options exhausts word-of-mouth networks and forces more active labor recruitment, which in turn reaches inner-city minorities.

In either case, however, what exists is akin to an employment filtering process. Unlike housing markets, though, this process is much more responsive to cyclical fluctuations. When employment options narrow, whites re-enter the job spheres they had vacated and either ease the pressure on employers to recruit actively and/or re-assert their statistical racial attractiveness. Thus seen, the inner-city minorities are in the familiar role of membership in the industrial reserve army: mobilized in periods of expansion to fill less desirable jobs in the consumer services sector and then cast out of the labor force when contraction makes those jobs relatively more desirable to whites (Gordon, et al., 1982:206-210).[10] This situation is in a way analogous to that of "guest workers" in the more dynamic economies of Western and Central Europe. Suburbanites can exploit the advantages of having a nearby pool of underutilized labor while deflecting as many of the social and fiscal costs as possible onto other jurisdictions.

All of these conditions contribute to the high, chronic unemployment that prevails in central cities in general and in black-led cities in particular. In a comparison of changes in unemployment rates between central cities and suburbs in ten SMSAs between 1971-76, cities presently governed by black regimes scored four of the five most significant instances of widening gap (Black, 1980:111).[11] With unemployment and income inequality comes increased criminal activity (Rosenfeld, 1979), which often enough victimizes participants in the office economy and other upper-income wayfarers into the central city. The rational response from a revenue and image conscious municipal administration is to mobilize police power to provide a *cordon sanitaire* to protect revenue-producing, upper-income consumers from potentially hostile -- or at least worrisome-- confrontation by an indigenous rabble. Thus Andrew Young's attempt to create a "vagrant-free" zone in downtown Atlanta is a mild, if gratuitous and odious, expression of a deeper logic.[12] The script for this scene was written when Great Britain marched into Calcutta and France sailed into Algiers, and it is replicated daily in the Third World. The irony here, as there, is that the black regime seems unable to generate remedies.

The economic forces that have produced this situation are national and international in scope, and to that extent they are largely beyond the effective influence of local government. The loci of pertinent decision-making are else-where -- Congress, the White House, corporate board rooms, international currency markets, the Federal Reserve Board, etc. In that context the municipal regime has few systemic levers with which to press the interests of its dis-possessed, marginalized citizens. Pursuit of economic growth on any terms looms as one of the few concrete options apparently open to local regimes, yet that orientation helps to reproduce the progrowth framework which has reinforced and exacerbated the dispersion processes underlying much of urban social and econ-omic marginalization. For the black regime this inherently contradictory condition is intensified because a) the level of need is likely to be greater among its citizenry, b) the dispossessed are a more central element of its electoral coalition, and c) it is likely to govern in circumstances of greater fiscal stress.

Fiscal Constraints

There is little need to detail the character of the fiscal issues that face urban administrations. Instead, we will simply highlight certain structurally embedded sources of the current relative fiscal straits and their particular implications for black regimes.

Municipal spending, like government spending at all levels, increased steadily over the two decades following the mid-1950s, with the greatest rates of increase occurring after the early 1960s (Schultze, et al., 1977:192-193; Lineberry and Sharkansky, 1978:225; Friedland, 1983:194). At the local level four main factors generated the growth in spending. First, increasing municipal size and complex-ity, as well as the changing socio-economic character of the urban population, naturally required city governments to take on new service functions and to expand on a per capita basis many services already provided. Second, the intrin-sically expansionist tendencies of bureaucratic and professionalizing subcultures exerted pressures both toward upgrading the quality and level of service delivery and toward organizational hypertrophy. Third, the proliferation of "pluralist budgeting" integrated coalition-building and conflict management into fiscal planning, thereby creating a situation in which "the dominant fiscal constraint is more likely to be one of meeting expenditure demands of key supporters and then redefining the revenue constraint in light of political commitments" (David and Kantor, 1979:191-192; Shefter, 1985). Finally, each of these tendencies was exacerbated by the progrowth framework that added to municipal functions, reinforced the propulsion of technical interests, and made federal resources available to institutionalize the strategy of guaranteeing social peace through budget allocations.

On the other side of the ledger, population and tax base loss and reductions in inter-governmental assistance combined with the relative fixity of prior expenditure commitments to send the specter of fiscal crisis haunting many cities. The cities governed by black regimes are among those most likely to be haunted.

The black-led cities are among the most likely to have experienced substantial losses of population, income and employment (Lowry, 1980:175; Bradbury, et al., 1982:6-7). In an examination by Garn and Ledebur of the 147 largest U.S. cities (excluding Washington, D.C.) 42 percent of the black-led cities ranked among those that had experienced "seriously adverse" income change between 1967-72 (compared to 13 percent of the total); 25 percent had had "seriously adverse" job change (compared to 3 percent of the total); and 33 percent experienced "seriously adverse" unemployment rate change (compared to 16 percent of the total) (Garn and Ledebur, 1980:216-218). In their composite ranking of economic performance from most to least distressed, 25 percent of the black-led cities were among the worst-off 6 percent of the total; 58 percent were among the worst-off 18 percent; and 83 percent fell within the worst-off 38 percent (Garn and Ledebur, 1980:210-211).[13] At the same time rates of public spending increased more in the black-led cities. Of the 37 central cities examined by Schultze, et al., the eight with black regimes had experienced an average per capita growth rate in government spending in 1957-70 of 199 percent, compared to an average 158 percent increase among the remaining 29 cities; in 1970 the cities now governed by black regimes received over 26 percent more than the others in per capita inter-governmental aid (1977:192-193; Bahl and Campbell, 1976), which suggests that they were more likely to feel the strain of subsequent federal retrenchment.[14] Indeed, black-governed cities are among those for which federal aid was most significant as a percentage of total general revenue as of 1978 (Oakland, 1979:350; Anton, 1983; Orlebeke, 1983; Fossett, 1983).

That the tendency toward fiscal stress is greater in the black-led cities is most significant not so much as a portent of imminent crisis or collapse; a more salient impact on municipal government is narrowing of the latitude open to regimes both objectively (by limiting their ability to engage in pluralistic budgeting) and subjectively (by articulating the vernacular baseline of the local political culture in the direction of "fiscal conservatism" and more stringent subordination of policy agendas to market imperatives) (Swanstrom, 1985; Monkkonen, 1984; Tabb, 1982; Clavel, 1986; Steinberger, 1985; Stein, et al., 1986; Shefter, 1985; Rubin and Rubin, 1986).

When consciousness of fiscal limitation is prominent in the local political culture, as it is likely to be in black-governed cities, local governments usually are faced with an unpalatable choice. One option is retrenchment which, as service reduction, affects most adversely those who lack resources to substitute in the private market for public services lost. Moreover, even when only "fat" is cut, some negative employment effect will likely be felt among the governing regime's electoral constituents. The other option is raising taxes, which business and financial interests oppose as "fiscally irresponsible" and harmful to the city's economic health. When those interests are relatively powerful, they "provide the city's politicians and public officials with a strong incentive to reach an accord with business and to pursue fiscal policies that are acceptable both to it and to participants in the public capital market" (Shefter, 1985:232). For black regimes, because of relations explained in the following section, this political tension is more acute than for others in similar circumstances. Thus, for example, Maynard Jackson, who long had cherished his identification as an advocate of the interests of the disadvantaged, was moved to fire 2,000 black sanitation workers, among the city's lowest-paid employees, in a 1977 labor dispute even as he acknowledged the legitimacy of their needs (Jones, 1978:114-115).

Competing Constituencies and Political Conflict

The black regime typically comes to power in a spirit of reform, surrounded by images of redress of long-standing inequities and breaking through walls of entrenched privilege (Nelson and Meranto, 1977:339-340). It is symbolically identified with advancement of the interests of racial democracy, or as Walters (1974) once claimed of black politicians in general, "fulfilling the legacy of black power." That symbolism, however, intensifies tensions on three terrains of political competition and conflict that the regime must somehow negotiate.

First, the election of the black regime destabilizes the "trench system" of ethnic/neighborhood interests that vie for shares of budget allocations, the terrain on which is decided who gets what, when and how in the context of implementing a dominant policy agenda. Location of public facilities and public works projects (both desirable and undesirable) and patterns of concentrating public service delivery most visibly define the spatial dimension of this terrain. Another dimension -- allocation of jobs and other patronage -- is only indirectly spatial, to the extent that ethnic or other group identity is overlapped by neighborhood identity.[15]

Peterson observes that this is the terrain on which relatively unfettered pluralist processes operate; however, he also notes that introduction of a racial component "changes the character" of the trench system. Discussing the trench phenomenon in relation to what he refers to as the "politics of allocation," Peterson lays out the problem succinctly:

Blacks themselves make redistributive demands as part of their claim for group recognition, and whites see even modest black allocational demands as redistributive in nature. What benefits blacks is perceived as damaging white interests -- thus it does. Token integration of community institutions is perceived by whites as the first step in an inevitable process of total change, and in what becomes a self-fulfilling prophecy whites stop using that community resource (1981:159).

Eisinger reports that whites perceived that the coming of black rule in Atlanta and Detroit somehow altered the "rules of the game" for local politics, though he contends that the transitions in those cities met less resistance than the earlier transition to Irish rule in Boston. However, the tension that Peterson attributes to a propensity of black demands to challenge inviolable, anti-redistributive principles and that Eisinger enfolds within a more general theory of variations in response to status displacement is also an artifact of the progrowth framework. It is, after all, only from that framework that Peterson's model derives. To the extent that the progrowth consensus in most cities has assumed blacks to occupy at best a subordinate status within the supportive coalition, the prospect of election of a black regime does imply the possibility of a substantive adjustment of the pattern of public resource allocation within the trench system. Anxiety among white voters is a predictable result; moreover, local media typically fuel that anxiety by carefully scrutinizing the actions of black candidates and officials for instances of temptation to play racial favoritism. That whites' anxiety is itself a function of anticipated loss of their own racial favoritism apparently does not mitigate the tension.

In this terrain the black regime is especially vulnerable to charges of inequitable practices because from the beginning it faces hostility and skepticism from white trenches fearful that governance by blacks will also be governance for blacks only. Even from the initial stages of campaigning, black aspirants to office must constantly reassure white voters that their interests will not be ignored. Thus a pundit was led to observe that a black candidate who needs 95 percent of the black vote and 5 percent of the white vote will spend 95 percent of the time trying to secure the 5 percent and 5 percent of the time campaigning for the 95 percent!

Once in power, the black regime is very much constrained, probably more than others because of the unyielding scrutiny to which it is subject, by the pluralist canon of maintaining equity within the ethnic and neighborhood trench system. In fact, the black regime often seems to go overboard; for example, Kenneth Gibson was indicted on felony charges that resulted from his having provided a public sinecure for a superannuated member of the Italian regime that he had displaced (Woody, 1982:190 and 202). However, neither altruism nor naivete nor "Uncle Tomism" is the effective source of this behavior; rather, it represents the pragmatic attempt to demonstrate good faith to potentially hostile forces in the white trenches. When those forces can not or will not be placated, as Harold Washington's experience in Chicago has shown, the regime's capacity to govern can be hindered severely. Such implacable hostility, in fact, was primarily responsible for the ouster of the Stokes regime after two terms in Cleveland (Swanstrom, 1985:100-107).

A second terrain on which the black regime faces the potential for considerable tension is its relationships with the different elements of its principal electoral constituency, although for the most part this tension has been far more potential than actual. Naturally, black expectations are raised by election of a black regime, but the structural and ideological constraints outlined here limit the extent to which those expectations can be met. Black regimes generally have been successful in curbing police brutality, which often has been prominent among black constituents' concerns. Hatcher in Gary, Wilson in Oakland, Gibson in Newark, Jackson in Atlanta and Young in Detroit were able to reduce significantly, if not eliminate altogether, the incidence of police terror (E. Greer, 1979:129-132; Woody, 1982:196; Guyot, 1983; Eisinger, 1980:85-90; Browning, et al., 1984:154-156). (Morial and Barthelemy have been less successful in New Orleans, which ranks among the national leaders in citizen complaints against police [Woody, 1982:39].) Not surprisingly, black regimes have made substantial gains in black police employment, which contributes to the reduction in police brutality (Eisinger, 1984:251).[16] However, that is one of the few areas in which black regimes have been able to deliver payoffs that filter down through the entire black constituency.

In the other areas in which black regimes clearly generate racially redistributive effects -- general municipal employment and contractual services-- benefits cluster disproportionately among middle and upper strata blacks. Increased access to municipal contracts practically by definition advantages upper income, upper strata individuals almost exclusively. At the same time, Eisinger finds that black regimes do increase black representation in municipal employment, over and above the effects of increased black proportion of city population, but that the greatest increases are in professional and administrative categories (ibid). That concentration occurs in part because upper-level positions are more likely to fall in unclassified service ranks, while most line and lower-level staff positions are likely to be covered by civil service rules and regulations, which constrain affirmative action efforts. However, even in the classified ranks the greatest gains seem to have been in managerial and professional positions (Eisinger, 1980:159-161; Woody, 1982:44-90). Moreover, while Eisinger finds that black-led cities also may increase the income level of black employees generally, even this effect is limited by the fact that those cities are among the most likely to exact personnel reductions or freezes induced by fiscal straits, thereby countering the regime's redistributive use of public employment (Eisinger, 1983:37-41; Ganz, 1986:47-50; Clark and Ferguson, 1983:138-144).

The symbolic benefits ensuing from election of a black regime arguably may constitute a public good for black constituents. If so, the potential for conflict resulting from the disproportionate concentration of material benefits may be lessened accordingly. In addition, the dominant practical discourse about and within black political activity posits the racial collectivity as its central agency and racial discrimination as its main analytical category. Within that discourse a benefit that accrues to any member of the group is a benefit to the entire group. This bias naturally obscures processes of intra-racial stratification and impedes critical response to policy agendas that are intra-racially regressive (Reed, 1986a:31-40). In local political cultures increasingly characterized by 1) diminishing expectations associated with retrenchment ideology, 2) a shrinking public realm, and 3) technicization of the framework for policy debate (Henig, 1986), the tension is all the more likely to be muted. Nevertheless, the bandwagon response that Jesse Jackson's dubious claims in 1984 to represent the alienated black "masses" elicited from many black elected officials suggests that they indeed may perceive a need to insulate themselves against disaffection and populist assault in the black community. Sharpe James' 1986 defeat of four-term incumbent Gibson in Newark certainly indicates that such assaults are possible and can topple even ostensibly well-entrenched regimes.

The problem is not that black regimes are led by inept, uncaring or mean-spirited elitists; in fact, black elected officials tend to be somewhat more attentive and liberal than their white counterparts in their attitudes about social welfare issues (Cole, 1976:147; Clark and Ferguson, 1983:133; Karnig and Welch, 1980:12-13). Nor is it necessarily the case that those regimes are so tightly hemmed in by absolute paucity of fiscal resources that they have no span for intervention; as we have seen, fiscal straits are defined within a configuration of ideological and programmatic priorities. It is within such a configuration that the policy relation between the regime and its electoral constituency is structured. The regime's operating context prohibits widespread redistribution, but it does provide space for meeting a more narrowly defined conception of black interest. Four factors ensure that the interests met are those of upper income, upper status blacks: 1) the conceptual bias in black political discourse against accounting for intra-racial stratification; 2) the sociological circumstance that black officials themselves are members of upper status communities and social networks and therefore are more likely to identify with upper strata agendas (Kilson, 1980:86-89; Karnig and Welch, 1980:11-12); 3) the pragmatic imperative to give priority to the most politically attentive constituents and most active supporters; and 4) the relatively low fiscal and political costs of defining black interests around incorporation into an existing elite allocation framework. Thus Conyers and Wallace found that the racial advancement strategies most frequently advocated by black officials included increasing black-owned business (86%) and increasing black involvement in white businesses (71%) (Conyers and Wallace, 1976:28). Those are strategies most compatible with the larger configuration of systemic power in which the black regime operates. They are also among the most important means the regimes deploy to negotiate the third major terrain of conflict, the relation between electoral constituency and governing coalition.

The black regime comes to power within a local system already organized around the progrowth framework. Indeed, the regime is itself most often an organic product of progrowth politics, the culmination of a dynamic of incorporation that began as a response to protest in the 1960s. To the extent that this dynamic has assumed the progrowth consensus as a backdrop, so does the kind of regime it produces. The regime forms and legitimizes itself (i.e., establishes its credibility as a contender for power, builds the allegiances required for winning office and governing, articulates its policy agenda) in a local political culture and system dominated hegemonically by the imperatives of the very "growth machine" that is the engine of black marginalization. That relation's practical consequences come into focus with consideration of the centripetal pressures that cement municipal governments into the progrowth coalition. Judd and Collins explain the logic that creates and undergirds the hegemony of local progrowth politics:

> the assumption is that investment leads to increased jobs and an increased tax base. This, in turn, raises the incomes for city residents and improves the public services which can be provided by city governments. Higher incomes lead to increased spending and consumption, which of course improves the general well-being of city residents. Better public services result in public improvements and neighborhood services such as police protection,

education, streets, and so forth. This, in turn, results in a general improvement in the quality of neighborhood life. Increased spending and consumption creates a favorable business environment which, of course, encourages investment, and on around the cycle again (1979:182-183).

The logic of growth is propagated and reinforced by the actions of interested parties and percolates throughout the local polity. It comes to set the terms for discussion of public policy and, typically spearheaded by metropolitan newspapers and civic boosterism, becomes one of the community's central normative conventions about the ends of local politics and the basis of municipal wellbeing (Molotch, 1980). Local officials are no less likely than other citizens to adhere to that convention, and one who appears to break with it runs the risk of general repudiation as an irresponsible maverick. Dennis Kucinich's stormy tenure in Cleveland offers perhaps the most dramatic recent example of the potential dangers of deviating from the growth logic; as Swanstrom observes in assessing the consequences of Kucinich's refusal to go along with a proposed tax-abatement giveaway, "[c]ontrol over the public's impression of the business climate is a potent weapon in growth politics" (1985:152).

The importance of controlling public perception of the business climate implies the subordination of public policy to business interests and is an artifact of the growth logic's hegemony. Assumption of the priority of business interests in the polity is what allows the counter-Keynesian policy orientation to take hold at the local level.

In addition, at least two other factors dispose local regimes to accept the de facto cue-taking role assigned to them in the progrowth framework. First, because of their command of information and other useful resources, business interests are likely to be especially attractive as partners in durable governing coalitions (C.N. Stone, 1986).[17] Second, business interests are attractive as partners not only to regimes in power but also to candidates seeking power; they can give valuable material and ideological assistance to candidates (and potential candidates) they support and can do considerable harm, particularly given the active agency of local media in progrowth politics, to those they oppose. Thus, for a regime to come to power more often than not means that it already shares the outlook and has the imprimatur of progrowth forces. Black regimes do not differ from others in this respect.

Coleman Young's accommodation to business interests in Detroit stands out both because of his candor in acknowledging its extent and because of the irony posed by his apparently left-activist background. He has, for example, quipped that there "is nothing wrong with Detroit that three or four factories can't solve" and has attempted whenever possible to act accordingly; he has shown little hesitation in giving priority to economic development interests over any others with which they might conflict (Judd, 1986:146; Eisinger, 1980:91-92; Swanstrom, 1985:3; Jones and Bachelor, 1986:38-39; Hill, 1983). However, Young's case is neither unique nor extreme. Atlanta's Andrew Young has been even more flamboyant a booster of business interests than his Detroit namesake; the former SCLC activist has aligned himself with conservative Republicans on business issues and extols the merits of unrestrained development with an often ecclesiastical rhetoric that harkens back to the Gilded Age (Harris, 1985; Stone, 1984a). Washington's Marion Barry, another former civil rights activist, likewise has been disposed to give development interests free rein over his regime's policy agenda, with little regard to disadvantageous impact on other elements of his constituency. Kenneth Gibson and Sharpe James in Newark, Lionel Wilson in Oakland, Morial and Barthelemy in New Orleans, Goode in Philadelphia, and Arrington in Birmingham all have come into office and governed on programs centered around making local government the handmaiden to private development interests (Woody, 1982; Bush, 1984; Clark and Ferguson, 1983:140-142).

My point here is not really to imply that black regimes have "sold out" or betrayed a special racial obligation by their association with progrowth politics. However, they are more likely than others to be beset with a chronic tension between satisfying the expectations of their governing and electoral constituencies. Their tension is greater not so much because they have an intrinsically greater moral obligation, though credible arguments to that effect might be made, but because a) they govern in cities whose populations include relatively great proportions of those citizens most likely to be adversely affected by progrowth politics, b) those citizens are most likely to be black or Hispanic, and c) the regimes tend to validate themselves to minority electoral constituents by invoking an image of progressive redistribution, while progrowth politics is grounded on a more regressive principle.

To the extent that it fuels industrial deconcentration and the other dispersive tendencies described here, the progrowth framework combines with sociological imperatives driving suburbanization (including the racial component of real estate value) at least to intensify black economic marginalization in central cities. The extent of how the "post-industrial" or corporate city has been effected at the expense of black citizens in general has already been noted, and the histories of cities with black regimes reveal a common pattern of displacement and ghettoization as products of the growth machine (Hill, 1983:94-98; Stone, 1976; Hayes, 1972:75-127; Clavel, 1986:21-22; Jones, 1978; Abbott, 1981:102 and 143-166; Taeuber and Taeuber, 1965). In addition, inner-city blacks suffer from progrowth politics insofar as it reinforces the tendencies to extreme labor market segmentation that characterize the "post-industrial" office economy. The regressive impact, furthermore, is heightened by the use of public resources to underwrite it. The progrowth logic rests on a trickle-down ideology that is faulty on two counts. First, even in the best-case scenario the benefits do not trickle very well, very far or very efficiently. The big winners are the developers and locating firms who garner public subsidies and the suburbanites who take the relatively high-paying jobs created by office economy growth. What trickles to a growing share of the electoral constituency are low-paying, consumer service sector jobs and not very many of those per dollar investment. Moreover, growth may even increase certain material costs for city residents across the board (Stone, 1984b; M.P. Smith, 1987; Muzzio and Bailey, 1986). Second, mounting evidence indicates that the array of subsidies that local governments offer to stimulate economic development may only needlessly underwrite development that would occur anyway. Local tax breaks and other fiscal inducements offered by municipalities appear to have little impact on business location and investment decisions, except perhaps insofar as they convey an ideological message concerning the city's "business climate" (Moriarty, 1980:246-257; Bluestone and Harrison, 1981:185-187; Smith, et al., 1985; Wasylenko, 1981; Schmenner, 1980; Swanstrom, 1985:141-155 and 232-239).[18]

Therein lies the central contradiction facing the black regime; it is caught between the expectations of its principally black electoral constituency, which implies downward redistribution, and those of its governing coalition, which converge around the use of public policy as a mechanism for upward redistribution. This tension has been a part of progrowth politics all along. It is neither accidental nor the product of some latter day natural law that "it is the interests of the disadvantaged which consistently come into conflict with economically productive policies" (Peterson, 1981:129). Friedland expresses the critical essence of the situation succinctly: "The policies necessary to growth have high social costs while the policies necessary to social control cut into the revenues necessary to support growth" (1983:221).[19] However, this contradiction is sharper in black-governed cities, both because the disparity between the two poles is greater and because the current mood of fiscal conservatism and retrenchment inhibits use of the standard palliative device of compensatory public spending.

The black regimes have responded to this contradictory situation in two ways. They tend to cling dogmatically, even in the face of evidence to the contrary, to progrowth trickle-down ideology, typically recycling the simplistic formula that growth → jobs → reduced inner city unemployment. Defense of specific projects of any sort proceeds by citing the general cant, with an occasional admonition that the city is in effect the hostage of mobile wealth and therefore must allow private capital to loot the public treasury, unfair as that may be, in order to prove itself competitive in a dog-eat-dog world (Swanstrom, 1985:3;

Gibson, 1979:110). The other response entails defining black interests in such a way as to fit them into the given growth agenda and reinventing elements of the latter rhetorically as distinctively black preferences. Elsewhere I have examined how Maynard Jackson, when confronted by pressure to show his loyalty to the black community's concerns about a police issue and from the business elite (which simultaneously was pressuring him not to show "racial favoritism" in the police controversy) to take a stand on an airport construction controversy, split the difference by arbitrarily and on specious grounds defining and arguing for one of the possible airport sites as the "black" choice. He was thereby able to reduce the pressure from both camps; however, it is instructive that while this reinvention was substantively meaningful to business concerns, it addressed black concerns only symbolically (Reed, 1987).[20]

These two responses, which are by no means mutually exclusive, are more effective now than they might have been several years ago because the program-matic discourse and thrust of progrowth politics have become more technical and thus relatively less accessible to precisely those groups most likely to be adversely affected. As Judd (1986:164) notes:

> Most of the growth strategies of the 1980s have not been as divisive as the urban renewal clearance programs. Tax abatements, industrial development bonds, tax increment financing, enterprise zones, loan programs -- all seem to be economic and not political in character. In most cases they involve quiet, behind-the-scenes transactions between a public authority and private institutions. Discussion of their merits and mechanisms usually proceed (sic) in a market language -- for example, their effect on interest rates or investment (1986:164).

The terms of general discourse in local politics likewise have been tech-nicized in a way that helps to contain the tension between elite and electoral constituencies' interests. Henig observes that:

> Today's urban crisis...is discussed in terms of bond ratings, investment tax credits, infrastructure, business climate, and efficiency. To many Americans, these terms are unfamiliar and forbidding. The message they carry is that these are complicated matters, that decisions should be deferred to those with expertise (Henig, 1986:236; Swanstrom, 1986; C.N. Stone, 1986).

In this context, the racial symbolism that mediates the black regime's relation to its black electoral constituency may make it an especially attractive partner in the progrowth coalition. The same racially evocative discourse that occasionally unsettles white elites can be instrumental in enlisting black support for progrowth initiatives whose regressiveness otherwise might generate controversy and opposition. Focus on such issues as minority set-asides in effect pushes questions of the propriety and impact of the growth agenda into the background; at the same time, the regime can appeal rather effectively to obligations of race loyalty to bind constituent support for growth-related projects it endorses, even those that are clearly regressive.

For similar reasons black regimes may be peculiarly well-suited to implement the draconian retrenchment policies said to instill fiscal confidence. Andrew Young, for example, generated enough black support to pass a sales tax referendum engineered by the Atlanta business elite. Two previous efforts had failed under Maynard Jackson, one when Jackson refused to endorse the referendum for fear of reprisal from blacks. Young overcame that obstacle by waving the "bloody shirt" of his past as one of Martin Luther King Jr.'s lieutenants. "Dutch" Morial also convinced black voters to pass a sales tax referendum in New Orleans (Schexnider, 1982:232-23).[21] Gibson, Coleman Young, Goode and others have effected substantial service and personnel reductions without protest. Indeed, cities governed by blacks seem to be particularly likely to experience significant retrenchment (Clark and Ferguson, 1983:138 ff; Eisinger, 1980:197-198).[22]

It may be that black regimes are "cautious about any controversial policy initiatives...[because]...the coalitions that elect them are usually so tenuous" (Judd, 1986:148). Those coalitions are tenuous because the relationship of their two principal components is or is very nearly zero-sum in many important policy areas. However, it is also the case that the black urban regimes are firmly rooted in the ideological and programmatic orientations of progrowth politics. In each of the main areas in which the regime faces competing pressures within the local polity its tendency is to respond in ways that preserve and privilege the growth agenda. Moreover, as the central city increasingly assumes the dual character of vibrant locale for a glitzy office economy and reservation for marginalized, dispossessed minorities, the black regime takes on a special ideological function. "Protecting development activities from popular pressures" (C.N. Stone, 1986:100) becomes an increasingly salient project as the uneven development of the city intensifies (Peterson, 1981:121 ff).

Empowerment of a black regime contributes to that project in two unique ways, both of which derive from its ability to effect Schattschneider's (1960:71) famous "mobilization of bias" in the black community. First, it provides a mechanism for incorporating upper status, upwardly mobile blacks more autonomously (and thus more reliably) into the growth machine. This not only reduces the likelihood of disruption by the most vocal and attentive elements in the black community; when filtered through the discourse of symbolic racial collectivism, it also becomes a proxy for broader racial redistribution. Second, the dominance of that discourse allows the black regime to claim in effect that whatever stances it takes on growth-related issues are *ipso facto* expressions of generic black interests. Certainly the success of those devices depends on the magical power of the growth/jobs incantation, which Molotch (1980:137) describes as the "key ideological prop for the growth machine," and the generally obfuscating and immobilizing consequences of the technicization of local political debate. Nevertheless, the promise held out by the black regime's special attributes is sufficiently attractive to prompt conservative business elites in such unlikely cities as Birmingham, Atlanta and New Orleans to support them and to endorse them enthusiastically over other possibilities.

Summary and Conclusions

It is now possible to pull together several threads of argument and thus draw some tentative conclusions about the character of the black urban regime. Moreover, once the black regime has been situated within its structural and historical contexts of origin and with respect to its immediate sphere of operation, we can discern at least an outline of expectations that reasonably can be held of it. One element of the concluding observations, therefore, consists of generalizations about: 1) the apparent state of "really existing" black municipal governance in relation to 2) the scope and span of intervention likely to be possible in cities governed by black regimes; and 3) the kinds of standards that realistically might be brought to bear on evaluating these regimes' performances as agencies of social melioration.

The Black Regime and the Corporate City

The most consequential characteristic of the black urban regime is that it is an artifact of the changing socio-economic functions and demographic composition of the central city. Specifically, it is a product of the following factors: 1) the economic dynamics that have constituted the transition from "industrial" to "corporate" city; 2) the long-term pattern of residential suburbanization and the attendant phenomenon of "white flight"; 3) the relative autonomy of local governments -- chiefly a product of slack in the federal system and the "home rule" movement -- that has enabled suburban jurisdictions to engage in zoning and other practices which in effect concentrate black metropolitan population growth in central cities; 4) consolidation of the progrowth framework as the basis and medium for both binding political loyalty and directing local public policy; and 5) the rise of black political assertiveness in the 1950s and 1960s.

Because those regimes are artifacts of progrowth politics, they tend to accept its imperatives as given and tend therefore both to underestimate the latitude open to them in their efforts to support economic development and to overestimate the extent to which fiscal straits hamper their capacities for deploying public policy in pursuit of redistributive goals. In fact the fear of fiscal crisis may induce, or at least rationalize, the regimes' acceptance of a cue-taking role. Rubin and Rubin (1986:190) have found that cities with higher property tax rates, lower median family income, larger number of families below the poverty line and higher unemployment -- all characteristics of both fiscally strained and black-governed cities -- tend more than others to engage in municipally sponsored economic development activity. As Swanstrom notes, though:

> Even the most depressed industrial cities ... are enjoying substantial growth in downtown service employment, which offers opportunities for redistributive reforms. Cities do not have to offer tax abatements to attract this investment; they can do just the opposite: Cities can tax this sector to provide funds to ameliorate the problems of uneven development such as neighborhood decay and a shortage of low-income housing (1986a:103).

A regime's ability to exact concessions varies with the extent to which the city's attractiveness limits capital's relative mobility (M.P. Smith, 1987; Smith, et al., 1985). However, in many instances the desirability of being in a given central city and being able to draw on its agglomeration of financial, information and other support services gives the municipality enough leverage to enforce "linkage" policies that steer growth and capture a share of its proceeds for progressively redistributive purposes (Swanstrom, 1986:225-245; Ganz, 1986). Nearly all of the big-city black regimes govern in cities that are advantageously situated as national or regional economic/administrative centers. Therefore those regimes should be capable of generating and enforcing measures aimed at channeling some of the proceeds of growth to address the needs of their electoral constituency. So far, however, none of the black regimes seems to have made genuine strides in that direction. Instead, they have only recycled the bankrupt growth/jobs formula, usually grafting on provisions for affirmative action and local small business development.[23] In fact, they tend to extrapolate immediately from their constituency's depressed economic condition to an urgency for strengthening standard public/private development partnerships, which are little more than mechanisms for co-opting public policy and resources for the risk management functions of private capital (Swanstrom, 1985:236).

Ironically, if the black regimes' failure to seek political leverage in development activity grows from an exaggerated sense of futility owing to the specter of fiscal stress, the development programs they endorse -- as was the case with another "supply-side" economic strategy applied at the national level in the first Reagan term -- may exacerbate stress by reducing revenues; in addition, development often actually increases service demand. Moreover, stress is a function of the relationship between potential revenues and expenditure commitments, and improving the "business climate" is only one -- and a rather indirect and remote one at that -- mechanism available for improving municipal revenue potential. That it is the primary option chosen by the black regimes is instructive.

Judd suggests that these regimes may be trapped in a structural dilemma: "They wanted to implement policies to promote their constituents' material interests, but they faced declining local economies and tax bases, crumbling infrastructures, white flight, and deteriorating neighborhoods...In response many of these mayors capitulated to the demands of the local corporate sector" (Judd, 1986:165). The problem with that view is that, in relying too much on Bush's provocative but simplistic "quasi-neocolonial" interpretation (Bush, 1984:4), it overlooks the fact that other options may exist but have not been chosen.[24] A result is that the black regimes are depicted as entirely passive. They are thereby left out of consideration of the reproduction of the corporate city altogether, except insofar as they are seen as duped, coerced or bought off -- depending on the normative predilections attached to one or another group of politicians -- by progrowth interests. Thus the endemic characteristics of the regime remain opaque, and discussion of it is imprisoned in a frame which is ultimately inadequate because it does not account for the regime's active agency.

Little evidence exists that black regimes have "capitulated" to "corporate sector demands" to implement the regressive progrowth agenda; Bush acknowledges that it is not difficult to find black mayors who have "always been enthusiastic supporters of corporate interests" (Bush, 1984:4; Dye, 1986:46-47). No black regime has had to be forced into a showdown similar to that which occurred in Cleveland under Kucinich. Maynard Jackson, in the incident to which Bush refers, was not pressured into firing sanitation workers; he did so voluntarily, even if unhappily, because the action seemed decreed by a specific logic of fiscal responsibility to which he adhered. Coleman Young was not pressured to generate a package of regressive fiscal incentives for the Poletown and Renaissance Center projects; he proposed them without reservation because he accepts the progrowth logic on which they are based.

That is the key to penetrating the character of the "really existing" black urban regime. Black regimes adhere to the progrowth framework for the same reasons that other regimes do: it seems reasonable and proper ideologically; it conforms to a familiar sense of rationality; and it promises to deliver practical, empirical benefits. The regime does not step outside the framework or attempt to create leverage for redistribution because there is no need to do so; not only does "business climate" rhetoric apparently seem intrinsically reasonable, but the interests to which the regime is most attentive are included among the framework's beneficiaries. In addition to the business community, which is the principal beneficiary, middle and upper-middle class blacks receive set-aside contracts, support for small business and private "neighborhood economic development" activity, and improved access to professional and administrative employment in both public and private sectors. Through the legerdemain of symbolic racial collectivism those benefits are purported to represent general social and racial redistribution, which, buttressed by a rhetoric of race loyalty, either palliates or defuses counter-mobilization by the larger black electoral constituency that is disadvantaged by progrowth politics.

The degree to which assumption of the growth/jobs logic engenders an exaggerated sense of helplessness before the prerogatives of private capital or reflects the extent to which the regime is simply the "executive committee" of private growth interests may differ from one regime to another. In any case the outcome is the same; the regime carries forward the pretense that providing a public safety net for private profiteering is in the long-term interest of those already marginalized people whose needs are sacrificed to make the netting. Thus in 1984, the National Conference of Black Mayors, on the pretext of accommodating the developmental *realpolitik*, endorsed the Reaganite enterprise zone stratagem, even though it is socially and economically regressive and is unlikely to stimulate any appreciable economic growth (*New York Times*, 1984; Bluestone and Harrison, 1981:228; Goldsmith, 1984; Sloan, 1985).

Although those last remarks may appear somewhat harsh, my intention is not so much to deprecate the black regime. Nor is it particularly useful at this point to denounce it as a class regime, though it certainly is an embodiment of the contingent class power of post-civil rights era black professional, managerial and entrepreneurial strata. After all, the black regime's class character is not really a shocking discovery; it is a natural outcropping of the class basis of black protest activity for nearly a century. Furthermore, those regimes do deliver payoffs to the general black constituency in some areas such as police/community relations and probably marginal improvement in the routine civility of client-serving bureaucracies. In any case, it does not appear plausible that a substantially more egalitarian regime could be elected in black-led cities at present, given requirements for campaign funding, the power of hegemonic ideologies and opinion-shaping media, and the absence of organized, popularly entrenched movements that might overcome those other obstacles. Nor is it likely, given experiences in Burlington, VT, Santa Monica, and elsewhere that such a regime, if it were to come to power, could expand its policy horizon radically (Clavel, 1986). It is more appropriate in this context to ask whether the "really existing" black regime maximizes the options open to it, within its limited sphere, to press the interests of the rank and file black constituency. This is a modest standard that entails adoption of neither a reflexive opposition to economic growth nor an adversarial relationship with concrete business interests. It does mean that black regimes should be assessed with respect to their use of public authority to articulate policy agendas that accommodate economic growth as much as possible to the needs of the municipality and its citizenry rather than vice versa. A prerequisite for effective performance according to that standard is repudiation of the growth/ jobs, trickle-down mystification. Once that is jettisoned, the regime should be expected to give its support to development projects on a more reasoned and conditional basis, reflective of its public charge.

I have referred to discussions of several strategies adopted by municipalities to accommodate the growth imperative to social purposes. Local conditions vary, and no blueprints are possible; however, experiences in Hartford, Berkeley and other cities suggest that municipal regimes are not inevitably the hostages of private economic activity. Moreover, black regimes generally may enjoy greater autonomy than others because of the loyalty of their black electoral support; a rebellious black regime, for example, would probably be less vulnerable to ideological assault from business elites than was Kucinich's, whose support among white ethnics declined in the face of a business propaganda campaign (Swanstrom, 1985). Given the characteristics of the cities they govern, black regimes should be among the most likely to seek to manage growth and its proceeds for the ends of social justice and equality. In addition, other means besides elaborate planning mechanisms and direct or indirect taxation schemes are available, though those are the most concrete and most immediately productive. Regimes can use the cultural authority of office to draw attention to unpalatable conditions that affect constituents but are beyond the scope of municipal control or formal influence. They can also take outrageous stands, e.g., passing unconstitutional tax ordinances, to dramatize existing inequities, thereby opening them to public awareness and debate and providing opportunities for political mobilization.[25] Along each of those dimensions of advocacy for justice and equity, the record of black regimes is poor. They are by and large only black versions of the progrowth regimes that they have replaced, distinguished in part by the asymmetry of their campaign rhetoric and their practice of governance. They are in one sense even more attractive as junior members in the progrowth coalition because of their peculiar skill at derailing opposition to development initiatives and cultivating the loyalty or acquiescence of the growth machine's victims. For that pattern to change will

require greatly increased and informed pressure from the black electoral constituency; which in turn implies proliferation of public, policy-focused debate. I hope
that this account can help to fuel that discourse.

Implications for Urban Theory and the Study of Afro-American Politics

This account of the black urban regime also throws into relief a problematic
tendency current in the study of both black urban politics and Afro-American
political activity more broadly. That tendency is important and troubling enough
to warrant brief comment.

Recent, properly influential scholarly interpretations of different epicycles in
Afro-American politics converge to imply a rather panglossian view of the status
of blacks in the American political system. This problem seems to be rooted in
the structuralist and what might be called neo-pluralist biases of that scholarship.[26] The scholarship in question has produced important insights, is often
engaging and has contributed much to our understanding of its subject matter.
However, that work is beset with a subtle but insidious flaw: failure to examine
adequately the theoretical and public policy implications of black political strategies and agendas. As a result, those interpretations produce one-dimensional
conclusions that are too neat and simplistically upbeat. Taken together, they
authorize disturbingly superficial pictures of the dynamics and outcomes of black
political activity in general and in cities in particular. This is not the place for
a thorough review of that scholarship. Therefore, I shall limit. myself to
illustrating the problem I have identified as it appears in the work of Doug
McAdam, Eisinger, and Browning, Marshall and Tabb, who present the most intel-
lectually rigorous and useful, as well as the most influential, examples of this
interpretive tendency.

McAdam (1982), building through dialogue with a line of research on social
movements initiated by Piven and Cloward, examines developments in the structural foundations of black protest activity over the period from 1930-1970
(also see Piven and Cloward, 1979). His account argues in general very
convincingly about the role of changes in the "structure of political
opportunities," changes in blacks' "sense of political efficacy," and institutional
articulation within the black community as important conditions influencing the
rise of mass protest activity. Even though he flirts with structural determinism
and occasionally succumbs to a questionable inference in order to fit the world to
theory -- e.g. taking the decline in officially recorded lynchings as an indication
of relaxation of the segregation system (p. 97) -- his study is the most important
examination to date of the background influences that shaped the civil rights

movement. The problem is that the heavy structural-functional bias of his interpretive lens glosses the internal dynamics of the movement itself and sees a smooth consensus on objectives, at least until the black power era. His account is thus blinded to the struggle over ultimate goals and contending political visions that also shaped the movement and gave it its historical contingency. For that reason McAdam does not undertake any critical consideration of the substantive significance and implications of different elements of the movement's program; instead, he sees after 1966 only a "proliferation of issues," deviation from the "single issue of integration," and not the culmination of an internal debate of considerable duration concerning the movement's normative and programmatic trajectory. He contends glibly that those factors, along with abandonment of "limited-reform goals" contributed to the movement's decline because he makes no reasoned judgment concerning the efficacy of any of its goals (p. 186 ff). His failure to link either programmatic differentiation within the movement or its substantive outcomes to any broader theory of power and stratification in American society renders his account utterly mute with respect to how we should apprehend the forms of black political activity that have become dominant since 1970. All he can say is that we might anticipate the occurrence of insurgency at some point because "institutional racism" remains entrenched.

The thrust of McAdam's interpretation is compatible, no doubt unintentionally, with the prevailing view that collapses the broad ideals and aspirations expressed in 1960s activism entirely into the incremental framework driving the regular systemic processes of interest-group politics. Their compatibility is visible in his critique of pluralist theory; he argues in effect for amending pluralist orthodoxy to include a systemically functional role for "noninstitutionalized," insurgent activity (pp. 231-234). That notion converges on the naive evolutionary perspective that sees the role of 1960s activism simply as preparing for regular systemic participation, which is understood as the only truly proper and most efficient arena for articulation and pursuit of group interests. McAdam's account in this respect reinforces the tendency to focalize black political objectives, and to define black interests, entirely in terms subordinate to entrenched system priorities, which are deeply implicated in the continuing disadvantagement and advancing marginalization among black citizens.

Eisinger's account of the transition to black rule and the impact of black mayors presents a somewhat clearer version of this problem. First of all, his comparisons of the transitions to black rule in Detroit and Atlanta with the Irish experience in Boston suffers from an ahistoricism that already shows the embedded flaw. Because he allows neither for the considerable changes that have occurred in the economic functions of central cities between the Boston case and the more recent ones nor the greatly changed set of actors and issues that constitute the local policy context, Eisinger's view is predisposed to see the black regime as the latest stage in a relatively uniform process of ethnic group succession in local politics. However, the contexts within which the black regime assumes power and governs greatly limit any such comparison's persuasiveness or usefulness. Black regimes take power in a city quite different from that in which earlier groups governed, and the needs of their constituents differ in relation to inherited system priorities. Eisinger's failure to acknowledge those differences leads him to suggest -- after noting that "city governments...cannot fashion thorough, successful and speedy policies to deal with...poverty, discrimination, unemployment, housing, or the quality of life" -- that electing "their own to city hall" may well have gotten blacks rolling along the upward mobility track already traversed by the comparable Irish (1980:194-196).

There is much in Eisinger's account that is sound and refreshing. His attempt to locate the black regime within a broader pattern of local ethnic group dominance brings discussion of black governance more centrally into the purview of the American politics field, and his focus on the regime's interaction with "displaced" elites illuminates certain constraining effects of political environment with much care and intelligence. However, in assuming *a priori* an identity of black interests and the racial agendas of black administrations (ibid:167), Eisinger eliminates any need to consider the operation of politics *within* the black community, and he renders himself blind to structurally-induced intraracial tensions. This failing combines with his acceptance of progrowth orthodoxy to underwrite an inverted argument that black regimes actually may "harness white economic power rather than vice versa" (ibid). Once he defines the affirmative action, minority set-aside agenda as the beginning and end of specifically black interests in development activity, then it does appear that blacks derive relatively great payoffs from progrowth politics. There is no critical space for him to consider the impact of the growth machine on different elements of the black community and at the same time no space to consider the intraracial implications of the regime's agendas. As with McAdam, we have an account from the outside, one that cannot bring into focus the self-driving tensions in black politics.

Browning, Marshall and Tabb (1984) bridge the gap between considerations of protest and electoral strategies in their study of minority political "incorporation" in ten Bay Area cities. In charting the relationships between political mobilization, response from other groups, organizational development and political experience, and size of minority population, they provide an impressively thorough explanation of the "steps that are necessary if excluded groups are to move toward political equality" (p. 241). However, their notion of incorporation, though empirically sound and important, also has a darker theoretical dimension that surfaces only with consideration of the tension between black or Hispanic interests and the entrenched priorities that constitute the prevailing configuration of systemic power. In light of that tension "incorporation" resonates with Peterson's observation that in local political systems potentially redistributive demands tend to be converted into symbolic ones. Thus incorporation may come at the price of making peace with the regressive policy framework that stimulates protest and mobilization in the first place.

The authors' choice of indicators of incorporation's policy impact sidesteps this critical issue. City employment, police review boards, minority contractors and commission appointments, while certainly significant in their own right, are policy areas that have little bearing on the systemic inequality reproduced through the logic of progrowth politics. Nor for that matter are patterns of federal program implementation much more instructive. Model Cities and Great Society programs facilitated mobilization, but toward what ultimate policy ends? Toward what uses are CDBG allocations directed?

The three studies share a common disposition to conceptualize black politics one-dimensionally on an exclusion/inclusion axis. While that perspective can organize very useful investigations of the nature of black political incorporation, as it does in different ways in each of these studies, it has serious limitations. It tends to assume uniform interests and agendas among blacks because incorporation itself is a universally shared value, insofar as incorporation is construed broadly as the antithesis of exclusion. It also tends toward an analytic exceptionalism which ironically reproduces an exclusionist bias within the study of black politics; to the extent that blacks are seen as excluded from the mainstream of American institutional processes, the latter are seen as relevant to blacks only as focal points in the struggle for inclusion. This view forgets that it is suffering the regressive impact of those processes that initially precipitates the demand for access.

In this sense a neo-pluralist bias is tacit in this scholarship; it picks up and responds to pluralism's original bracketing of race as an unhappy appendage on a system that allegedly worked well for everyone else -- the ubiquitous "except for the Negroes" clause in pluralist studies in the 1950s and 1960s. This new scholarship has found ways, with the assistance of changes in the world, to dissolve the brackets. Noninstitutionalized activity, ethno-racial transition and political incorporation all are accurate, important descriptions of what is occurring on one level in Afro-American politics. Moreover, those descriptions enhance our view of the changing urban political terrain. Despite being apparently well-intentioned politically, however, they are also intellectual devices for accommodating discussion of the political condition of blacks to a pluralist frame of reference which obscures the cumulatively redistributive outcomes of public policy in general and of the distinctive, progrowth policy consensus into which blacks are incorporated in cities in particular. As a result, they produce accounts that are incomplete and disturbing to the democratic temper.

Those problems can be overcome by grounding the exclusion/inclusion axis as an epicycle within broader configurations of systemic power and by bringing political dynamics within the black community into the foreground of analysis. I believe that at the urban level sharpening focus on differential impacts of policies and political agendas within the black community and examination of the tensions between regimes' electoral and governing coalitions are useful avenues toward that end. In the event, I hope that I have suggested a useful orientation for more detailed case studies and aggregate analyses of black urban regimes.

Implications for Democracy in Urban Life

The most salient implications of the view of the black regime put forward here have to do with the need to compensate for reinforcement and perpetuation of injustice produced through the federal system, either directly or by manipulation of slack. Most immediate is the need to offset federal and state policies that stimulate economic deconcentration and allow suburban jurisdictions to freeload on municipal services and cultural amenities while undergirding the bantustanization of inner-city minority populations.

Metropolitan tax base sharing is one technique that may offer a way to help balance two democratic values which appear to conflict in this case: equitable allocation of the costs of metropolitan life and representative government that is equitable along racial lines. Given the difficulty blacks experience in electing representatives in non-black majority jurisdictions (Karnig & Welch, 1980:54-55; Keech, 1968), simple annexation or metro consolidation alternatives generally would sacrifice the value of equitable representation. Nationally coordinated industrial policy aimed at smoothing out the imbalances of uneven regional development also seems to be called for, as does a national incomes policy that may both retard and help offset the disruptive effects of productive capital's mobility by bolstering the social wage.

In a similar vein, a concerted strategy of reindustrialization seems to be important for several reasons, including foreign policy. The vision of a "postindustrial" or "information economy" as the basis of the American future presumes an industrial foundation somewhere. To the extent that the "information" that drives our office economy is information about production or what to do with the proceeds of production, a strategy of concentrating a Ricardian advantage in "postindustrial" activity implies maintenance of the costly and dangerous "defense" apparatus required to make certain that repressive regimes remain in power in Third World countries to ensure their comparative advantage in providing low-wage labor and minimally regulated production processes. Concern with humane and democratic interests must oppose that international division of labor. Moreover, the increased transnational mobility of capital has meant that suppression of wages and standard of living in the underdeveloped countries now reverberates into the advanced countries as well. So far in the United States the reverberation has been felt disproportionately by blacks and other minorities who are pushed progressively farther onto the margins of the social order.

All the aforementioned suggestions of areas in which to focus strategy are well beyond the scope of effective municipal intervention. However, both individually and collectively -- through lobbies such as the National Conference of Black Mayors, U.S. Conference of Mayors and National League of Cities-- regimes can push public discourse about these areas of concern and can agitate for reform. Within their domain, as I have indicated, it is possible to break with slavish adherence to progrowth ideology and to assert public authority to limit the socially and culturally disruptive effects of development. It is also possible to insist that public resources are deployed on behalf of development in central cities in ways that optimize downward redistribution.

Should a truly democratic citizenry settle for anything less?

Notes

1. This manuscript has been improved by criticisms, comments, suggestions and reassurances from several individuals at various stages of its production. Among those whose efforts should be noted are: Claude Barnes, Demetrios Caraley, Ester Fuchs, Jennifer Hochschild, Dennis Judd, Willie Legette, John Hull Mollenkopf, David Plotke, Stephen Skowronek, Michael Peter Smith, Clarence Stone, Linda Williams, Rhonda Williams and Kathryn Yatrakis.

2. Those cities are: Chicago, Philadelphia, Detroit, Washington, D.C., New Orleans, Atlanta, Newark, Oakland, Birmingham, Richmond, VA, Gary, Hartford, and Portsmouth, VA. Seven other regimes are governed in cities between 50,000 and 100,000 in population. All of them, for example East St. Louis, IL, East Orange, NJ and Mt. Vernon, NY, are small cities adjacent to a major central city. This definition of the black urban regime does not include black mayors who lead administrations and govern coalitions in which blacks are not the dominant or principle group - e.g., Tom Bradley in Los Angeles.

3. Orfield concludes that "economics cannot begin to explain the present extreme pattern of separation" because he uses "economics" somewhat

narrowly to refer to dynamics of segregation by income. That conclusion, therefore, is not necessarily inconsistent with the view that a racial element is embedded in the "natural" operation of residential real estate markets.

4. An apparent exception is Atlanta, where it appears that a city/county consolidation may be on the horizon. However, it is not clear whether a) consolidation actually will occur or b) what the net revenue implications-- after factoring in the costs of extending municipal services to the remainder of the county -- of consolidation would be. The county already is predominantly black, which makes the plan credible to several black officials, but projections done in 1975 by Atlanta's Departments of Budget & Planning and Finance, which assumed a best-case scenario for consolidation, showed the city incurring a net revenue loss until the 21st century (Reed, 1975).

5. This claim is a source of controversy among economists. One view contends that plant closings indicate "creative destruction," the flow of capital from less to more productive uses in the domestic economy (Leroy, 1987). In that view what appears to be atrophy is actually a sign of economic health. Another view -- focused on absolute changes in domestic manufacturing employment and comparison of aggregate output, investment and employment trends in the U.S. and other industrialized nations -- questions whether deindustrialization is even occurring at all (Lawrence, 1987). However, declines in actual manufacturing *production* employment indicate that domestic labor markets are deindustrializing; furthermore, increases in structural unemployment and the overall decline in real wages suggest that those labor markets do not have sufficient absorptive capacities to compensate for the mobility of capital at its present velocity. That implies, in turn, that the social costs of capital restructuring -- along sectoral, regional and global lines -- are concentrated in the ways that deindustrialization theorists argue: in urban areas, among blue collar workers, in the Northeast and North Central regions, among minorities and in labor-intensive industries (Bluestone, 1987; R.L. Smith, 1985:214-17).

6. Stone defines systemic power as "that dimension of power in which durable features of the socioeconomic system (the *situational* element) confer advantages and disadvantages on groups (the *intergroup* element) in ways predisposing public officials to favor some interests at the expense of others (the *indirect* element)." The coalition of selected interest groups forming a durable hierarchy in support of pro-growth politics is an instance of systemic power.

7. Portsmouth and Oakland were not ranked, presumably because they are not clearly the dominant cities in their SMSAs. Of the total 121 cities listed, 36 percent were growing and 35 percent were stagnant.

8. One-third of the total of 153 cities ranked scored in the three worst categories on the disparity index, compared to 11 out of 13 black-led cities. Nearly one-third of the 153 scored in the three best categories. On the divergence index, five of 13 black-led cities scored in the three worst categories, compared to 11 of the total sample.

9. Between 1970-1975, four of the cities currently governed by black regimes (Atlanta, New Orleans, Philadelphia and Washington) lost 78,500 manufacturing jobs and gained 36,200 in the service sector.

10. Although Smith and Welch (1979:54) suggest that blacks may be becoming less vulnerable to business cycles relative to whites, that effect reflects the progress of an intraracial labor segmentation; the marginalized inner-city population remains as vulnerable as ever, as was indicated in the tremendous increases in black unemployment during the early 1980s.

11. The four cities were Chicago, Detroit, Philadelphia and Washington. The other six were Baltimore, Cleveland, Milwaukee, New York and St. Louis. Of those, only St. Louis, which actually had the most disadvantageous divergence of any of the central cities, was comparable to the other four. In Dallas and Cleveland the gap between central city and suburban unemployment rates even narrowed.

12. In fairness to Young, the desire to purify a sector of the CBD has been a recurring theme in Atlanta politics. Earlier attempts (in the Maynard Jackson administration) included restrictions on consumption of alcohol near liquor stores (to remove winos from view) and two attempts to establish curfews on adolescents (to clear them from downtown). The second curfew attempt, which originated from the same council member who proposed the earlier one, succeeded because its proponents grafted it on public concern over the then current missing and murdered children issue (Reed, 1981).

13. On their index of "Changes in Urban Conditions, 1960-1977," Fossett and Nathan (1981:66) rank 53 of the largest 57 U.S. cities on the basis on amount of older housing population loss and concentration of poverty; 88

percent of the black-led cities ranked fell in the worst-off 40 percent of the total.

14. In every region except the mid-west, the sample for which excluded Gary, the mean percentage increase for black-led cities was higher than that for the region as a whole; in all four regions black-led cities received more intergovernmental assistance.

15. Of course, the trenches themselves are products of political competition for uses of urban space and therefore reflect a hierarchy already influenced by direction of public policy and patterns of service delivery (Kaufman, 1974; Rich, 1979).

16. Eisinger's study of six cities with black mayors highlights a distinction between black regimes and individual black mayors in this respect. In each of the five cities with black regimes (Newark, Atlanta, Detroit, Washington DC, and Gary) black representation on police forces increased by at least 100 percent. By contrast, in Los Angeles the increase was negligible.

17. Stone develops this point in relation to explaining a notion of "ecological power," i.e., "the capacity to reshape the context -- that is, the social ecology -- within which one operates," or, more specifically, the ability "to enlist government in restructuring the terms under which social interactions occur."

18. In addition to other limitations on the growth/jobs/reduced inner-city unemployment formula, Harrison cites evidence indicating that even the low-wage, secondary labor market employment that the growth agenda generates in the central city goes disproportionately to white suburbanites (B. Harrison, 1974:52-53).

19. Recognition of this tension may be a main reason that local elites often suspect first-time black regimes of being vaguely and generically "anti-business" (see Judd, 1986:145-146; Levine, 1974:76-77 and passim; Eisinger, 1980:81 ff; Henson and King, 1982:306-307).

20. Jackson eventually settled on insistence on a minority set-aside and joint-venture program for airport construction and operation as his administration's "black" position.

21. The sales tax in New Orleans, however, replaced two flat-rate service taxes that were even more regressive (also see Eisinger, 1980:175-180).

22. Many critics have contended that a white mayor who acted as Wilson Goode did in the infamous MOVE incident in Philadelphia would be met by tremendous outrage from blacks. While the nature of the MOVE case is considerably more complex than most of Goode's critics have acknowledged, the suggestion that more voluble reaction would have greeted a white mayor almost certainly is sound (see, for example, C. Stone, 1986).

23. Harold Washington's ambitious-sounding development plan is one of the more recent and clearest cases in point. The centerpiece of this plan is public-private cooperation to generate some 8,000 jobs through the use of tax and rent giveaways. Despite formal stipulation of preferential hiring for city residents (which in most instances is unenforceable), the general thrust of the plan is to provide public subsidies for private development and to concentrate municipal purchasing as much as possible with local and minority firms (Judd, 1986:157-160). Moreover, linkage policies, by settling for front-end side-payments, actually may not be very good alternatives to taxation after all. In addition to not adequately compensating for the costs of growth, they may have a demobilizing effect on those groups in local politics who would press for more equitable compensation (M.P. Smith, 1987).

24. The Bush volume suffers from a general failure to examine carefully the policy contexts within which the regimes operate and a naivete about local public policy that at times slides into complete avoidance. For example, Bush's 43-page essay on black politics in Oakland devotes less than four pages to discussion of the Wilson regime, and over a page of that concerns how he came to be elected.

25. In this respect I recall arguing as a functionary in the Maynard Jackson administration that we should lobby for passage of a point-of-earnings income tax ordinance even though it was clearly in violation of the Georgia constitution. By passing it and forcing the state to react, we could at least have precipitated public debate on the issue and on the problem of service-delivery strain created by freeloading commuters. The argument fell on deaf ears.

26. By "neo-pluralist" I refer to versions of pluralist theory that have been amended to provide a role for extra systemic activity (usually construed as

systemic activity by other means, when regular channels are blocked) and to acknowledge that different groups possess different degrees of concentrated power and access to systemic channels. For a debate over neo pluralism's character and content, see Manley (1983).

References

Abbott, C. (1981) *The New Urban America: Growth and Politics in Sunbelt Cities.* Chapel Hill: University of North Carolina Press.

Abney, G.F. and Hutcheson, Jr. (1981) Race, representation and trust: Changes in attitudes after the election of a black mayor, *Public Opinion Quarterly* 45, (Spring): 91-101.

Anderson, M. (1964) *The Federal Bulldozer: A Critical Analysis of Urban Renewal, 1949-1962.* Cambridge, MA: MIT Press.

Anton, T.J. (1983) *Federal Aid to Detroit.* Washington, D.C.: Brookings.

Ashton, P.J. (1978) The Political Economy of Suburban Development. In W. Tabb and L. Sawers (Eds.), *Marxism and the Metropolis.* New York: Oxford University Press.

Babcock, R. (1973) Exclusionary zoning: A code phrase for a notable legal struggle. In L. Masotti and J. Hadden (Eds.), *The Urbanization of the Suburbs.* Beverly Hills: Sage.

Bahl, R.W. and A. Campbell (1976) City budgets and the black constituency. In H. Bryce (Ed.), *Urban Governance and Minorities.* New York: Praeger.

Baraka, I.A., Ed. (1972) *African Congress: A Documentary of the First Modern Pan-African Congress.* New York: William Morrow.

Birch, D.L. (1981) Who creates jobs? *Public Interest* (Fall): 3-14.

Black, J.T. (1980) The changing economic role of central cities and suburbs. In A.P. Solomon (Ed.), *The Prospective City.* Cambridge, MA: MIT Press.

Bledstein, Burton J. (1976) *The Culture of Professionalism.* New York: W.W. Norton.

Bluestone, B. (1987) In support of the deindustrialization thesis. In P.D. Staudohar and H.E. Brown (Eds.), *Deindustrialization and Plant Closure.* Lexington, MA: D.C. Heath.

Bluestone, B.A. and B. Harrison (1981) *The Deindustrialization of America: Plant Closings, Community Abandonment and the Dismantling of Basic Industry.* New York: Basic Books.

Bowles, S., D. Gordon, and T. Weisskopf (1982) *Beyond the Wasteland: A Democratic Alternative to Economic Decline.* New York: Random House.

Bradbury, K., A. Downs, and K. Small (1982) *Urban Decline and the Future of American Cities.* Washington, D.C.: Brookings.

Braverman, H. (1974) *Labor and Monopoly Capital: The Degradation of Work in the Twentieth Century.* New York: Monthly Review.

Brown, M.K. and S.P. Erie (1981) Blacks and the legacy of the Great Society: The economic and political impact of federal social policy. *Public Policy* (Summer): 299-330.

Browning, R.P., D.R. Marshall, and D.H. Tabb (1984) *Protest is not Enough: The Struggle of Blacks and Hispanics for Equality in Urban Politics.* Berkeley: University of California Press.

Bush, R. (1984) Oakland; grassroots organizing against Reagan. In R. Bush (Ed.), *The New Black Vote: Politics and Power in Four American Cities.* San Francisco: Synthesis.

Button, J. (1978) *Black Violence: Political Impact of the 1960s Riots.* Princeton: Princeton University Press.

Carnoy, M., D. Shearer, and R. Rumberger (1983) *A New Social Contract: The Economy and Government after Reagan.* New York: Harper and Row.

Center on Budget and Policy Priorities (1984) *Falling Behind: A Report on How Blacks have Fared Under the Reagan Policies.* Washington, D.C.: Center on Budget & Policies Priorities.

Clark, T.N., and L.C. Ferguson (1983) *City Money: Political Processes, Fiscal Strain and Retrenchment.* New York: Columbia University Press.

Clavel, P. (1986) *The Progressive City: Planning and Participation, 1969-84.* New Brunswick, NJ: Rutgers University Press.

Cohen, R.B. (1981) The new international division of labor, multinational corporations and urban hierarchy. In M. Dear and A.J. Scott, (Eds.), *Urbanization and Urban Planning in Capitalist Society.* London & New York: Methuen.

Cole, L. (1976) *Blacks in Power: A Comparative Study of Black and White Elected Officials.* Princeton: Princeton University Press.

Conyers, J.E., & W.L. Wallace (1976) *Black Elected Officials: A Study of Black Americans Holding Governmental Office.* New York: Russell Sage Foundation.

Crenson, M.A. (1982) Urban bureaucracy in urban politics: Notes toward a developmental theory. In J.D. Greenstone (Ed.), *Public Values and Private Power in American Politics.* Chicago: University of Chicago Press.

Darden, J.T. (1986) The significance of race and class in residential segregation, *Journal of Urban Affairs, 8* (Winter): 49-55.

David, S.M., and P. Kantor (1979) Political theory and transformations in urban budgetary arenas: The case of New York City. In D.R. Marshall (Ed.), *Urban Policy Making.* Beverly Hills: Sage.

Downs, A. (1981) *Neighborhoods and Urban Development.* Washington, DC: Brookings.

Dye, T.R. (1964) Urban political integration: Conditions associated with annexation in American cities, *Midwest Journal of Political Science, 8* (November): 430-446.

Dye, T.R. (1986) Community power and public policy. In R.J. Waste (Ed.), *Community Power: Directions for Future Research.* Beverly Hills: Sage.

Eisinger, P.K. (1979) The community action program and the development of black political leadership. In D.R. Marshall (Ed.), *Urban Policy Making.* Beverly Hills: Sage.

Eisinger, P.K. (1980) *The Politics of Displacement.* New York: Academic Press.

Eisinger, P.K. (1982) Black employment in municipal jobs: The impact of black political power, *American Political Science Review, 76* (June): 380-392.

Eisinger, P.K. (1983) *Black Employment in City Government, 1973-1980.* Washington, D.C.: Joint Center for Political Studies.

Eisinger, P.K. (1984) Black mayors and the politics of racial economic advancement. In H. Hahn and C.H. Levine (Eds.), *Readings in Urban Politics: Past, Present and Future,* 2nd edition. New York: Longman.

Fainstein, N., and S. Fainstein (1983) New Haven: The limits of the local state. In Fainstein, et al., *Restructuring the City: The Political Economy of Urban Development.* New York: Longman.

Fossett, J.W. (1983) *Federal Aid to Big Cities: The Politics of Dependence.* Washington, D.C.: Brookings

Fossett, J.W., and R.P. Nathan (1981) The prospects for urban revival. In R. Bahl (Ed.), *Urban Government Finance.* Beverly Hills: Sage.

Friedland, R. (1983) *Power and Crisis in the City: Corporations, Unions and Urban Politics.* New York: Macmillan.

Ganz, A. (1986) Where has the urban crisis gone? How Boston and other large cities have stemmed economic decline. In M. Gottdiener (Ed.), *Cities in Stress.* Beverly Hills: Sage.

Garn, H.A., and L.C. Ledebur (1980) The economic performance and prospects of cities. In A.P. Solomon (Ed.), *The Prospective City.* Cambridge, MA: MIT.

Gibson, K. (1979) Managing a metropolis: Philosophy and practice. In G.A. Tobin (Ed.), *The Changing Structure of the City: What Happened to the Urban Crisis.* Beverly Hills: Sage.

Goldsmith, W.W. (1984) Bringing the third world home: Enterprise zones for America? In L. Sawers and W. Tabb (Eds.), *Sunbelt/Snowbelt: Urban Development and Regional Restructuring.* New York: Oxford University Press.

Goodman, R. (1979) *The Last Entrepreneurs: America's Regional Wars for Jobs and Dollars.* Boston: South End.

Gordon, D. (1977) Class struggle and the stages of American urban development. In D.C. Perry and A.J. Watkins (Eds.), *Rise of the Sunbelt Cities.* Beverly Hills: Sage.

Gordon, D. (1978) Capitalist development and the history of American cities. In W. Tabb and L. Sawers (Eds.), *Marxism and the Metropolis.* New York: Oxford University Press.

Gordon, D., R. Edwards, and M. Reich (1982) *Segmented Work, Divided Workers: The Historical Transformation of Labor in the U.S.* London and New York: Cambridge University Press.

Greer, E. (1979) *Big Steel: Black Politics and Corporate Power in Gary, Indiana.* New York: Monthly Review.

Greer, S. (1979) Bureaucratization of the emerging city. In J.P. Blair and D. Nachmias (Eds.), *Fiscal Retrenchment and Urban Policy.* Beverly Hills: Sage.

Guyot, D.H. (1983) Newark: Crime and politics in a declining city. In A. Heinz, H. Jacob, and R.L. Lineberry (Eds.), *Crime in City Politics.* New York: Longman.

Hadden, J., L. Masotti, and V. Thiessen (1969) The making of the Negro mayors, 1967. In L. Ruchelman (Ed.), *Big City Mayors: The Crisis in Urban Politics.* Bloomington: University of Indiana Press.

Harrigan, J.J. (1984) *Political Change in the Metropolis, 3rd edition.* Boston: Little, Brown.

Harris, A. (1985) The capitalistic gospel according to Rev. Young, *The Atlanta Journal-Constitution* (September 22).

Harrison, B. (1974) *Urban Economic Development.* Washington, D.C.: Urban Institute.

Harrison, R.S. (1982) The effects of exclusionary zoning and residential segregation on urban-service distributions. In R.C. Rich (Ed.), *The Politics of Urban Public Services.* Lexington, MA: D.C. Heath.

Harvey, D. (1973) *Social Justice and the City.* Baltimore: Johns Hopkins University Press.

Hayes, E.C. (1972) *Power Structure and Urban Policy: Who Rules in Oakland.* New York: McGraw-Hill.

Henig, J.R. (1986) Collective responses to the urban crisis: Ideology and mobilization. In M. Gottdiener (Ed.), *Cities in Stress.* Beverly Hills: Sage.

Henson, M.D., and J. King (1982) The Atlanta public-private romance: An abrupt transformation. In R.S. Fosler and R.A. Berger (Eds.), *Public-Private Partnership in American Cities: Seven Case Studies.* Lexington, MA: Lexington Books.

Hill, R.C. (1983) Crisis in the Motor City: The politics of economic development in Detroit. In Fainstein, et al., *Restructuring the City*. New York: Longman.

Hirsch, A.R. (1983) New Orleans: Sunbelt in the swamp. In B. Rice and R.M. Bernard (Eds.), *Sunbelt Cities: Politics and Growth since WW II*. Austin: University of Texas Press.

Holden, M. (1971) Black politicians in the time of the 'new' urban politics, *Review of Black Political Economy 2* (Fall).

Hout, M. (1984) Occupational mobility of black men: 1962 to 1973, *American Sociological Review, 49* (June): 308-322.

Jaynes, G.D. (1984) Urban policy and economic reform, *review of Black Political Economy, 13* (Summer/Fall): 103f.

Jencks, C. (1985) Affirmative action for blacks: Past, present and future, *American Behavioral Scientist* (July/August): 731-760.

Joint Center for Political Studies (1986) *Black Elected Officials: A National Roster*. Washington, D.C.: JCPS.

Jones, B.D., and L.W. Bachelor with C. Wilson (1986) *The Sustaining Hand: Community Leadership and Corporate Power*. Lawrence: University of Kansas.

Jones, M.H. (1978) Black political empowerment in Atlanta: Myth and reality, *Annals of the American Academy of Political and Social Science, 439* (September): 90-117.

Judd, D.R. (1979) *The Politics of American Cities: Private Power and Public Policy*. Boston: Little, Brown.

Judd, D.R. (1986) Electoral coalitions, minority mayors, and the contradictions in the municipal policy agenda. In M. Gottdiener (Ed.), *Cities in Stress*. Beverly Hills: Sage.

Judd, D.R., and M. Collins (1979) The case of tourism: Political coalitions and redevelopment in the central cities. In G. Tobin (Ed.), *Changing Structure of the City*. Beverly Hills: Sage.

Kain, J. (1968) The distribution and movement of jobs and industry. In J.Q. Wilson (Ed.), *The Metropolitan Enigma*. Garden City, NY: Doubleday.

Karnig, A., and S. Welch (1980) *Black Representation and Urban Policy*. Chicago: University of Chicago.

Kasarda, J.D. (1985) Urban change and minority opportunities. In P. Peterson (Ed.), *New Urban Reality*. Washington, D.C.: Brookings.

Katznelson, I. (1981) *City Trenches: Urban Policy and the Patterning of Class in the United States*. New York: Pantheon.

Kaufman, C. (1974) Political urbanism: Urban spatial organization, policy and politics, *Urban Affairs Quarterly, 9* (June): 421-436.

Keech, W. (1968) *The Impact of Negro Voting.* Chicago: Rand McNally.

Keller, E.J. (1978) The impact of black mayors on urban policy, Annals, *American Academy of Political and Social Science, 439* (September): 40-52.

Kilson, M.L. (1971) Political change in the Negro ghetto, 1900-1940s. In N. Huggins, M. Kilson, and D. Fox (Eds.), *Key Issues in the Afro-American Experience, v. II.* New York: Harcourt, Brace, Jovanovich.

Kilson, M.L. (1980) The new black political class. In J. Washington (Ed.), *Dilemmas of the Black Middle Class.* Philadelphia: J. Washington.

Larson, M.S. (1977) *The Rise of Professionalism.* Berkeley: University of California Press.

Lawrence, R.Z. (1987) Is deindustrialization a myth? In P.D. Staudohar and H.E. Brown, (Eds.), *Deindustrialization and Plant Closure.* Lexington, MA: D.C. Heath.

Leroy, H.C. (1987) The free market approach. In P.D. Staudohar and H.E. Brown (Eds.), *Deindistrialization and Plant Closure.* Lexington, MA: D.C. Heath.

Levine, C.H. (1974) *Racial Conflict and the American Mayor.* Lexington, MA: Lexington Books.

Lineberry, R. and L. Masotti (1976) Introduction. In R. Lineberry and L. Masotti (Eds.), *The New Urban Politics.* Boston: Ballinger.

Lineberry, R. and I. Sharkansky (1978) *Urban Politics and Public Policy,* 3rd Edition. New York: Harper and Row.

Lipsky, M. (1980) *Street Level Bureaucracy: Dilemmas of the Individual in Public Services.* New York: Russell Sage Foundation.

Lowi, T. (1967) Machine politics -- old and new, *Public Interest, 9* (Fall): 83-92.

Lowry, I.S. (1980) The dismal future of central cities. In A.P. Solomon (Ed.), *The Prospective City.* Cambridge: MIT.

Luke, T.L. (1986) The modern service state: Public power in American from the New Deal to the New Beginning. In A. Reed (Ed.), *Race, Politics and Culture: Critical Essays on the Radicalism of the 1960s.* Westport, CT: Greenwood.

Manley, J.F. (1983) Neo-pluralism: A class analysis of pluralism I and pluralism II (with comments by C.E. Lindblom and R.A. Dahl), *American Political Science Review, 77* (June): 368-389.

Markusen, A. (1978) Class and urban social expenditure: A Marxist theory of metropolitan government. In W. Tabb and L. Sawers (Eds.), *Marxism and the Metropolis.* New York: Oxford University Press.

McAdam, D. (1982) *Political Process and Black Insurgency, 1930-1970.* Chicago: University of Chicago Press.

Miller, S.M., and D. Tomaskovic-Devey (1983) *Recapitalizing America.* Boston and London: Routledge and Kegan Paul.

Mollenkopf, J. (1983) *The Contested City.* Princeton: Princeton University Press.

Molotch, H. (1980) The city as a growth machine: Toward a political economy of place. In H. Hahn and C. Levine (Eds.), *Urban Politics: Past, Present and Future,* 1st edition. New York: Longman.

Monkkonen, E.H. (1984) The politics of municipal indebtedness and default, 1850-1936. In S.K. Ward and T.J. McDonald (Eds.), *The Politics of Urban Fiscal Policy.* Beverly Hills: Sage.

Moriarty, B.M., et al. (1980) *Industrial Location and Community Development.* Chapel Hill: University of North Carolina Press.

Muzzio, D., and R.W. Bailey (1986) Economic development, housing and zoning: A tale of two cities, *Journal of Urban Affairs, 8* (Winter): 1-18.

Nathan, R.P., and C. Adams (1976) Understanding central city hardship, *Political Science Quarterly, 91* (Spring): 47-62.

Nelson, W.E., Jr. (1987) Cleveland: The evolution of black political power. In M. Preston, L. Henderson, and P. Puryear (Eds.), *The New Black Politics.* New York: Longman.

Nelson, W.E., Jr. and P.J. Meranto (1977) *Electing Black Mayors: Political Action in the Black Community.* Columbus: Ohio State University Press.

Newton, K. (1975) American urban politics: Social class, political structure and public goods, *Urban Affairs Quarterly, 11* (December): 241-264.

New York Times (May 6, 1984) Black mayors back subminimum wage for youth.

O'Brien, D., and J. Lange (1986) Racial composition and neighborhood evaluation, *Journal of Urban Affairs, 8* (Summer): 43-61.

Oakland, W.H. (1979) Central cities: Fiscal plight and prospects for reform. In P. Mieskowski and M. Straszheim (Eds.), *Current Issues in Urban Economics.* Baltimore: John Hopkins.

Orfield, G. (1985) Ghettoization and its alternatives. In P. Peterson (Ed.), *New Urban Reality.* Washington, D.C.: Brookings.

Orlebeke, C.J. (1983) *Federal Aid to Chicago.* Washington, D.C.: Brookings.

Peterson, P. (1981) *City Limits.* Chicago: University of Chicago Press.

Pettigrew, T. (1980) Racial change and the intrametropolitan distribution of black Americans. In A.P. Solomon (Ed.), *The Prospective City.* Cambridge: MIT.

Piven, F.F., and R.A. Cloward (1974) *The Politics of Turmoil: Race, Poverty and the Urban Crisis.* New York: Pantheon.

Piven, F.F., and R.A. Cloward (1979) *Poor People's Movements: Why They Succeed, How They Fail.* New York: Pantheon.

Preston, M. (1976) Limitations of black urban power: The case of black mayors. In L. Masotti and R. Lineberry (Eds.), *The New Urban Politics.* Boston: Ballinger.

Reed, A. Jr. (1975) Annexation and consolidation options for Atlanta: An evaluative report. Unpublished staff paper, Department of Budget & Planning, City of Atlanta.

Reed, A. Jr. (1981) Narcissistic politics in Atlanta, *Telos* (Summer): 97-105.

Reed, A. Jr. (1986a) *The Jesse Jackson Phenomenon: The Crisis of Purpose in Afro-American Politics.* New Haven and London: Yale University Press.

Reed, A. Jr. (1986b) The 'black revolution' and the reconstitution of domination. In A. Reed, Jr. (Ed.), *Race, Politics and Culture: Critical Essays on the Radicalism of the 1960s.* Westport, CT: Greenwood.

Reed, A. Jr. (1987) A critique of neo-progressivism in theorizing about local development policy: A case from Atlanta. In C.N. Stone and H. Sanders (Eds.), *The Politics of Urban Economic Development.* Lawrence: University of Kansas Press.

Rice, B., and R.M. Bernard (1983) Introduction. In B. Rice and R.M. Bernard (Eds.), *Sunbelt Cities: Politics and Growth Since WWII.* Austin: University of Texas Press.

Rich, R.C. (1979) Distribution of services: Studying the products of urban policy making. In D.R. Marshall (Ed.), *Urban Policy Making.* Beverly Hills: Sage.

Rosenfeld, R. (1979) Income inequality and crime. In G.A. Tobin (Ed.), *The Changing Structure of the City.* Beverly Hills: Sage.

Rubin, I.S., and R.J. Rubin (1986) Structural theories and urban fiscal stress. In M. Gottdiener (Ed.), *Cities in Stress.* Beverly Hills: Sage.

Salisbury, R. (1964) The new convergence of power, *Journal of Politics* (November): 775-797.

Sanders, H.T. (1980) Urban renewal and the revitalized city: A reconsideration of recent history. In D.B. Rosenthal (Ed.), *Urban Revitalization.* Beverly Hills: Sage.

Sayre, W., and H. Kaufman (1960) *Governing New York City.* New York: W.W. Norton.

Schattschneider, E.E. (1960) *The Semi-Sovereign People.* New York: Holt, Rhinehart & Winston.

Schexnider, A.J. (1982) Political mobilization in the South: The election of a black mayor in New Orleans. In M. Preston, L.J. Henderson, and P. Puryear (Eds.), *The New Black Politics,* 1st edition. New York: Longman.

Schlay, A.B., and P.H. Rossi (1981) Putting politics into urban ecology: Estimating the net effects of zoning. In T.N. Clark (Ed.), *Urban Policy Analysis: Directions for Future Research.* Beverly Hills: Sage.

Schmenner, R.W. (1980) Industrial location and urban public management. In A.P. Solomon (Ed.), *The Prospective City.* Cambridge: MIT.

Schultze, C.L., E.R. Fried, A.M. Rivlin, N. Teeters, and R.D. Reischauer (1977) Fiscal problems of cities. In R. Alcaly and D. Mermelstein (Eds.), *The Fiscal Crisis of American Cities*. New York: Random House.

Shefter, M. (1985) *Political Crisis/Fiscal Crisis: The Collapse and Revival of New York City*. New York: Basic Books.

Sloan, J. (1985) Enterprise zones may not be the bargain that's advertised, *Wall Street Journal* (March 26)

Sloan, L., and R. French (1973) Black rule in the urban South? In A. Shank (Ed.), *Political Power and the Urban Crisis,* 2nd edition. Boston: Little, Brown.

Smith, J.P., and F. Welch (1979) Race differences in earnings: A survey of new evidence. In P. Mieskowski and M. Straszheim (Eds.), *Current Issues in Urban Economics*. Baltimore: Johns Hopkins.

Smith, M.P. (1984) Urban structure, social theory and political power. In M.P. Smith (Ed.), *Cities in Transformation*. Beverly Hills: Sage.

Smith, M.P. (1987) The uses of linked development policies in U.S. cities. In M. Parkinson, et al. (Eds.), *Regenerating the Cities: The U.K. Crisis and the American Experience*. Manchester: University of Manchester Press.

Smith, M.P., and M. Keller (1983) 'Managed growth' and the politics of uneven development in New Orleans. In Fainstein, et al., *Restructuring the City*. New York: Longman.

Smith, M.P., R.L. Ready, and D.R. Judd (1985) Capital flight, tax incentives and the marginalization of American states and localities. In D.R. Judd (Ed.), *Public Policy Across States and Communities*. Greenwich, CT: JAI Press.

Smith, R. (1981) Black power and the transformation from protest to politics, *Political Science Quarterly, 96* (Fall): 431-443.

Smith, R.L. (1985) Interdependencies in urban economic development: The role of multi-establishment corporations. In D.R. Judd (Ed.), *Public Policy across States and Communities*. Greenwich, CT: JAI Press.

Solomon, A.P. (1980) The emerging metropolis. In A.P. Solomon (Ed.), *The Prospective City*. Cambridge: MIT.

Squires, G.D. (1984) Capital mobility versus upward mobility: The racially discriminatory consequences of plant closings and corporate relocations. In L. Sawers and W. Tabb (Eds.), *Sunbelt/Snowbelt*. New York: Oxford University Press.

Stein, R.M., E.G. Sinclair, and M. Neiman (1986) Local government and fiscal stress: An exploration into spending and public employment decisions. In M. Gottdiener (Ed.), *Cities in Stress*. Beverly Hills: Sage.

Steinberger, P.J. (1985) *Ideology and the Urban Crisis*. Albany: SUNY Press.

Sternlieb, G., and J.W. Hughes (1977) Metropolitan decline and inter-regional job shifts. In R. Alcaly and D. Mermelstein (Eds.), *The Fiscal Crisis of American Cities*. New York: Random House.

Stokes, C. (1973) *Promises of Power*. New York: Simon and Schuster.

Stone, C. (1986) Goode: Bad and indifferent, *Washington Monthly* (July/August): 27-28.

Stone, C.N. (1976) *Economic Growth and Neighborhood Discontent: System-Bias in the Urban Reviewal Program of Atlanta*. Chapel Hill: University of North Carolina Press.

Stone, C.N. (1980) Systemic power in community decision-making: A restatement of stratification theory, *American Political Science Review, 74* (December): 978-990.

Stone, C.N. (1983) Whither the welfare state: Professionalism, bureaucracy and the market alternative, *Ethics, 93* (April): 588-595.

Stone, C.N. (1984) New class or convergence: Competing interpretations of social complexity on the structure of urban power, *Power and Elites, 1* (Fall): 1-22.

Stone, C.N. (1984b) City politics and economic development: Political economy perspectives, *Journal of Politics, 46* (February): 286-299.

Stone, C.N. (1986) Power and social complexity. In R.J. Waste (Ed.), *Community Power: Direction for Future Research*. Beverly Hills: Sage.

Swanstrom, T. (1985) *The Crisis of Growth Politics: Cleveland, Kucinich and the Challenge of Urban Populism*. Philadelphia: Temple University Press.

Swanstrom, T. (1986) Urban populism, fiscal crisis, and the new political economy. In M. Gottdiener (Ed.), *Cities in Stress*. Beverly Hills: Sage.

Swanstrom, T. (1986b) Semisovereign cities: The political logic of urban development. Unpublished American Political Science Association conference paper.

Tabb, W.K. (1982) *The Long Default*. New York: Monthly Review.

Taeuber, K.E., and A.F. Taeuber (1965) *Negroes in Cities*. Chicago: Aldine.

Thurow, L. (1975) *Generating Inequality*. New York: Basic.

Tilly, C. (1968) Race and migration to the American city. In J.Q. Wilson (Ed.), *Metropolitan Enigma*. Garden City: Doubleday.

Walker, R.A. (1981) A theory of suburbanization: Capitalism and the construction of urban space in the U.S. In M. Dear and A. Scott (Eds.), *Urbanization and Urban Planning in Capitalist Society*. London and New York: Methuen.

Walters, R.W. (1974) The black politician: Fulfilling the legacy of black power, *Current History, 67* (November): 200f.

Warner, S.B. (1978) *Streetcar Suburbs*. Cambridge: Harvard University Press.

Wasylenko, M. (1981) The location of firms: The role of taxes and fiscal incentives. In R. Bahl (Ed.), *Urban Government Finance*. Beverly Hills: Sage.

Watson, S. (1980) Do mayors matter? The role of leadership in urban policy. Unpublished American Political Science Association conference paper.

Whelan, R.K. (1987) New Orleans: Mayoral politics and economic development policies in the postwar years, 1945-1986. In C.N. Stone and H.T. Sanders (Eds.), *The Politics of Urban Economic Development*. Lawrence: University of Kansas Press.

Williams, J. (1986) A dream deferred: A black mayor betrays the faith, *The Washington Monthly* (July-August): 24f.

Wolfe, A. (1981) *America's Impasse: The Rise and Fall of the Politics of Growth*. Boston: South End.

Woody, B. (1982) *Managing Urban Crises: The New Black Leadership and the Politics of Resource Allocation*. Westport, CT: Greenwood.

Yates, Douglas (1977) *The Ungovernable City: The Politics of Urban Problems and Policy Making*. Cambridge, MA: MIT.

Comparative Urban and Community Research is grateful to the following people for their reviews of manuscripts. Their time, effort, and especially their constructive comments, have been invaluable in the publication of this first issue of the Review.

Janet Abu-Lughod
Northwestern University
Evanston, IL

Roger Friedland
University of California
Santa Barbara

Enzo Mingione
University of Messina
Italy

Richard P. Appelbaum
University of California
Santa Barbara

John Friedmann
University of California
Los Angeles

Ben Orlove
University of California
Davis

Stephen Barton
University of California
Berkeley

M. Gottdiener
University of California
Riverside

B. Guy Peters
University of Pittsburgh

Christopher Chase-Dunn
Johns Hopkins Univ.
Baltimore

Greg Guagnano
University of California
Davis

Ernesto Pollitt
University of California
Davis

Steve Brush
University of California
Davis

William John Hanna
University of Maryland
College Park

Helen Roland
University of California
Davis

Phil Coulter
University of Alabama
University

Bryan Jones
Texas A & M
University

Carol Smith
Duke University
Durham, NC

Dennis J. Dingemans
University of California
Davis

Dennis Judd
University of Missouri
St. Louis

Richard Tardanico
Florida
International
University

Norman Fainstein
City University of
New York

Lyn H. Lofland
University of California
Davis

Michael Timberlake
Memphis State
University

Susan S. Fainstein
Rutgers University
New Brunswick, NJ

Dean MacCannell
University of California
Davis

John Walton
University of California
Davis

Joe R. Feagin
University of Texas
Austin

Dario Melossi
University of California
Davis

Patricia Wilson
University of Texas
Austin